CRIMINALISING CONTAGION

The use of the criminal law to punish those who transmit disease is a topical and controversial issue. To date, the law (and the related academic literature) has largely focused on HIV transmission. With contributions from leading practitioners and international scholars from a variety of disciplines, this book explores the broader question of if and when it is appropriate to criminalise the transmission of contagion. The scope and application of the laws in jurisdictions such as Canada, England and Wales, and Norway are considered; historical comparisons are examined; and options for the further development of the law are proposed.

CATHERINE STANTON is Lecturer in Law at the University of Manchester.

HANNAH QUIRK is Senior Lecturer in Criminal Law and Justice at the University of Manchester.

CAMBRIDGE BIOETHICS AND LAW

This series of books was founded by Cambridge University Press with Alexander McCall Smith as its first editor in 2003. It focuses on the law's complex and troubled relationship with medicine across both the developed and the developing worlds. Since the early 1990s, we have seen in many countries increasing resort to the courts by dissatisfied patients and a growing use of the courts to attempt to resolve intractable ethical dilemmas. At the same time, legislatures across the world have struggled to address the questions posed by both the successes and the failures of modern medicine, while international organisations such as the WHO and UNESCO now regularly address issues of medical law.

It follows that we would expect ethical and policy questions to be integral to the analysis of the legal issues discussed in this series. The series responds to the high profile of medical law in universities, in legal and medical practice, as well as in public and political affairs. We seek to reflect the evidence that many major health-related policy debates in the United Kingdom, Europe, and the international community involve a strong medical law dimension. With that in mind, we seek to address how legal analysis might have a trans-jurisdictional and international relevance. Organ retention, embryonic stem cell research, physician-assisted suicide, and the allocation of resources to fund healthcare are but a few examples among many. The emphasis of this series is thus on matters of public concern and/or practical significance. We look for books that could make a difference to the development of medical law and enhance the role of medico-legal debate in policy circles. That is not to say that we lack interest in the important theoretical dimensions of the subject, but we aim to ensure that theoretical debate is grounded in the realities of how the law does and should interact with medicine and healthcare.

Series Editors

Professor Margaret Brazier, *University of Manchester*

Professor Graeme Laurie, *University of Edinburgh*

Professor Richard Ashcroft, Queen Mary, *University of London*

Professor Eric M. Meslin, *Indiana University*

Books in the series

Marcus Radetzki, Marian Radetzki, Niklas Juth
Genes and Insurance: Ethical, Legal and Economic Issues

Ruth Macklin
Double Standards in Medical Research in Developing Countries

(*continued after Index*)

CRIMINALISING CONTAGION

Legal and Ethical Challenges of Disease
Transmission and the Criminal Law

Edited by

CATHERINE STANTON and
HANNAH QUIRK

CAMBRIDGE
UNIVERSITY PRESS

CAMBRIDGE
UNIVERSITY PRESS

University Printing House, Cambridge CB2 8BS, United Kingdom

Cambridge University Press is part of the University of Cambridge.

It furthers the University's mission by disseminating knowledge in the pursuit of education, learning and research at the highest international levels of excellence.

www.cambridge.org
Information on this title: www.cambridge.org/9781107091825

© Cambridge University Press 2016

First published 2016

A catalogue record for this publication is available from the British Library

Library of Congress Cataloguing in Publication data
Names: Stanton, Catherine, editor. | Quirk, Hannah, editor.
Title: Criminalising contagion: legal and ethical challenges of disease transmission and the criminal law / edited by Catherine Stanton and Hannah Quirk.
Description: Cambridge: Cambridge University Press, 2016. |
Series: Cambridge Bioethics and Law |
Includes bibliographical references and index.
Identifiers: LCCN 2015039550 | ISBN 9781107091825 (hardback)
Subjects: LCSH: Communicable diseases – Prevention. | Epidemics – Prevention. |
Communicable diseases – Prevention – Moral and ethical aspects. |
Epidemics – Prevention – Moral and ethical aspects. | Public health laws. |
Biological weapons. | Criminal law.
Classification: LCC RA644.3 C75 2016 | DDC 616.9–dc23
LC record available at http://lccn.loc.gov/2015039550

ISBN 978-1-107-09182-5 Hardback

For Margot
and
In Memory of T. E. Yates

CONTENTS

ix

CONTRIBUTORS

MARGARET BRAZIER, Professor of Law, School of Law, University of Manchester, UK

CERI EVANS, Senior Sexual Health Adviser, West London Centre for Sexual Health, (part of Chelsea and Westminster Healthcare NHS Foundation Trust), Charing Cross Hospital, London, UK

LAWRENCE O. GOSTIN, University Professor and Founding Linda D. and Timothy J. O'Neill Professor of Global Health Law, Georgetown Law, Washington D.C., USA

MICHAEL HANNE, Associate Professor of Comparative Literature, Faculty of Arts, University of Auckland, New Zealand

KERRI A. INGLIS, Associate Professor of History, University of Hawai'i at Hilo, USA

ALANA KLEIN, Assistant Professor, Faculty of Law, McGill University, Montreal, Canada

KARL LAIRD, Lecturer in Law, St. John's College, Oxford, UK; Teaching Associate, Faculty of Law, University of Cambridge, UK

ERIC MYKHALOVSKIY, Associate Professor, Department of Sociology, York University, Canada

HANNAH QUIRK, Senior Lecturer in Criminal Law and Justice, School of Criminal Law and Justice, University of Manchester, UK

CATHERINE STANTON, Lecturer in Law, School of Law, University of Manchester, UK

ASLAK SYSE, Professor of Law, Department of Public and International Law, Faculty of Law, University of Oslo, Norway

MATTHEW WEAIT, Professor and Dean of the Faculty of Humanities and Social Sciences, University of Portsmouth, UK

LESLIE E. WOLF, Professor and Director of the Center for Law, Health & Society at Georgia State University College of Law, USA

FOREWORD

MARGARET BRAZIER AND LAWRENCE O. GOSTIN

Not so very long ago, when the authors of this Foreword were young lawyers, the notion of a book on criminal liability and disease transmission would have been close to risible for two reasons. First, in the richer and developed parts of the world, scientists were claiming that we had all but conquered deadly threats of contagious diseases. Vaccinations, better public health measures, and above all the magical anti-microbial medications had reduced contagious diseases to little more than inconveniences. (This idea turned out to be badly flawed, as the world has continued to experience successive threats of novel infections, most recently the Ebola virus.) Second, even if a wiser medically qualified friend had pointed out to us the hubris of any view that humankind had defeated all the viruses and bacteria that share our planet, we would have given short shrift to any suggestion that infected individuals should be subject to criminal penalties for risking transmission of the infection to others. How wrong we were.

In 2016 it is all too clear that contagious diseases never went away and continue to ravage much of the world, particularly affecting lower-income countries in sub-Saharan Africa, Asia, and Latin America. Little has been done to research vaccines and treatments for endemic diseases (such as malaria, tuberculosis, and yellow fever) or emerging threats such as novel influenzas, corona viruses (e.g., SARS and the currently circulating Middle East Respiratory Disease), and haemorrhagic fevers (such as Ebola virus). In the fortunate West, which could afford potentially expensive medical interventions, for several decades killer diseases such as septicaemia, and once-fatal scarlet fever responded to antibiotics whilst the viral killers such as polio and influenza were combated with vaccinations and anti-viral drugs. Now, travel and the mass movement of people bring the killer diseases of the developing world to the doorsteps of Europe and North America. Our profligate use of antibiotics has led the Chief Medical Officer of England to warn that all too soon antibiotic resistance will render many infectious diseases untreatable – a view shared by the World Health Organization. The emergence of antibiotic-resistant staphylococcal infections means that a septic scratch may kill again and routine surgery will become more dangerous. Too many viruses as yet do not respond to vaccination, and at the same time growing numbers of people reject vaccination for themselves and their children. Diseases are dangerous.

Protecting citizens from danger is one of the functions of the criminal law. Prohibitions preventing the editors of this work taking out their anger at our delay in producing this Foreword by punching us in the nose are central to criminal laws dealing with offences against the person. So, given what we have said about the resurgent danger of infectious disease, maybe it is no more than common sense to say that if the weapon is disease, rather than a fist, that should not matter too much. If we know we have a virulent strain of influenza and still go to visit our frail Aunt Doris, then embrace her, and thus fatally infect her, is our gross negligence any less culpable than if we had shoved past her on the stairs and knocked her down, as a result of which she died of her injuries? As the chapters in this book demonstrate, the relationship between criminal law and contagion is much more complex than our simple example suggests, and the imposition of criminal sanctions can drive epidemics underground, actually increasing the threat to wider populations.

Until repealed in 2010, public health legislation in the United Kingdom included a criminal sanction where the accused exposed another to a notifiable disease in a public place. That sanction to our knowledge was little used, if at all, in modern times. The trigger for resort to the criminal law to combat contagion was the emergence of the HIV pandemic and the international moral panic to which the pandemic gave rise. Across the world, prosecutions were brought against people who it was alleged had intentionally or recklessly infected another, usually a lover, with HIV. Worse yet, many criminal laws penalized behaviour risking transmission, even if the partner or contact never became infected.

The contributors to this work offer a number of different accounts and perspectives on the role of the criminal process in relation both to HIV and other infections more broadly. The very nature of the HIV pandemic, however, has distorted fundamental conceptions of risk behaviours and the law. In its early years, representations of individuals living with HIV/ AIDS as dangerous and irresponsible, and sent to wreak vengeance on humankind inspired fear and horror. Misunderstandings of HIV/AIDS led many to think that it could be spread with the ease of the common cold: by a handshake or a kiss or even by using the same toilet seat. The initial presence of HIV among the gay community, and among people from, or who had had sexual relations with people from, a number of African countries created racial and sexual stereotypes. Above all, the fact that HIV was a sexually transmitted disease resulted in the stigmatisation of those who contracted and carried this virus. People living with HIV were seen as dangerous. The gradual realisation by the public and the media that HIV could be contracted by means other than sexual intercourse (e.g., from childbirth, contaminated blood products, contaminated drug injection equipment, or even in the course of certain kinds of surgery) did little to diminish the perception that many people living with HIV/AIDS were somehow blameworthy. The stereotypes led to two distinct visions of persons living with HIV/AIDS: the 'guilty', who contracted HIV from sex or by sharing drug injection equipment, and the 'innocent' who were infected by say Factor 8, as part of treatment for haemophilia or through perinatal transmission.

Against this background, as the chapters in this book show, the criminal process intruded on disease prevention and control. The book contains diverse views and marries theoretical analysis with practical critique. The authors challenge understandings of criminal law's norms and process, as well as the motivations behind the stances of those who applaud the role of the criminal law and those who decry it. In examining the work as whole, the questions raised take us well beyond the starting point for this insightful work, leading us to reflect on the emphasis on individual responsibility rather than on governmental duty. It forces us to ponder whether solutions are merely a matter of national sovereignty, or whether there should be a global norm against the criminalisation of individuals who risk transmission of infection – as UNAIDS powerfully urges. Criminalising a person living with HIV/AIDS or the frightened family concealing a sick relative with Ebola remains deeply controversial. Even in cases where the individual acts with malice, the mere fact that society resorts to the criminal law draws attention away from the responsibility of governments and all-of-society, especially the most powerful. Following the tragic cases of those infected with HIV after receiving medical treatment with infected blood products, in the United Kingdom, a brief investigation by the Crown Prosecution Service resulted in no criminal proceedings. In France, senior doctors and managers were held criminally responsible for the delays and cover-ups that resulted in more people being infected by HIV-contaminated blood products, but their political masters were for the most part exonerated. The resort to the criminal process in France does not seem to have prevented other similar scandals.

Individuals bear responsibility for actions that endanger others. Individuals equally bear responsibility to protect their own health, and thus, as we shall see in the context of the chapters on HIV transmission, the question is not only whether X should have acted to protect Y, but also what should Y have done to protect herself? Again, UNAIDS counsels everyone to protect themselves against sexual transmission or sharing injection equipment. In an inter-connected world, health is the responsibility not only of governments primarily but also of national and international organisations. Should one be tempted to blame the family who fails to report their fears that a child has Ebola, one first needs to reflect on how well the local, national, and global community will care for the child and family? Will the child be treated insofar as treatment is accessible? Will the family be protected or driven out of their community? The questions are not that different from those which have plagued the debate on HIV transmission. If X agrees to be tested, if X discloses his sero-positive status to those who need to know, will his privacy be safeguarded and will his job be safe? If X is in treatment with a negligible viral load or if X wears a condom, is there any role for the criminal law?

The public health community often thinks of disease prevention and control as primarily, if not solely, a scientific concern. We must also consider if there is a role for law, particularly criminal law, and, if so, in what limited circumstances? The role of the criminal law in public health at one time was unthinkable. Today, it is a matter of major national and global importance.

~

Disease Transmission and the Criminal Law: A Growing Concern?

HANNAH QUIRK AND CATHERINE STANTON

States have a responsibility to protect their citizens and at times have to take coercive action to isolate or incapacitate those who carry infectious diseases and threaten the health of others. Such measures have included the fourteenth-century Venetian requirement for ships arriving from plague infected ports to sit at anchor for forty days[1] before landing; the forcible medical examination and detention of female sex workers under the Contagious Diseases Act 1864 in England;[2] and the closure of businesses and the cancellation of Christmas celebrations in Sierra Leone in 2014 in response to the Ebola epidemic.[3] Article 5 of the European Convention on Human Rights (the right to liberty and security) provides an exemption for 'the lawful detention of persons for the prevention of the spreading of infectious diseases…'.[4] There are many methods that states can deploy for dissuading individuals from spreading infection, including providing education, offering encouragement or incentives, and imposing civil regulations.[5] Until recently, few societies have attached criminal liability to disease transmission.[6] Whilst public health orders lack the expression

---

[1] The word 'quarantine' is derived from the Italian words *quaranta giorni* meaning 'forty days' (E. Tognotti, 'Lessons from the history of quarantine, from plague to influenza A', *Emerging Infectious Diseases*, 19: 2 (2013), 254.

[2] Similar versions were enacted in most of the colonies, see, for example, P. Levine, 'Venereal disease, prostitution, and the politics of Empire: the case of British India', *Journal of the History of Sexuality*, 4 (1994), 579.

[3] 'Ebola crisis: Sierra Leone bans Christmas celebrations'. www.bbc.co.uk/news/world-africa-30455248, 12 December 2014.

[4] Article 5(1)(e) European Convention on Human Rights and Fundamental Freedoms.

[5] State action is not always necessary. The villagers of Eyam in Derbyshire, England, heroically isolated themselves in 1665–6 to stop the spread of the plague (W. Wood, *The History and Antiquities of Eyam* (London: Thomas Miller, 1842)).

[6] The Canadian Criminal Code included an offence of knowingly transmitting a venereal disease, but this was repealed in 1985, largely because it had not been used since 1922 (J. Chalmers, 'Ethics, law, and medicine: the criminalisation of HIV transmission', *Sexually Transmitted Infections*, 78: 6 (2002), 448–51).

1

of censure and imposition of punishment that characterise a criminal conviction, this may be of cold comfort to those who experience such measures as repressive, demeaning, discriminatory or unjust. The powers exercised by public health authorities, such as the use of quarantine or enforced treatment, can be equally or even more draconian than the punishments imposed by the criminal courts, and may be applied without the due process safeguards that apply to trials. Nevertheless, the professed aim of the authorities is to curb the spread of disease – usually only those that are incurable or highly injurious – rather than to punish or to condemn the person spreading the disease. For reasons that are not entirely clear, there has been a shift from the use of public health legislation to that of the criminal law in response to HIV transmission. The lack of clarity in the law in many jurisdictions, and the uncertainty as to how it may develop, makes this fertile ground for scholars and practitioners.

There is no straightforward definition of what behaviours should constitute crimes. The extensive literature around criminalisation discusses the various rationales for criminalisation; a process that has become so chaotic that Ashworth dismisses it as a 'lost cause'.[7] There are certain broad characteristics, however. Crime is regarded as having a public quality (the wrong done is deemed harmful to society as a whole, rather than just to the individual 'victim') – this is why the state prosecutes criminal cases[8] – and there is a symbolic or expressive function to its exercise. The classic liberal position of John Stuart Mill is that '[t]he only purpose for which power can be rightfully exercised over any member of a civilised community against his will is to prevent harm to others',[9] thus the criminal law might appear an appropriate tool to deter or to sanction[10] the transmission of disease. Harm, of itself, is not a sufficient reason to prosecute, however: '[t]here are principled reasons not to criminalize all wrongful and blameworthy conduct, even if the practical difficulties of enforcement could be overcome'.[11] Culpability is usually essential in establishing criminal liability – not just that an individual caused harm, but that he or she was blameworthy in so doing.[12] It would be unfair to punish those who did

---

[7] A. Ashworth, 'Is criminal law a lost cause', *Law Quarterly Review*, 116 (2000), 225.
[8] R. A. Duff, *Answering for Crime* (Oxford: Hart, 2007).
[9] J. S. Mill, 'On liberty', in J. Mill, *On Liberty and Other Essays* (ed. J. Gray) (Oxford: Oxford University Press, 1991), p. 14.
[10] A. von Hirsch, *Censure and Sanctions* (Oxford: Oxford University Press, 1993).
[11] D. Husak, 'The nature and justifiability of non-commensurate offenses', *Arizona Law Review*, 37 (1995), 151, 155.
[12] A. Honoré, *Responsibility and Fault* (Oxford: Hart, 1998).

not know that they were ill for example, or did not understand how they might transmit an infection. Yet even if moral culpability for causing harm is present, many of those opposed to the criminalisation of disease transmission argue against adding the stigma of criminalisation to that already faced by the sick.[13] Many prioritise the protection of public health over the attribution of criminal liability, arguing that a criminalisation strategy is counter-productive as it may discourage engagement with healthcare providers which may increase the risk of disease transmission.[14] Weait argues that 'if we start from a set of *a priori* assumptions about the function(s) of the criminal law in this context, and treat incidents of HIV transmission simply as an opportunity to apply the principles which have traditionally informed the law relating to non-fatal offences against the person, we risk doing more harm than good'.[15] It has also been argued that using the criminal law in this way, putting the onus upon the HIV positive partner, detracts from the public health message of encouraging notions of shared responsibility for 'safer sex'.[16]

States have adopted a variety of approaches to criminalisation. Some jurisdictions have enacted HIV-specific statutes; others have applied existing criminal laws (primarily offences against the person acts). The wrong that is being punished varies; it can require the actual transmission of disease, which may be a matter of (bad) luck: as in England; or merely the reckless exposure of another to the disease, regardless of the outcome, as in Canada. There is no consistent rationale as to which types of disease transmission are deemed appropriate for a criminal sanction. HIV and syphilis can both be life threatening if left untreated but, to take three examples from the United States of America, only the transmission of HIV is criminalised in Colorado; Alabama does not differentiate between sexually transmitted diseases; but in Louisiana, HIV exposure is a felony, whereas exposure to other sexually transmitted diseases is a misdemeanor.[17]

---

[13] R. Jürgens, J. Cohen, E. Cameron, S. Burris, M. Clayton, R. Elliott, R. Pearshouse, A. Gathumbi and D. Cupido, 'Ten reasons to oppose the criminalization of HIV exposure or transmission', *Reproductive Health Matters*, 17: 34 (2009), 163–72, 166.

[14] C. L. Galletly and S. D. Pinkerton, 'Conflicting messages: how criminal HIV disclosure laws undermine public health efforts to control the spread of HIV', *AIDS and Behavior*, 10 (2006), 451–61.

[15] M. Weait, 'Knowledge, autonomy and consent: *R v Konzani*', *Criminal Law Review*, (October 2005), 763–72.

[16] M. Weait, 'Taking the blame: criminal law, social responsibility and the sexual transmission of HIV', *Journal of Social Welfare and Family Law*, 23 (2001), 441–57.

[17] See www.criminaldefenselawyer.com/resources/transmitting-std-criminal-laws-penalties .htm, last accessed 5 July 2015.

Chlamydia can cause arguably more serious harm than herpes as it can lead to infertility but thus far only HIV and herpes transmission have been prosecuted in England.[18] We are not aware of any prosecutions for disease transmission arising from intravenous drug users sharing infected needles in England and Wales, but fourteen US states have requirements for disclosure between needle sharers.[19] There are immense practical difficulties in proving to a criminal standard that a defendant intentionally or recklessly transmitted a disease to the victim, in particular, establishing causation; just because A discovers that she is HIV positive after having sex with B, does not prove that B is the source. As with other sexual offences, cases involving stereotypical ('innocent') victims and predatory or promiscuous defendants may be more likely to result in convictions. This may be why groups seen as 'Other', such as migrants and sex workers, appear to have been prosecuted disproportionately.[20] While the problems and solutions in individual countries may differ, the underlying principles require similar attention.

This edited collection arose from a series of four seminars funded by the Economic and Social Research Council (ESRC)[21] held between January 2013 and September 2014 which were hosted by the University of Manchester and the University of Southampton (after our project partner David Gurnham moved there).[22] We would like to thank the ESRC for its assistance and David for his input in the early stages of the development of this collection. As with so much research at the intersection of medical and criminal law, this project was the brainchild of Professor Margot Brazier and one of the offshoots of the many investigations she has led at the Centre for Social Ethics and Policy at the University of Manchester.[23]

---

[18] *R v Golding* [2014] EWCA Crim 889.

[19] J. S. Lehman, M. H. Carr, A. J. Nichol, A. Ruisanchez, D. W. Knight, A. E. Langford, S. C. Gray and J. H. Mermin, 'Prevalence and public health implications of state laws that criminalize potential HIV exposure in the United States', *AIDS and Behavior*, 18 (2014), 724.

[20] H. Worth, C. Patton and D. Goldstein, 'Introduction to special issue: reckless vectors: the infecting "other" in HIV/AIDS law', *Sexuality Research and Social Policy*, 2: 2 (2005), 3–14.

[21] ES/J021555/1 *Criminalising Contagion: Legal and Ethical Challenges of Disease Transmission and the Criminal Law*.

[22] *Criminalising Contagion: Legal and Ethical Challenges of Disease Transmission and the Criminal Law*. Final Report available at www.southampton.ac.uk/icjr/news/2014/11/25_criminalising_contagion_summary.page?

[23] Inter alia, M. Brazier and S. Ost (eds.), *Medicine and Bioethics in the Theatre of the Criminal Process. Bioethics and the Criminal Process* (Cambridge: Cambridge University Press, 2013); A. Alghrani, R. Bennett and S. Ost (eds.), *The Criminal Law and Bioethical Conflict: Walking the Tightrope* (Cambridge: Cambridge University Press, 2012); D. Griffiths and A. Sanders (eds.), *Bioethics, Medicine and the Criminal Law* (Cambridge: Cambridge University Press, 2013).

We are indebted to her for her intellectual generosity and support. Much of the debate in this area focuses on whether disease transmission should be addressed from a criminal or public health perspective. We are thus delighted, that Margot and Professor Larry Gostin, one of the leading international scholars in public health, have written the foreword for this collection and we would like to thank them both for that.

We sought a range of inter-disciplinary and international perspectives on these issues. Seminar participants included lawyers, ethicists, social scientists, journalists, criminal justice and healthcare practitioners from the United Kingdom, Norway, the United States of America and Canada. We are grateful to all those who presented their work[24] and also to those who attended and contributed to the discussions. The chapters in this book by Ceri Evans, Alana Klein, Karl Laird and Aslak Syse are based on papers given at these seminars. A number of additional publications resulted from the seminars and all benefitted from the lively exchange of ideas that occurred there. Each chapter in this book was reviewed by both editors and was sent to an external 'blind' reviewer. Whilst we cannot name the reviewers here, we would like to record our appreciation and that of our contributors for their efforts which have strengthened this collection.

A UK-based seminar series is necessarily constrained in its range of delegates. To counterbalance this, we put out a call for publications as part of a series of three special issues across the *British Medical Journal* publications[25] to include the perspectives of some of those who were unable to join the seminars. This widened the debate to include areas such as United Nations' policy and legislation in Africa, which are not covered in this volume.[26] Most of the literature in this area focuses on HIV and

---

[24] James Chalmers (University of Glasgow), John Coggon (University of Southampton), Sharon Cowan (University of Edinburgh), John Dilworth (CPS), Ceri Evans (Society of Sexual Health Advisers), Steven Evans (36 Bedford Row Chambers), David Fenton (BBC), John G. Francis (University of Utah), Peter Greenhouse (BASHH), David Gurnham (University of Southampton), Imogen Jones (University of Birmingham) Alana Klein (McGill University), Karl Laird (University of Oxford), Maggie O'Neill (Durham University), Matthew Phillips (Manchester Centre for Sexual Health), Leslie Picking Francis (University of Utah), James Slater (University of Buckingham), Lucy Stackpool-Moore (SOAS), Aslak Syse (University of Oslo) and Matthew Weait (Birkbeck School of Law) (affiliations stated are those which applied at the time of the seminars)

[25] *Sexually Transmitted Infections*, 89:4 (2013), 274–94 (edited by David Gurnham); *Medical Humanities*, 39:2 (2013), 75–84 (edited by Hannah Quirk); *Journal of Medical Ethics*, 40:12 (2014), 792–801 (edited by Catherine Stanton). We were sorry to hear of the death of Sue Eckstein, the editor of *Medical Humanities*, just before the special issue was printed.

[26] D. Grace, 'Legislative epidemics: the role of model law in the transnational trend to criminalise HIV transmission', *Medical Humanities*, 39 (2013), 77–84; P. O'Byrne, A. Bryan and

other sexually transmitted infections. We found it difficult to move as far beyond this as we had initially intended, but most of the arguments and ideas raised can be extrapolated to other diseases.

We quickly found this topic is like no other area of criminal law. It was striking throughout the seminar series how differently most academics and practitioners regarded the reckless transmission of HIV to other crimes; as Mawhinney observes, '[a] culture of sympathy comes through much of the research critical of criminalisation of HIV transmission'.[27] In recent years, criminal justice scholarship and policy has taken a much greater interest in the victims of crime.[28] In the United States and the United Kingdom, funding has been increased for victim support groups, which have been given greater involvement in policymaking. Evidential changes have been made, such as the use of victim impact statements, in order to 'rebalance' a criminal justice system which has been criticised for overly favouring the rights of defendants.[29] In the area of disease transmission, however, it appears that the experience of the victims is often underplayed – it was noteworthy throughout the seminars how often the effects of HIV and a lifetime on medication were minimised, and how the boundaries between offender and victim were blurred, as the 'offender' was, of course, also victimised when infected. One seminar attendee recalled a newly diagnosed 'angry young man' wanting the person who had infected him to be prosecuted, and how instead he was counselled to address his responsibility for exposing himself to infection. Such 'victim blaming' is increasingly out of favour in criminal justice policy, particularly in relation to sexual offences. Unlike other crimes, which are often justified as protecting the freedoms of others, autonomy was discussed primarily in terms of those with HIV – their right to have sex and not to have to disclose their status – with

M. Roy, 'HIV criminal prosecutions and public health: an examination of the empirical research', *Medical Humanities*, 39 (2013), 85–90. On the use of model law see also: D. Grace, 'Criminalizing HIV transmission using model law: troubling best practice standardizations in the global HIV/AIDS response', *Critical Public Health*, 25: 4 (2015), 441–54.

[27] G. R. Mawhinney, 'To be ill or to kill: the criminality of contagion', *Journal of Criminal Law*, 77:3 (2013), 202, 203.

[28] United Nations A/RES/40/34, 29 November 1985, Declaration of Basic Principles of Justice for Victims of Crime and Abuse of Power; Council of Europe Framework Decision of 15 March 2001 on the standing of victims in criminal proceedings (2001/220/JHA); Directive 2012/29/EU; J. Doak, *Victims' Rights, Human Rights and Criminal Justice: Reconceiving the Role of Third Parties* (Oxford: Hart Publishing, 2008); I. Vanfraechem, A. Pemberton and F. Mukwiza Ndahinda (eds.), *Justice for Victims: Perspectives on Rights, Transition and Reconciliation* (Abingdon: Routledge, 2014).

[29] J. D. Jackson, 'Justice for all: putting victims at the heart of criminal justice?', *Journal of Law and Society*, 30: 2 (2003), 309.

much less consideration given to the right of 'victims' to (refuse) consent to exposure to any risk, however slight. The majority view was clearly that criminalising disease transmission was unfair, counter-productive in public health terms, and potentially discriminatory.

This collection begins with a provocative suggestion by Matthew Weait that HIV should not be thought of as a 'harm' for the purposes of the criminal law. Weait argues that the debate has become frozen between two conflicting perspectives – those who object to criminalisation by focusing on its negative effects in terms of stigmatisation and public health campaigns, and those who adopt the orthodox approach that HIV is a criminally significant harm. While acknowledging 'the seriously adverse physical, psychological and social impact that HIV may have on people',[30] he offers a bold attempt to reframe the debate by reassessing what is meant by harm. He explains how the conceptualisation of the body in criminal law has developed from a porous entity at the whim of the gods in medieval times, to a molar single entity today. Weait argues that 'the bodily integrity assumed by the criminal law is illusory' and that by deconstructing notions of 'the body' and taking a 'post-human' approach, the idea of harm can be reassessed. He argues that '[t]he bodies of people living with HIV are merely composite in a different way from those not living with HIV... People living with HIV are normal, in this sense, in the same way that people living without HIV are normal.'[31] Weait contends that the decision to criminalise an activity is a political choice, and that any argument for or against criminalising the transmission of disease, must acknowledge this and interrogate the assumptions that underlie it.

Such definitional issues are important, as how a subject is conceptualised sets the parameters for debate and the possibilities for action. Michael Hanne's chapter examines the use of metaphor in relation to illness and crime. He explores the associations between the two concepts, the overlaps and shifting boundaries, over time and between cultures, and the ways in which societies seek to correct or to cure both problems. Using a range of sociological and historical examples, he explains how illness and criminality are regarded by most societies as a form of social deviance – the former generally being regarded more sympathetically, but sometimes as a punishment for the latter (see, for example, the startling campaigns of the Westboro Baptist Church in the United States that views AIDS and war as

---

[30] Weait, Chapter 1, this volume, at 19.
[31] Ibid., at 32.

God's punishment for society permitting homosexuality[32]). As Weait does, he argues that there are political factors that contribute to how notions of blame, culpability and criminal justice policies are constructed, such as policies that criminalise the transmission of HIV, but not the businesses that damage life expectancy through pollution or fast food. In all these discussions, Hanne argues that it is important to understand the role of the language used and how this in turn can influence the debate. He examines the widespread use of both 'disease as crime' and 'crime as disease' metaphors, and the danger that this may lead to the collapse of the boundary between the two concepts. There are often overlaps between the populations most susceptible to disease and those with the highest crime rates. He urges therefore that, while the use of metaphor should not be abandoned, there is a need to be critical about its usage.

Words are enormously important, and how a disease is named is also significant. When clusters of Kaposi's sarcoma and pneumocystis pneumonia were noted among gay males in Southern California and New York City in the early 1980s, it was proposed to call the condition that became known as HIV-AIDS, 'Gay-Related Immune Deficiency' (GRID).[33] In the British press – broadsheet as well as tabloid – the disease was dubbed a 'gay plague'.[34] This labelling of the disease appeared to affect public responses to it – from, British Prime Minister, Margaret Thatcher's reluctance to run a public information campaign that might risk offending public sensibilities,[35] to the outright discrimination that many HIV positive (and gay people generally) suffered as a result. A leader in *The Times* newspaper opined that 'the infection's origins and means of propagation excites repugnance, moral and physical, at promiscuous male homosexuality'.[36] The World Health Organisation recently called upon scientists, national authorities and the media to avoiding giving diseases names associated with places or species (such as Spanish or bird flu) or groups (such as Legionnaires' Disease). It reasoned that certain disease names may 'provoke a backlash against members of particular religious or ethnic communities, create unjustified barriers to travel, commerce and trade,

---

[32] www.godhatesfags.com.

[33] www.cdc.gov/mmwr/preview/mmwrhtml/00001114.htm.

[34] 'Spread of the "Gay Plague"' *Mail on Sunday* 1 May 1983; ' "Gay Plague" may lead to blood ban on homosexuals' *Daily Telegraph*, 2 May 1983; 'Alert over "Gay Plague"' *Daily Mirror* 2 May 1983; ' "Watchdogs in "Gay Plague" probe' *The Sun* 2 May 1983.

[35] S. Garfield 'Saying the Unsayable' *The Independent*, 11 November 1995.

[36] *The Times*, 21 November 1984. Newspaper details reported in A. McSmith, *No Such Thing as Society* (London: Constable, 2011).

and trigger needless slaughtering of animals. This can have serious consequences for peoples' lives and livelihoods'.[37] As Kerri Inglis explains in her chapter, leprosy was renamed Hansen's Disease in an effort to reduce the associated stigma but, as she notes, the naming is of significance, not just to the wider community, but to those with the condition as 'naming or labelling of course brings with it implications of identity'.[38]

We soon realised that it was almost impossible to separate the debate around criminalising disease transmission from these notions of identity and the experiences of those who have lived with and/or campaigned against the stigma faced by those with HIV. To newcomers to the debate, it seems perfectly possible not to be homophobic or racist, yet to advocate criminalisation of HIV transmission, but for many of those with longer or personal experience in this area, the terms of the debate appear to have been set by its history. Inglis's chapter offers a fascinating historical perspective on this issue by examining the use of the law to prevent the spread of Leprosy in Hawai'i between the mid-nineteenth and twentieth centuries. She draws upon moving personal testimony and contemporaneous accounts to illustrate how a policy with benign original intentions came to be experienced as oppressive, humiliating and racist. It was imposed by a colonial authority on primarily indigenous patients. In the face of an incurable epidemic of unknown origin, the authorities set up a quarantine regime: 'Geographically and culturally, this was to be a land "set apart".[39] The language used became increasingly punitive – patients became prisoners and the way in which the inmates were treated and regarded carried as much stigma as those subject to the criminal law. Patients were subject to compulsory sterilisation, degrading physical examinations and were separated from their families. Medical advancements ended the need for these 'geographies of exclusion',[40] but former patients continue to work to address the additional stigma imposed on them by the law.

Several of our contributors emphasised this importance of examining the effects of the criminal law in practice. Ceri Evans, a sexual health adviser in London notes in her chapter how, just as lawyers and legislators struggle keeping up to date with medical advances, healthcare professionals now have to understand and communicate accurately to their patients the current state of a complex, changing area of law. Although

---

[37] www.who.int/mediacentre/news/notes/2015/naming-new-diseases/en/
[38] Inglis, Chapter 3, this volume, at 58.
[39] Ibid., at 56.
[40] Ibid.

transmission of herpes and HIV would be charged under the same law by prosecutors, the populations affected by, and the clinical differences between, the two viruses require very different responses from healthcare practitioners. Evans details the significant practical challenges she and her colleagues have to navigate with the newly diagnosed, including judging when to mention potential criminal liability. Staff may 'sigh with relief once the potentially tricky area of criminalisation has been navigated for the first time',[41] but their responsibilities do not end there. The increased life expectancy of those complying with their treatment means that their situations and relationship statuses are likely to change. Whilst 'being ill does not absolve a person of her normal legal and moral responsibilities to other people',[42] following the shock of diagnosis, people may be unable to understand, retain or process such information.[43] Healthcare professionals may be called upon to testify in criminal proceedings – for the prosecution or defence – about the patient's understanding of any advice given.[44] A sense of divided loyalties between their patients and members of the public[45] is not unique to sexual healthcare workers, but Evans argues that the imposition on them is particularly difficult. She explains that the history of HIV and the stigma these patients continue to face has forged a distinct professional sense of self, in particular as protectors of their patients. There is a special relationship between healthcare professionals and their clients, and '[i]t may then feel like a betrayal for those patients and staff to acknowledge that issues of criminalisation, safer sex and partner notification may need to be discussed.'[46]

Globally, there has been a range of approaches to the use of the criminal law in relation to HIV transmission. The first prosecution in Scotland for the sexual transmission of disease for over a century occurred in February 2001, in relation to transmitting HIV.[47] In England and Wales,

---

[41] Evans, Chapter 4, this volume, at 87.

[42] M. Brazier, 'Do no harm – do patients have responsibilities too?' *The Cambridge Law Journal* (2006), 397 at 406.

[43] M. D. Phillips and G. Schembri, 'Narratives of HIV: measuring understanding of HIV and the law in HIV positive patients', *Journal of Family Planning and Reproductive Health Care*, online, 14 January 2015, doi:10.1136/jfprhc-2013–100789.

[44] For a recent study examining the impact of the criminal law on how public health nurses in Ontario record their consultations with HIV positive clients see: C. Sanders, ' "Examining public health nurses" documentary practices: the impact of criminalizing HIV non-disclosure on inscription styles', *Critical Public Health*, 25:4 (2015), 398–409.

[45] See C. Dodds et al., *Keeping Confidence: Responsibility and Public Health* (Sigma Research, 2013).

[46] Evans, Chapter 4, this volume, at 92.

[47] Chalmers, 'Ethics law and medicine'.

the government rejected the proposals of its law reform body[48] to create specific offences of disease transmission on the basis that it was not satisfied that 'it would be right or appropriate to make the range of normal everyday activities during which illness could be transmitted potentially criminal'.[49] In the lacuna that followed, the courts developed the common law on a seemingly *ad hoc* basis, following the Scottish decision. Thus a significant change in criminal law – and indeed public health – was introduced with no discussion, consultation or guidance. Across the world, laws continue to be enacted, most recently in Uganda in 2014[50], and, once passed, tend to 'be sticky'.[51] To date, the only country to de-criminalise HIV transmission is Denmark, where the Minister of Justice suspended its HIV-specific law in 2011.[52] Nevertheless, there have been some reviews of the law and two examples are discussed in this volume.

Following the Danish decision, a Law Commission, chaired by Aslak Syse, was charged with reviewing the Norwegian position. Syse's chapter explores the factual, historical and cultural influences on the responses that different jurisdictions have adopted, and sets out the practical difficulties that his commission faced. Of particular significance is his finding that much of the 'evidence' on which policy is based turned out not to rest on secure foundations ('[w]hat were presented as general "facts" often turn out to be just key persons' personal beliefs, or results from studies that were biased or not representative for other reasons.'[53]) He argues that this, coupled with the limited public discussion of the issue, means that the debate has been dominated by those with a personal interest in the field, many of whom 'seem to function mainly as advocates for a de-criminalisation policy'.[54] Whether or not one agrees with the conclusion of the Norwegian Commission that the criminal law does still have a role to

---

[48] *Legislating the Criminal Code: Offences against the Person and General Principles* (1993) Law Com No 218 (Cm. 2370).

[49] Home Office, *Violence: Reforming the Offences against the Person Act 1861* (London: HMSO, 1998). In the late 1980s, West Midlands Police and the Crown Prosecution Service claimed that they 'were powerless to act' against a man who continued to have sexual relationships with women after he was diagnosed as HIV positive and was accused of deliberately infecting four of them with HIV, one of whom later died of AIDS (*Guardian*, London, 23 June 1992).

[50] The HIV and AIDS Prevention and Control Act 2014. www.hivlawandpolicy.org/sites/www.hivlawandpolicy.org/files/Ugandan-HIV%20Law.pdf.

[51] Wolf, Chapter 6, this volume, at 143.

[52] www.hivjustice.net/news/denmark-justice-minister-suspends-hiv-specific-criminal-law-sets-up-working-group/.

[53] Syse, Chapter 5, this volume, at 101–102.

[54] Ibid., at 101.

play in this context, these concerns are important for the quality and terms of public, scholarly and policymaking debate on this issue.

As Leslie Wolf sets out in her chapter, the United States of America has seen the widespread adoption of statutes criminalising both exposure to and transmission of the HIV virus. Thirty-three states have at least one HIV-specific criminal law, the provisions of which are 'disheartening'[55] in their breadth and disproportionate effects. Reiterating the importance of definitions, she notes the difficulties caused by many of these offences replicating the broad definitions used in sexual offences, thus – probably unintentionally – bringing 'safer sex' practices, such as use of sex toys within their remit. Wolf highlights the difficulties the law has had in keeping pace with improvements in medical and scientific knowledge, for example, eleven states in the United States criminalise spitting or the throwing of bodily fluid, despite the fact that these pose a 'negligible' risk of infection.[56] Most statutes fail to account for prevention measures (only five states include condom use as a defence against reckless transmission). The US Department of Justice has recently issued guidance suggesting that states should review their legislation in light of current scientific knowledge, commenting that:

> While HIV-specific state criminal laws may be viewed as initially well-intentioned and necessary law enforcement tools, the vast majority do not reflect the current state of the science of HIV and, as a result, place unique and additional burdens on individuals living with HIV.[57]

Wolf notes the high level of public support that such statutes enjoy and the practical difficulties in removing them, but is optimistic that there may be changes in the future. She suggests a pragmatic strategy of seeking amendments that are more supportive of public health measures and details an unsuccessful Congressional effort to review this area. The federal government has moved from supporting the use of criminal HIV exposure statutes to calling into question their continued existence. The Iowa legislature has substantially revised its criminal exposure statute and Wolf argues that this provides a model for other states.

---

[55] Wolf, Chapter 6, this volume, at 148.
[56] US Centers for Disease Control and Prevention, 'HIV transmission'. www.cdc.gov/hiv/basics/transmission.html.
[57] US Department of Justice, Civil Rights Division, *Best Practices Guide to Reform HIV-Specific Criminal Laws to Align with Scientifically-Supported Factors* www.hivjustice.net/news/us-department-of-justice-releases-guidance-to-eliminate-or-reform-hiv-criminalisation-laws/.

Further chapters offer detailed critiques of how the law is working in different jurisdictions. Canada is the world leader in HIV transmission prosecutions. Eric Mykhalovskiy's chapter offers a reflexive analysis of his work with activists belonging to two organisations that have led local campaigns against these prosecutions: the Ontario Working Group on Criminal Law and HIV Exposure; and the Canadian HIV/AIDS Legal Network. He uses an institutional ethnography of HIV criminalisation to explore how lawyers and activists responded to the Supreme Court of Canada decision in *Cuerrier*.[58] In this case, it was held that failure by HIV positive individuals to disclose their HIV status can vitiate consent to sexual activity (and thereby cause them to commit a sexual assault) where there is a 'significant risk of serious bodily harm'[59] to their partners, whether or not transmission occurs. As Mykhalovskiy explains, the Court did not draw explicitly on any scientific evidence as to the risks of transmission in coming to its decision. In response to this judgment, the groups sought to intervene in the 'text-mediated relations of criminal law' using 'science-based activism' to assist criminal justice actors with understanding and managing epidemiological notions of risk. This occurred at a time when new and much more effective drug regimens were being introduced that were transforming HIV into a chronic manageable condition and reducing the risk of transmission. The Legal Network produced a widely cited critique of *Cuerrier* that argued for legal assessments of risk to be empirically based which the Supreme Court of Canada considered in the case of *Mabior*.[60] Again this emphasises the importance of acknowledging the politics of criminalisation – and indeed scientific interpretation. The activists had to 'write science for jurists in ways that would not disavow advocacy goals but, at the same time, would not colonise science for political ends',[61] and the Court gave less weight to the data than it did to appeals to the normative Constitutional values of equality, autonomy and human dignity. In addition, Mykhalovskiy argues that '[t]hrough the intersection of activism, science and the criminal law, a novel form of biological citizenship has arisen'[62] among those living with HIV.

None of the decisions around criminalisation is neutral. *Mabior* was unusual in that the Supreme Court of Canada made explicit some of these value judgements. It explained its decision to expand the scope of liability

---

[58] *R v Cuerrier* [1998] 2 SCR 371.
[59] Ibid., para. 129.
[60] *R v Mabior* [2012] 2 SCR 584.
[61] Mykhalovskiy, Chapter 7, this volume, at 164.
[62] Ibid., at 174.

for failing to disclose HIV status to a sexual partner as part of a series of feminist-driven reforms to purge gender stereotypes and misogyny from the law.[63] The Court held that an obligation to disclose HIV positive status protects the autonomy of HIV negative women, who can then decide whether to engage in risky sex. Alana Klein offers a competing feminist account of this decision, arguing that the essentialist account of the Court fails to take into account 'the complex power dynamics where HIV and sex interact'.[64] She emphasises more recent feminist critiques of notions of agency and autonomy and the value of sex as a personal and social good for women. She argues that competing anti-subordination goals and 'the multiple intersecting forms of oppression that women experience'[65] must also be considered. These include the needs of HIV positive women who may fear abandonment or violence upon disclosure, or the threat of the criminal law if their relationship breaks down, even if they used adequate protection. She contends that those who have unprotected sex without knowing their partner's HIV status may be agents choosing to take risks as well as potential victims. Stigmatising only the HIV positive individual undermines notions of shared responsibility, with both the HIV negative partner and wider society. She addresses the scepticism in feminist scholarship about the use of the criminal law to achieve feminist goals, in particular when the effects of these laws are examined in the context of the lives of marginalised women, rather than in the abstract. She concludes that judgments such as those in *Mabior* must explain why they are 'placing a fragile notion of autonomy for HIV negative people ahead of competing anti-subordination goals'.[66]

Rather than introducing specific legislation, jurisdictions such as England and Wales have used pre-existing criminal laws to prosecute intentional and reckless transmission of disease. Karl Laird's chapter explores the evolution of the common law which has enabled prosecutions for disease transmission to be brought under the Offences Against the Person Act 1861. Laird notes that the potentially expansive nature of the common law, which could stretch to encompass all types of disease, has been overlooked, even though the only prosecutions to date have been for sexual transmission. He suggests that this omission is because criminalisation has the greatest effect on minority or 'Other' groups. The focus

---

[63] *Mabior* at paras 46–48.
[64] Klein, Chapter 8, this volume, at 178.
[65] Ibid., at 184.
[66] Ibid., at 200.

on the sexual transmission of disease has meant that important issues have been neglected and that this failure has 'allowed the law to stagnate'.[67] It has allowed policymakers to avoid considering the broader issue of whether disease transmission should be criminalised at all. The current low threshold for the harm caused (any level of risk above *de minimis*) opens 'a broad vista of potential criminal liability'.[68] Prosecutorial discretion plays a significant role and it is for the jury to assess the harm done 'applying contemporary social standards'.[69] Laird examines possible explanations for the exclusive focus on sexually transmitted disease: the problems of proving causation and *mens rea*; the breach of trust not present in non-sexual transmission; and the 'feelings of disgust and shame associated with the transmission of an STD'.[70] Laird concludes, however, that none of these explanations justifies a paradigm whereby only the sexual transmission of diseases is prosecuted. As he argues, '[a]lthough evidential difficulties and the public interest might preclude prosecution in the vast majority of instances of non-STD transmission, it is possible to conceive of circumstances in which prosecution would be both possible and justified'.[71] He concludes that such a complex and policy-laden issue 'is not one that lends itself well to the incremental method of the common law'[72] and emphasises the need to reignite the debate around disease transmission.

We hope that this volume contributes a spark to this process. Bronit argued in 1994 that 'the United Kingdom has not confronted the difficult issues of legal principle and policy surrounding criminal liability for transmitting disease';[73] twenty years later, Mawhinney states that, broadly this remains the case.[74] The United Kingdom is not alone in its failure to address these issues adequately and the time is ripe for a reappraisal of both how the law has developed and how it should treat disease transmission in future.[75]

---

[67] Laird, Chapter 9, this volume, at 228.
[68] Ibid., at 211.
[69] *R v Golding* at [64].
[70] Laird, Chapter 9, this volume, at 214.
[71] Ibid., at 227.
[72] Ibid., at 210–211.
[73] S. Bronit 'Spreading disease and the criminal law', *Criminal Law Review* (1994), 21.
[74] B. Mawhinney, 'To be ill or to kill: the criminality of contagion', *Criminal Law Review* (2013), 202.
[75] We agree with Laird that this is too complex a topic to be left to the common law to develop. As this book went to press, The Law Commission published its report into reforming offences against the person in England and Wales (Law Commission, 'Reform of Offences

Epidemics and illness have recurred throughout history – the Black Death killed an estimated 60 per cent of Europe's population between 1346 and 1353.[76] In First World countries, HIV is now largely treatable but threats remain from the periodic influenza pandemics, Severe Acute Respiratory Syndrome (SARS), Ebola and strains of tuberculosis which are resistant to many of the traditionally used drugs. England's Chief Medical Officer has warned of the danger of antimicrobial resistance which may mean that currently treatable infections become life threatening.[77] The nature and scale of the threat to public health changes but the underlying question remains, namely, what role (if any) should the criminal law have in promoting responsible behaviour and sanctioning those who do not comply with this?

Epidemics and the (re-)emergence of diseases understandably cause panic and distress among the public and policymakers. As Bronit notes, '[g]enerations through the centuries have periodically been threatened with annihilation by the uncontrolled spread of incurable diseases. Community responses to such epidemics are invariably marked by fear, anger, paranoia and a desire to attribute blame for the spread of the disease.'[78] In the United Kingdom and United States in recent years, there has been a tendency to resort to the criminal law when a problem needs addressing[79] and 'knee-jerk reactions to the problem invariably produce poorly drafted provisions which leave many issues unresolved.'[80] This suggests that the thinking should take place 'between the wars' rather than in the face of the latest panic.

---

against the Person' (Law Com No 361 HC 555, 2015) available at: www.lawcom.gov.uk/wp-content/uploads/2015/11/51950-LC-HC555_Web.pdf (accessed 19 November 2015)). It is disappointing that, despite having raised the issue of disease transmission in its scoping paper (Law Commission, Reform of Offences Against the Person: A Scoping Consultation Paper (Consultation Paper No. 217) (HMSO, 2014), chapter 6, 'Transmission of Disease'), the Commission did not have time to consider this issue. It therefore recommended that the present legal position should be preserved in a modified version of the draft bill under consideration, pending any wider review.

[76] For a useful historical and scientific overview of infectious disease see: D. H. Crawford, *Deadly Companions: How Microbes Shaped Our History* (Oxford: Oxford University Press, 2007).

[77] S Davies, *The Drugs Don't Work: A Global Threat* (London: Penguin Books, 2013).

[78] Bronit, 'Spreading disease and the criminal law'. For example, in response to the outbreak, Sierra Leone introduced a criminal offence of hiding an individual suffering from ebola: 'Hiding Ebola patients now a crime in Sierra Leone'. www.dw.de/hiding-ebola-patients-now-a-crime-in-sierra-leone/a-17873804 (accessed 9 October 2014).

[79] J. Chalmers, ' "Frenzied law making": overcriminalization by numbers', *Current Legal Problems*, 67:(1) (2014), 483–502.

[80] Bronit, 'Spreading disease and the criminal law'.

Any decision making needs to begin by interrogating the appropriate role of the criminal law. To start with Weait's contention, is a criminal response appropriate at all? This is not a neutral decision; criminologists have long examined the process and effects of criminalisation and the unequal attention the criminal law gives to the marginalised and the powerful.[81] Nicola Lacey has called for 'a multi-disciplinary criminalisation research agenda informed by history, sociology and political science as much as by law, criminology and philosophy',[82] and each of these disciplines, together with others,[83] undoubtedly has a contribution to make. It is a mark of how topical and complex the issues involved are that after three years, four seminars, three special issues and an edited collection, we find ourselves still intrigued by the subject.

---

[81] See S. Box, *Power, Crime and Mystification* (London: Tavistock, 1983); C. Pantazis 'The problem with criminalisation', *Criminal Justice Matters*, 74: 1 (2008), 10–12; P. Scraton, *Law, Order and the Authoritarian State* (Milton Keynes: Open University Press, 1987); J. Simon *Governing through Crime: How the War on Crime Transformed American Democracy and Created a Culture of Fear* (Oxford: Oxford University Press, 2007).

[82] N. Lacey, 'Historicising criminalisation: conceptual and empirical issues', *The Modern Law Review*, 72 (2009), 936–60.

[83] E. Mykhalovskiy, 'The public health implications of HIV criminalization: past, current, and future research directions', *Critical Public Health*, 25:4 (2015), 373–85, 380.

1

HIV and the Meaning of Harm

MATTHEW WEAIT

Introduction

To date, the approach of scholars and activists interested in the criminalisation of HIV transmission, exposure and non-disclosure has, typically, been to criticise its over-inclusiveness, and to argue that anything other than purposeful transmission (or, in some cases, deliberate attempts to transmit) should not be a criminal offence. Interventions of this kind have, variously, explored principled moral-philosophical objections, doctrinal problems relating to criminal fault requirements and consent, practical evidential issues and, to a somewhat lesser extent, the effects of criminalisation as regards deterrence.[1] It is also fair to say that where these contributions have engaged with public health policy – and many have – the drive has overwhelmingly been to demonstrate that over-extensive criminalisation has, or may have, an adverse impact on HIV prevention efforts and on the lives of people living with HIV (PLHIV).[2]

---

[1] Z. Lazzarini, S. Bray and B. Burris, 'Evaluating the impact of criminal laws on HIV risk behavior', *Journal of Law and Medical Ethics*, 30:2 (2002), 239–53; C. Galletly and L. Pinkerton, 'Conflicting messages: how criminal HIV disclosure laws undermine public health efforts to control the spread of HIV', *AIDS and Behavior*, 10: 5 (2006), 451–61; S. Burris, L. Beletsky, J. Burleson, P. Case and Z. Lazzarini, 'Do criminal laws influence HIV risk behavior? An empirical trial', *Arizona State Law Journal*, 39 (2007), 467–517; M. Kaplan, 'Re-thinking HIV exposure crimes', *Indiana Law Journal*, 87 (2012), 15–17; S. Burris and M. Weait, 'Criminalization and the moral responsibility for sexual transmission of HIV', in N. Priaulx and A. Wrigley (eds.), *Ethics, Law and Society*, Vol. 5 (Farnham: Ashgate, 2013), pp. 133–52.

[2] UNAIDS, *The Criminalization of HIV Transmission: Policy Brief* (Geneva: UNAIDS, 2008); E. Mykhalovskiy, 'The problem of "significant risk": exploring the public health impact of criminalizing HIV non-disclosure', *Social Science & Medicine*, 73 (2011), 670–7; Global Commission on HIV and the Law, *Risks, Rights and Health* (New York: UNDP, 2012).

I would like to thank Hannah Quirk, Elena Loizidou, Daniel Monk and an anonymous reviewer for their comments. Errors of fact and analysis that remain are mine.

This chapter does not rehearse in any detail the arguments that have been made in these contributions. Rather, it tackles a question that is rarely, if ever, addressed explicitly by such scholars: must HIV necessarily be treated as a harm for the purposes of the criminal law? To many, especially those working in the field of HIV criminalisation (a group which includes not only academic lawyers but also international policy experts, activists, virologists, epidemiologists, clinicians and others), this is, paradoxically, both a stale and persistent issue; stale in the sense that it is a question that has been around for as long as people have been subjected to state punishment for transmission, exposure and non-disclosure (more than three decades now), and persistent in that it still exercises those who have advocated against criminalisation, or at least against its more extravagant versions. It exercises because, to put it simply, it is hard to acknowledge the seriously adverse physical, psychological and social impact that HIV may have on people and at the same time to argue against including its (avoidable) transmission within the category of bodily harms with which criminal law has traditionally concerned itself.

At one level the source of this paradox is the fact that the criminalisation of HIV transmission is framed within two seemingly incommensurable 'ways of seeing'. One perspective (the one favoured by most opponents of criminalisation) centres either on the adverse, or potentially adverse, impact that criminalisation may have on prevention efforts and HIV-related stigma and discrimination (a concern that has rested, to date, more on intuitive appeal than on strong empirical evidence,[3] or, at the very least, that criminalisation does no positive good as far as these important matters are concerned. This way of seeing is instrumental in that the objection to criminalisation focuses on what it does, or does not, achieve and/or how it may, or may not, hinder goals and objectives which are seen as more important than the public censure and condemnation of particular individuals.

The other, fundamentally different perspective, is one that draws on a tradition of liberal legal and criminal justice theorising which treats as irrelevant or secondary the instrumental justification or otherwise for criminalisation.[4] Instead, there is a focus on the symbolic and expressive

---

[3] See, however, Lazzarini et al., 'Evaluating the impact'; Galletly and Pinkerton, 'Conflicting messages'; C. Dodds, A. Bourne and M. Weait, 'Responses to criminal prosecutions for HIV transmission among gay men with HIV in England and Wales', *Reproductive Health Matters*, 17:34 (2009), 135–45; Mykhalovskiy, 'The problem of "significant risk"'.

[4] M. Moore, *Placing Blame: A General Theory of the Criminal Law* (Oxford: Oxford University Press, 1997).

dimensions and value of state punishment, and as such is concerned more with the intrinsic or immanent qualities of particular conduct and any consequences that conduct may have. If the conduct poses a sufficiently proximate risk of substantial harm,[5] is sufficiently egregious and unacceptable, or if its consequences sufficiently harmful (understood, for example, as a 'setback' to legitimate interests),[6] criminalisation is *prima facie* justifiable as a matter of principle. It does not matter that the application of the principle in practice as regards specific individuals will typically be subject to the exercise of discretion, or may appear in some cases to be capricious, illogical, or have unintended and unanticipated effects.[7]

While few criminal law theorists have advanced or defended pro-criminalisation arguments explicitly,[8] what these perspectives have in common, though, is an assumption – whether implicitly or explicitly articulated – that HIV is a criminally significant harm. (It is important to recognise, as a reviewer of this chapter noted, that what might be termed generalist criminal law theorists, for whom HIV is understood merely as exemplar of harm, rather than as a public health problem, have been far less sceptical about the legitimacy of criminalisation.) For the instrumentalists, there is no need to question harmfulness as such, since their arguments tend to focus on over-inclusive fault requirements ('only *intentional* transmission should be criminalised'), or on the way criminal law undermines messages of *shared* responsibility, or on the public health impact of criminalisation. None of these arguments requires that the harm of HIV be problematised as such. For their opponents, whose arguments assume that HIV is, in principle, no different from any other form of serious physical injury, the harmfulness of HIV is simply a given. When, for example, Feinberg suggests that harm may be understood in terms of impairment to 'normal functioning' (of an organism), by someone 'invading', and thus setting back, an interest in that functioning, the analysis can only proceed from, and make sense based on, an assumption that there exists something that can be called 'normal functioning'.[9]

I want to question this assumption because I think it is not only necessary, but also progressive, to do so: necessary, for reasons I shall explore

---

[5] R. Duff, 'Criminalizing endangerment', *Los Angeles Law Review*, 65 (2005), 941–65.

[6] J. Feinberg, *Harm to Others* (Oxford: Oxford University Press, 1984).

[7] Cf. D. Husak, *Overcriminalization: The Limits of the Criminal Law* (Oxford: Oxford University Press, 2008).

[8] See, for example, J. Spencer, 'Reckless infection in the Court of Appeal: R v Dica', *New Law Journal* (2004), 762.

[9] Feinberg, *Harm to Others*, 33–4.

in some detail, and progressive because it provides a way not only of re-imagining the way criminal law can and should comprehend the body, but also – potentially – of engaging effectively with the persistent, and seemingly intractable, problem of HIV-related stigma and discrimination. Put briefly, I want to suggest that what the criminal law treats as 'normal' about human bodies is something that should not be taken for granted, or without question. Specifically, I want to suggest that we need not, and should not, treat HIV – an environmental phenomenon that inhabits some people and not others – as something that is abnormal in any morally significant sense; and that we can, and should, cease treating it as an impairment for the purposes of justifying its criminalisation.

Legal Preliminaries

Given the number and variety of jurisdictions in which HIV is criminalised, it is impossible to provide a comprehensive account of the way criminal liability is structured, and other more detailed reviews are available.[10] Nevertheless, a brief overview will help provide a background to the issues explored in this chapter. HIV is typically criminalised in one of two ways, either under a country's general law concerning offences against the person, or under HIV- or disease-specific legislation. First, there may be liability for exposing someone to the risk of infection. For this offence, HIV need not be transmitted, the harm subsisting in the endangerment that the person living with HIV (PLHIV) has caused to another. Second, there may be liability for actually transmitting HIV. Here, the harm is causing the infection. In some jurisdictions, non-disclosure of status is an ancillary but important factor. For example, the Supreme Court of Canada has ruled that to avoid criminal liability for aggravated sexual assault, a PLHIV must disclose her or his status to a partner where there is a 'realistic possibility' of onward transmission.[11]

Where exposure and/or transmission are established, there will, in addition, be a need for proof of fault on the part of the defendant. A person who is unaware of her or his HIV positive status will not be liable,

---

[10] UNAIDS, *Expert Meeting on the Scientific, Medical, Legal and Human Rights Aspects of the Criminalisation of HIV Non-Disclosure, Exposure and Transmission.* (Geneva: UNAIDS, 2011); M. Weait, *The Criminalisation of HIV Exposure and Transmission: A Global Review. Working Paper Prepared for the Third Meeting of the Technical Advisory Group, Global Commission on HIV and the Law,* 7–9 July 2011 (New York: UNDP). www.hivlawcommission.org/index.php/working-papers?task=document.viewdoc&id=90

[11] *R v Mabior* 2012 S.C.C. 47; *R v D.C.* 2012 S.C.C. 48. See Klein, in this volume.

even if there is exposure or transmission, because there will be no legally recognised culpability. Fault may be established, depending on the jurisdiction, by proof that the defendant acted intentionally, recklessly or (more rarely) negligently. The terms mean different things in different legal systems, but intentionally is typically taken to mean 'on purpose', or 'deliberately'; recklessly to mean 'consciously taking an unjustifiable risk'; and negligently as 'breaching a duty of care'. It is relatively rare for defendants to be convicted of intentional transmission (though in exposure cases, knowledge of status is often equated with 'intentionally' exposing someone to risk, and sometimes with an attempt to infect), and far more common for convictions to be based on the defendant's recklessness.[12] In these latter cases, the relevance of condom use and/or effective anti-retroviral treatment (which makes onward transmission extremely unlikely) is significant, especially in exposure allegations.[13]

Where there is proof of exposure or infection, and of the requisite fault, a defendant may in some jurisdictions avoid liability because the complainant consented to the risk of transmission.[14] Such consent will typically be established only if the consent was "willing and conscious" (i.e., a complainant's general knowledge of the risks associated with unprotected sex will not establish the existence of consent – there must be actual knowledge, gained from disclosure by the defendant, or from a third party, that the defendant was living with HIV at the relevant time).[15]

The Body in Criminal Law

It should be self-evident that it is impossible to problematise the concept of bodily harm in criminal law, of which HIV infection is treated as an exemplar, without first engaging with the way in which criminal law conceptualises the body. Unless we are clear about what it is that can be the subject of harm, and what specifically about that thing may be harmed, there can be no critical engagement with the thing that is treated as harmful.

---

[12] For the most up-to-date record of, and legal basis for, criminal cases globally, see GNP+, *Global Criminalisation Scan* (Amsterdam: GNP+, 2010).

[13] M. S. Cohen, M. McCauley and T. R. Gamble, 'HIV treatment as prevention and HPTN 052', *Current Opinion in HIV and AIDS*, 7: 2 (2012), 99–105; M. Loutfy, M. Tyndall, J-G. Baril, J. S. Montaner, R. Kaul and C. Hankins, 'Canadian consensus statement on HIV and its transmission in the context of criminal law', *The Canadian Journal of Infectious Diseases & Medical Microbiology*, 225:3 (2014), 135–40.

[14] For example, *R v Dica* [2004] EWCA Crim 1103 (Court of Appeal, England and Wales).

[15] *R v Konzani* [2005] EWCA Crim 706 (Court of Appeal, England and Wales).

The first observation one might make, at the risk of banality, is that the human body of criminal law has qualities and characteristics that are not only physical and material, but also metaphysical and abstract. The empirically observable human being, made up of organs, muscles and bones, of neural, sensory, immunological, cardio-vascular and other systems and bounded by its skin, constitutes and comprises the material substance of the legal body – one which might variously be understood, depending on the prevailing socio-economic, cultural and political order, as capable of ownership or being owned, as racialised, as sexed and gendered, and as having – or not having – rights and interests, autonomy and integrity. It is not only the legal body whose defining characteristics shift with the times, the physical body onto which those qualities and characteristics are mapped, or in which they inhere, is unstable and contingent too. This is important, as we shall see, for the way harm to that body has been understood and why, as I hope to show, the concept of physical harm is capable of re-imagination and re-definition.

The medieval, pre-modern body, as Deborah Lupton has explained, was – in Europe at least – 'uncontrolled, sensuous, and volatile'.[16] It was understood as porous – as something that leaked things out and soaked things up. It was a body whose morbidity and mortality was determined by the gods, or fate, or the stars. With the coming of what we characterise as Modernity and the distinction between mind and body, this chaotic physicality came to be understood as bounded, individuated and capable of self-regulation through conscious reflection and act of will.[17] As Lupton puts it:

> The progressive change from the open 'grotesque' body to the closed or 'civilised' body ... resulted in the intensification of anxieties about the orifices of the body and what flows in and out of it. When the body was conceptualised as open to the world, as inevitably porous and only weakly subject to the control of the individual, pleasure as well as fear accompanied the flow of forces in and out of the body. The increasing emphasis on self-regulation, the closing off of the body as much as possible, resulted in greater anxiety about the possibility of the loss of self-control and the blurring of boundaries between inside and outside, and self and Other.[18]

This gradual process of individuation and responsibilisation finds articulation in Kant, who, according to Evelyn Fox Keller,[19] was one of the first to

[16] D. Lupton, *Risk* (London: Routledge, 1999), 125.
[17] N. Elias, *The Civilising Process* (Oxford: Blackwell, 1939/1994).
[18] Lupton, *Risk*, 26.
[19] E. F. Keller, *The Century of the Gene* (Cambridge, MA: Harvard University Press, 2000).

define an organism (of which the body is of course an exemplar) as something that was both end and means, properly defined by reference to its autonomous, self-organising properties.[20] It was also a process accompanied by the development of biopolitical technologies (such as statistical measurement of mortality and reproduction) that enabled bodily discipline in the interest of the health of the population,[21] while scientific and medical advances reframed the way that the body came to be understood:

> Under the clinical gaze, the body became a static entity that could be penetrated in order to find the 'real' cause of disease. The modern clinical body hereafter became a bounded living organism, made up of functionally connected components (such as organs and tissues) and internal systems and processes (such as feedbacks, rhythms, and circulations), an organic and functional unity that is at constant risk of disruption by disease.[22]

The body of the nineteenth and twentieth centuries thus came to be conceived of in terms of its stability and systematic unity – as homeostatic and 'molar', a whole rather than the sum of its parts.[23] Disease was something that undermined the unity and integrity of an individuated self, which in turn rendered the efficacy of the body's immune system, vital to combating allogenic threats, a matter of critical importance.[24]

It is this model of the body that has informed, and continues to inform, the criminal legal response to offences against the person. From at least the time of Blackstone, the body has been understood in a molar sense – as discrete and systemically coherent, bounded and differentiated from its environment, and separated from other bodies, by its skin/surface. These material qualities, defining the relevant characteristics of the physical body and limiting its reach, or extent, find normative expression in a legal body against which the 'slightest touching', unless consensual, justified or excused, constitutes an assault,[25] and which – in many jurisdictions – the person inhabiting the body is precluded from allowing others to damage for other than culturally legitimated reasons (such as surgery and sport).

---

[20] T. Sharon, *Human Nature in an Age of Biotechnology: The Case for Mediated Posthumanism* (Dordrecht: Springer, 2014), p. 123.

[21] M. Foucault, *The Birth of the Clinic* (London: Routledge Classics, 2003).

[22] Sharon, *Human Nature in an Age of Biotechnology*, 115.

[23] G. Deleuze and F. Guattari, *A Thousand Plateaus: Capitalism and Schizophrenia* (trans. B. Massumi) (Minneapolis: University of Minnesota Press, 1987).

[24] D. Haraway, 'The biopolitics of postmodern bodies: determinations of self in immune system discourse', in J. Price and M. Shildrick (eds.), *Feminist Theory and the Body: A Reader* (New York: Routledge, 1999), pp. 203–14; R. Esposito, *Immunitas: The Protection and Negation of Life* (Cambridge: Polity Press, 2011).

[25] W. Blackstone, *Commentaries*, Vol. 3 (Chicago: Chicago University Press, 1830/1979).

They are the qualities that, in the liberal legal tradition, are taken to constitute and affirm bodily autonomy, and in critical and feminist legal theory are the markers of (violable) bodily integrity.[26]

Given this, it is small wonder that HIV, against which there currently exists neither vaccine nor cure, is treated as a harm. Even where treatment is available and accessible, PLHIV may experience physically deleterious side effects, and, because of the stigma associated with the condition, experience violence, discrimination and psychological distress. Framed in this way, HIV infection is no different from any of the other kinds of physical injury which societies routinely include within the category of bodily harms and which may form the basis of a criminal charge. Some might even wish to argue that HIV is a particularly serious, if not *the* most, serious of bodily harms: worse than losing a limb, or one's sight or one's mobility – given that physiological integrity and the immunity which sustains it have become so profoundly identified with our understanding of unique selfhood.[27] HIV and the HIV positive person challenge the received assumptions we have about our bodies and how to regulate and defend them from existential threat. It is hardly surprising, then, that the transmission of a virus which – quite literally – breaks down our immunity and compromises our integrity should be something which falls squarely within the sights of criminal law. In legal, political and economic cultures that have come to treat personal autonomy and physical integrity as in some sense factual, as empirically observable truths, HIV reminds us that they are not in fact qualities of the physical and material world but rather theoretically useful phantasms and that HIV poses a threat which is not only physical, but also political, ontological and epistemological.

If this is the case, then the only way of challenging the characterisation of HIV as a criminally significant harm would be to attempt some kind of deconstruction of these fundamental assumptions – a deconstruction that, materially, challenges the way in which we understand and characterise the relationship between our embodied selves and the environment in which we exist, and, existentially, how we describe and analyse action and human subjectivity, both from a legal perspective and otherwise.

---

[26] M. Weait, *Intimacy and Responsibility: The Criminalisation of HIV Transmission* (Abingdon: Routledge, 2007), chapter 3.

[27] A. Tauber and L. Chernyak, *Metchnikoff and the Origins of Immunology: From Metaphor to Theory* (Oxford: Oxford University Press, 1991); A. Tauber, *The Immune Self: Theory or Metaphor* (Cambridge: Cambridge University Press, 1994); T. Pradeu, *The Limits of the Self: Immunology and Biological Identity* (Oxford: Oxford University Press, 2012).

Deconstructing Bodies, Deconstructing Harm

Consider, briefly, the (more or less obvious) criminal legal effects of the tradition of comprehending the individual human body both as molar, in the sense described earlier, and as subject to, and identifiable with, that particular body's mind and will.[28] First and foremost, it is a model that allows for, and justifies, accountability for the actions and conduct of the body and the effects that these produce. Identification between these physical, material, effects, and the will that is their source, is a pre-requisite for translating this accountability into moral responsibility, and *via* this into criminal fault. This much is uncontentious, but it raises two fundamental issues for just adjudication. First, a person alleged to have committed an offence requiring proof of *mens rea* (guilty mind) may deny the existence of that state of mind. In such cases, the only possible way of determining guilt or innocence is inference, based on conduct at the time, and (if available and admissible) other relevant evidence. Second, a person may deny that it was s/he who engaged in the prohibited conduct or was the author of the prohibited consequence. In some cases, this assertion may be refuted by the testimony of others, but in other cases the prosecution may need to rely on the probative value of markers, or traces. These markers may be molar in quality (e.g., teeth marks or fingerprints[29]) or molecular (e.g., DNA or an HIV sub-type[30]).

For my purposes, it is the possibility of molecular analysis and the use of the molecular trace that are significant; first, because they demonstrate the way in which the attribution of criminal responsibility may depend on our ability to analyse the material body at an ever-increasing level of specificity and detail, and to determine the risk (conventionally understood) that it presents to other bodies. Second, the critical relationship between will, act and consequence, on the one hand, and between agency and responsibility, on the other, is problematised. If it is not possible for a person to exercise a purposively directed will to determine whether HIV is transmitted

---

[28] See, generally, E. Grosz, *Volatile Bodies: Toward a Corporeal Feminism* (Sydney: Allen & Unwin, 1994).

[29] S. A. Cole, *Suspect Identities: A History of Criminal Identification and Fingerprinting* (Cambridge, MA: Harvard University Press, 2002).

[30] M. L. Metzker, D. P. Mindell, X.-M. Liu, R. G. Ptak, R. A. Gibbs and D. M. Hillis, 'Molecular evidence of HIV-1 transmission in a criminal case', *Proceedings of the National Academy of Sciences of the United States of America*, 99: 22 (2002), 14292–7; D. I. Scaduto et al., 'Source identification in two criminal cases using phylogenetic analysis of HIV-1 DNA sequences', *Proceedings of the National Academy of Sciences of the United States of America*, 107: 50 (2010), 21242–7.

on those occasions where there is the risk of transmission, or to 'know' whether s/he is exposing another to a risk substantial enough to be legally significant (i.e., where there is a real rather than a merely theoretical risk), then what, if any, is the legitimate basis for holding that person criminally responsible for transmission or exposure? As the Supreme Court of Iowa stated in 2014, allowing the appeal against conviction of Nick Rhoades (who had an undetectable viral load at the relevant time):

> [...] we would not want to deprive a person of his or her liberty on the basis he defendant's actions caused something that can only theoretically occur. Causation must be reasonably possible under the facts and circumstances of the case to convict a person of criminal transmission of HIV in violation of Iowa Code section 709C.1.[31]

Third, molecular analysis demonstrates the way the body lacks bounded integrity and distributes itself in time and place – that it in some sense, leaves itself behind. The body hosting HIV is living with a virus that has been 'left behind' by another body (as indeed is the case with all viruses and other humanly transmissible infections). Fourth, and relatedly, such analysis raises the possibility of exploring what is and is not properly understood as *of* a particular body. Is HIV properly to be understood as 'incorporated', in the sense of being definitional of a particular body, as an integral aspect of its physical identity, or existing independently within it? If the human body is conceived of in this context as simply the environment in which HIV is able to exist, as the biosphere is for the bodies which the virus inhabits, then what, precisely, is it that justifies the allocation to it of a normative quality, to wit 'harmfulness'?

A useful place to start unpacking these important questions is the concept of agency. Jane Bennett,[32] drawing on the actor network theory of Bruno Latour,[33] draws attention to the theoretical and political potential of re-imagining agency as something that extends beyond the human to non-human entities and assemblages of which human beings may, or may not, be a part. Starting from an assertion that agency may be conceived of as 'distributive and composite', she asks: 'Are there not human, biological, vegetal, pharmaceutical, and viral agents?', adding 'Is not the ability to

---

[31] *Rhoades v State of Iowa*, S.C. of Iowa, No. 12–0180.
[32] J. Bennett, 'The force of things: steps towards an ecology of matter', *Political Theory*, 32: 3 (2004), 347–72; J. Bennett, 'The agency of assemblages and the North American blackout', *Public Culture*, 7: 3 (2005), 42–65; J. Bennett, *Vibrant Matter: A Political Ecology of Things* (Durham, NC: Duke University Press, 2010).
[33] B. Latour, *Reassembling the Social – An Introduction to Actor Network Theory*, (Oxford: Oxford University Press, 2005).

make a difference, to produce effects, or even to initiate action distributed among an ontologically diverse range of actors – or actants?'[34] This 'way of seeing', is, of course unsettling to most social scientists, for whom the human being is at the centre of thought, theory and practice and who – while recognising the situatedness of human action – find it difficult to conceive of agency as being something that may be exercised other than through human will (however much that may be constrained by exogenous, environmental factors).

It is even more unsettling perhaps to lawyers and legal theorists who – even more than social scientists – place human beings at the centre of the action, and for whom the moral subject is the self-evident locus of discussions about responsibility, blame and harm. To displace the moral subject and intentionality as the *foci* of analysis is alien and unsettling because it calls into question the causal efficacy of purposively directed will by accepting that the power to make a difference is in fact distributed among a complex and diverse collective of actants and that outcomes are properly understood as the effect(s) of the interaction between these. Opening our mind to this way of thinking is, however, theoretically liberating – especially because (as Bennett affirms) it is an approach that does not *deny* the relevance or significance of human intentionality but rather asks us to acknowledge that this is not, in itself, determinative or decisive. Human beings do have agency, but it is an agency to be understood both as 'the sole and original author of an effect' and as 'vehicle or passive conduit' (someone through whom others act). Similarly, Bennett is keen to emphasise that the 'agency of assemblages … is not the strong kind of agency traditionally attributed exclusively to humans', which would be anthropomorphic, but rather that

> if one looks closely enough, the productive power behind effects is always a collectivity. Not only is human agency always already distributed in tools, microbes, minerals, and sounds, it only emerges as agentic *by way of* a distribution into the 'foreign' materialities its bearers are eager to exclude.[35]

With this in mind, let us return to HIV infection. Where it is the subject of a criminal charge, this is treated as an effect in person Y caused by a human agent X – an outcome that would not have happened but for the act of X. Assuming for the moment that we are dealing with transmission in the context of sexual activity and that there is sufficient evidence that X is (as far as law's logic operates) the source of Y's infection, the only

---

[34] Bennett, 'The agency of assemblages', 446.
[35] Bennett, 'The agency of assemblages', 463, emphasis in original.

other matters with which the law will be concerned are the state of mind of X (knowledge of HIV status, awareness of risk of transmission) and, in some jurisdictions, whether Y consented to the risk of transmission (whether after status disclosure by X or otherwise). If we set aside the mental/psychic states of X and Y at the moment HIV passed from X to Y, and focus specifically on the *material* dimensions of the process of infection, it becomes clear that the isomorphic identification of X's will with Y's infection is absurd. States of mind are not infectious. It is certainly true that X's (and indeed Y's) intentionality, as manifested in bodily movements and sexual preferences, are part of the story, but they are by no means the whole part.

Just as significant, depending on where we wish to focus our attention, is the assemblage comprising not only intentionality but also viral RNA, human DNA, osmotic membranes and dendritic cells (human cells targeted by HIV). To this we might add, and Bennett would surely argue that, there is no reason to exclude them, research laboratories, anti-retroviral drugs, clinical treatment protocols, healthcare systems, Big Pharma, HIV-related stigma and discrimination and any or all of the other institutional, social and economic phenomena and processes that impact on whether X, being a person living with HIV, is more or less likely to be infectious at the moment HIV is provided with the means of moving from his or her body to that of another and so begin its replication.

This way of seeing HIV infection – as an effect of distributive agency – takes us some way towards 'de-harming' HIV, but not all the way because, a pro-criminalisation advocate might well argue, human choice and agency are still implicated, and it is a legitimate moral, political and legal project to allocate responsibility to the human actant but for whom the new infection would not have taken place. However composite agency may be, there is still someone who may, and should be, punished. Let us accept that contention for the moment and agree on the presence of some moral agency and consequent responsibility. Is there a way of countering this?

Over the past two decades or so there has been an increasing interest among social theorists in the concept of trans/posthumanity and the trans/posthuman[36] (hereafter referred to as posthuman/posthumanity). Some scholars have focused on the ways in which the biological concept of 'man' (as we know it) is now so much dead meat, and that properly to understand our place in the world we must acknowledge the technologically intermediated/supplemented/integrated dimensions of much, if not

---

[36] C. Wolfe, *What Is Posthumanism?* (Minneapolis: University of Minnesota Press, 2010).

all, human existence.[37] Others draw attention to the exclusionary and socially marginalising effects of the humanistic ideal of 'the human' as male and Caucasian, not to mention gloriously muscular and disease-free. For scholars in the latter category, pre-eminent among whom is Rosi Braidotti,[38] there is an attractive, materially grounded, optimism (in stark contrast to some posthumanist doom-mongering) which recognises not only the importance of resisting classical humanism's value-laden anthropocentrism, but also the possibility of creating a new ecological politics in which the lived experience of and difference between humans is fully acknowledged, and the world properly understood as home to both the human and non-human. In other words, social theorists should move beyond analysis that prioritises the human and adopt a more holistic, environmentally aware, approach.

For the purposes of my argument here, what interests me about (some) posthumanist theory, including Braidotti's, is the way it complements Bennett's focus on distributive and composite agency and on 'vibrant matter'. Consider, for example, the idea that what characterises the posthuman is the ever-increasing structural elision between the organic human being and technology.[39] This elision may be described in neo-Darwinian evolutionary terms or, as some posthumanists would prefer, as descriptive of the emergent quality of the posthuman, whose identity is not, nor can be, fixed but is only ever in a process of becoming. In this schema, we are all posthuman now because we are all, to a greater or lesser extent, the product or effect of technological, especially medical, intervention. From a historical perspective, many of us here would not be alive but for penicillin and the early twentieth century advances in obstetrics and gynaecology that secured the births and health of our foremothers and of us; and thinking in contemporary terms, there are many who owe their health and lives to drugs, transfusions and transplants, who can see because of glasses and contact lenses, hear because of auditory aids and have mobility because of wheelchairs and prostheses. (The same observations could be made, of course, with respect to the improved nutrition provided by artificial fertilisers and genetically modified foodstuffs.)

---

[37] D. Haraway, *Simians, Cyborgs and Women: The Reinvention of Nature* (New York: Routledge, 1991), Haraway, 'The biopolitics of postmodern bodies'; M. More and N. Vita-More, *The Transhumanist Reader: Classical and Contemporary Essays on the Science, Technology, and Philosophy of the Human Future* (Oxford: Wiley-Blackwell, 2014).

[38] R. Braidotti, *The Posthuman* (Cambridge: Polity, 2013).

[39] Haraway, *Simians, Cyborgs and Women*.

The point is that it becomes increasingly difficult, if we adopt this way of seeing, to characterise human life (a particularly vivid form of Bennett's 'vibrant matter') as anything other than a composite, contingent, assemblage;[40] it is certainly not 'natural' (whatever that means). More significantly, it seems to me, that this assemblage must logically comprise not only the inorganic and organic pharmaceutical, nutritional and other supports upon which many human beings rely but those other elements, or actants, for whom we (*homo sapiens*) provide the environment in which existence and replication is possible. If we are willing to accept, as posthuman and actor network theorists urge us in their different ways, to think of ourselves as constituents (albeit important ones) in a complex ecology, then a number of things seem to follow.

We would have to accept, for example, that the 'normal' body is far from the ideal body of the humanist imaginary. Rather, the normal body is composite and contingent. Comprising both life-sustaining and life-compromising elements, or actants, to speak of the normal body as having integrity may be normatively attractive (and necessary, so far as traditional jurisprudential analysis is concerned) but is empirically false insofar as it claims to describe something pure and 'essentially' human. Put another way, human life – and the quality of that life for any particular individual – are ecological effects. Just as human life is dependent on, and potentially threatened by, the interaction of ecological phenomena, so those ecological phenomena are dependent on, and threatened by, us.

All of this brings us back to the original question of whether it is possible to question the harmfulness of HIV. There is, of course, no question that HIV compromises human life. To suggest otherwise would be absurd. Does it follow, however, that because it has this effect, this is sufficient for it to be defined as a harm with which the criminal law should be concerned? Setting aside for the moment the political or moral desirability of doing so, I think it may be possible and the argument, drawing on the material discussed in this chapter, would go something like this.

Human beings are composite entities. In both evolutionary and physiological terms, their existence has depended on and been affected (both

---

[40] Although the focus is different, this characterisation resonates with the position of 'holistic' or co-constructionist biologists concerned with finding ways of integrating molecular and evolutionary biology through a more expansive, environmentally responsive, definition of the organism (see, e.g., R. Lewontin, *The Triple Helix: Gene, Organism, and Environment* (Cambridge, MA: Harvard University Press, 2000); S. Gilbert, and D. Epel, *Ecological Developmental Biology: Integrating Epigenetics, Medicine, and Evolution* (Sunderland, MA: Sinauer Associates, 2008)).

advantageously and otherwise) by the environment in which they live. That environment comprises entities and institutions, simple and complex, which in varying and often unpredictable ways combine to produce effects and may therefore be described as actants. Agency is thus distributive. Human beings are actants to the extent that they have the capacity to, and do in fact, contribute to the production of such effects; but at this level of analysis they are no more and no less actants than anything else which have the capacity to, and do in fact, make such a contribution. Human life is not merely composite; it is itself an effect of distributive agency.

HIV is an actant. All existing HIV infections are an effect of the ecological assemblage of which HIV is a necessary but insufficient component. Any new HIV infection will be an effect, not merely of human agency and interaction, but of the existence, availability, accessibility and deployment of prevention and treatment technologies. These, in turn, are effects of political will and economic resource. From this perspective, new HIV infections are an effect of distributive agency.

All human life, and therefore each and every human being, is a composite effect of distributive agency. Thus, the 'normal' human body is composite and ecologically mediated and determined. The bodies of people living with HIV are merely composite in a different way from those not living with HIV, just as those able to manage their HIV and be less infectious because of pharmacological support are composite in a different way from those without that support. People living with HIV are normal, in this sense, in the same way that people living without HIV are normal.

Criminal law has treated HIV transmission as harmful conduct because it meets its criterion of serious physical interference. However, it is important to stress two important dimensions to this way of seeing. First, to those who might object that the argument advanced here is one that would in principle de-criminalise all forms of physical interference, I would suggest that there is, or could be argued to be, a qualitative difference between intentionally or recklessly using one's fist or a weapon to injure, and engaging in conduct that carries with it the risk of a naturally occurring infection being transmitted by and between people. There is, arguably, a much more direct relationship between a person's will and his/her actions in the former case than there is in the latter. Injuries caused by shooting, stabbing or punching are not, as I would suggest, an ecological or environmental phenomenon, which is the way I believe we should conceive the altered state which HIV infection represents. There are, admittedly, difficult cases, identified by a reviewer of this chapter. One (exemplified in the US case of *State v Schmidt* 771 So.

2d 131) concerns a physician who injected blood infected with HIV into a patient (his ex-girlfiend). The reviewer wondered whether the argument advanced here meant that we should ignore the fact of the HIV transmission and merely focus on the puncture wound – an approach that would bring the law into disrepute. My response to this has to be yes – we should ignore the fact that HIV was transmitted. What makes this culpable conduct need not be the fact of infection – we could perfectly well conceive of a criminal offence that focused on the perpetrator's heinous moral state at the time of acting. Indeed, this *is* what makes his conduct culpable – if he had not known the syringe contained HIV there could be no criminal liability, and yet the infection would still have occurred. What makes it a criminal 'harm' is not, therefore, the HIV infection but the thought processes of the defendant. It is worth remembering here that a particular physical act or course of conduct that is constructed as a harm may be identical to one that is of no interest whatsoever to the criminal law in other areas too. A cutting, sexual penetration, or the appropriation of property become an offence against the person, rape, theft or obtaining by deception only if certain contextual conditions, including the state of mind of the cutter, penetrator or appropriator, are also co-present. It follows that what we think of as harmful in criminal law is properly understood as a product of moral agency: it is the manner of its production that renders it so.

To summarise: what makes HIV a harm is not HIV *per se* but the moral context in which the infection occurs. Or, put another way, what makes an innately value-free fact in the world (a new infection) a legally significant harm is (1) the elision we choose to make, or the relationship we choose to construct, between the physiological and the normative dimensions of this altered state and (2) the analytical and theoretical prioritisation of human subjectivity and intentionality.

Concluding Observations

The admittedly provocative argument advanced in this chapter has two differing, but complementary, objectives. First, it offers a limited contribution to current theoretical scholarship in the wider field of biopolitics. Those working in this area have drawn our attention to the ways in which recent scientific and medical advances have changed the way we understand the human body and, indeed, 'life itself'. Genetic and other nano-technologies have only begun to impact on traditional bioethics[41]

41 Wolfe, *What Is Posthumanism?*

and their longer-term discursive and political effects can only be guessed at. It seems to me to be both important, and timely, that theorists begin to engage with their impact on the doctrinal assumptions and presuppositions of criminal, and other areas, of law. In a molecular world, questions such as those explored here could, and should, be complemented with others addressing issues such as the nature of legal subjectivity, responsibility and fault, as well as their implications for procedure and evidence (especially expert scientific evidence).[42]

Second, the essay has, categorically, not sought to suggest that HIV does not for many result in illness and death, nor that it does not contribute to economic loss in regions where it is endemic, nor that its effective treatment is a significant financial burden for countries. In these senses of course it is harmful. Simply because something has these effects, however, does not in and of itself justify treating it as *necessarily* a harm for the purposes of criminal law. We know that alcohol and cigarettes heighten the risk of cirrhosis and lung cancer; we know that excess salt, sugar and fat in processed foods contribute to obesity, diabetes and heart disease. Although countries regulate the availability and accessibility of these things through pricing, taxation, licensing and so on, there are few (other than for religious reasons as far as alcohol is concerned) that criminalise their sale or purchase. Criminalisation of HIV is a choice, and what I hope to have done in this chapter is at least to have provoked some questions as to the assumed justification for that choice. It may be that we, as moral subjects in community, wish publicly to denounce those who, living with HIV, lie to, and deceive, others as an indirect consequence of which HIV is passed on; but there may be stronger arguments for criminalising the lie and the deception than the fact of transmission. We may also be better served by putting our efforts into the prevention and elimination of HIV through evidence-based public health initiatives, rather than into the denunciation of a small minority of individuals whose criminalisation perpetuates the stigma and shame that impedes those efforts. HIV serves to demonstrate that the bodily integrity assumed by the criminal law is illusory. As to moral integrity, that is something else entirely.

[42] T. Lemke, *Bio-Politics: An Advanced Introduction* (New York: New York University Press, 2011).

2

Crime and Disease: Contagion by Metaphor

MICHAEL HANNE

To see, as we do in many of the cases cited in this volume, the actions of a person known to be suffering from a serious, indeed potentially terminal, physical illness such as HIV-AIDS being categorised as criminal is, in principle, deeply shocking. On further investigation, however, it becomes clear that there has always been a close association between the concepts and categories 'illness' and 'crime' and that our thinking, and so our public policies, in the two domains run closely parallel. This chapter explores the nature of the association between them, employing a range of disciplinary perspectives. In addition, it highlights the extent to which an uncritical use of metaphor around both 'crime' and 'disease' contributes to a worrisome tendency towards a collapse of the conceptual boundary between the two domains.

The Shifting Boundary between Illness and Crime

As sociologists since Talcott Parsons in the 1950s have pointed out, illness and crime are regarded by most societies as forms of social deviance, in the sense that those who are sick and those who commit crimes disrupt normal social functioning in ways which are considered undesirable.[1] Correction of both kinds of deviance, as far as that is possible, is seen as a priority in most societies. Of course, the deviance of those who are sick is in most cases socially sanctioned, whereas the deviance of those who commit crimes is not.[2] Indeed, we often use the terms in a contrastive way, for instance, in judicial decisions about whether a person should or should not be held criminally responsible on the basis of their mental

---

[1] See, for instance, G. L. Weiss and L. Lonnquist, *The Sociology of Health, Healing, and Illness* (Upper Saddle River, NJ: Prentice Hall, 2003), especially chapter 7.
[2] A. C. Twaddle, 'Illness and deviance', *Social Science and Medicine*, 7 (1973), 751–62 at 755; P. Conrad and J. Schneider, *Deviance and Medicalization: From Badness to Sickness* (Philadelphia: Temple University Press, 2012).

health for the act which brings them before the court. Debate in such cases has become increasingly complex.[3]

As this last point suggests, it is not just that sickness and crime are close neighbours, but that the boundary between the two categories has been fluid over time and across cultures; interactions between the categories have been frequent and varied. Anthropologists, theologians, historians, political scientists and sociologists have much to say about the overlap between thinking around sickness and thinking around crime.[4]

Blaming for Illness

In certain cultures and eras, sickness has been seen as stemming primarily from the commission of some kind of offence. In many indigenous cultures, sickness is viewed as the consequence either of the infringement of a taboo by the sick person or a member of their family or of a curse uttered by an enemy.[5] It was a fundamental tenet of ancient Jewish thought that sickness, whether individual or in epidemics, was a punishment sent by God for impurity or sin (Leviticus 26:21, 25; Numbers 16:49 and 25:9; Deuteronomy 28:22). Leprosy was singled out as unclean and a punishment for sin (Leviticus 3 and 14).[6,7] In the Christian Middle Ages, syphilis,

---

[3] T. R. Medina and A. McCranie, 'Layering control: medicalization, psychopathy, and the increasing multi-institutional management of social problems', in B. A. Pescosolido, J. K. Martin, J. D. McLeod and A. Rogers (eds.), *Handbook of the Sociology of Health, Illness, and Healing: A Blueprint for the Twenty-First Century* (New York: Springer, 2011), pp. 139–62.

[4] An outstanding recent example of a collection of essays which explores this overlap from a historical perspective, and in contexts ranging from nineteenth-century London to Nazi Germany and contemporary China is R. Peckham (ed.), *Disease and Crime: A History of Social Pathologies and the New Politics of Health* (New York; Abingdon; Oxon: Routledge, 2014).

[5] See, for instance, R. Griffith Jones, 'Rongoa Maori and primary health care', unpublished Master of Public Health thesis, University of Auckland, 2000, pp. 25–7 on understandings of the origins of sickness in traditional Maori society.

[6] Kerri Inglis's chapter in this volume refers in detail to the mix of motives, treatment and punishment, with which leprosy was handled in Hawai'i from the mid-nineteenth century to the mid-twentieth century.

[7] It should be noted that those biblical commentators who, in other respects, insist on a literal interpretation of the text, tend to reframe the Bible's clear identification of leprosy with sin as a merely metaphorical relationship. So, on a website entitled 'The Bible Says' (http://biblesays .faithsite.com/content.asp?CID=23981, accessed 18 May 2015) James T. Heron, in an article entitled 'Comparing Leprosy and Sin' declares: 'Leprosy is a physical disease, while sin is a spiritual disease … Sin, like leprosy, is contagious … Sin, like leprosy, is deceptive' to which James C. Guy adds: 'Leprosy was one of the most highly feared diseases in times of old, and still is in many places. The similarities to sin are interesting. If only sin were feared as much as leprosy!' See also the blog by Mike Boldea, entitled 'The Leprosy of Sin', *Homeward Bound* (Friday 22 May 2009). http://Mikeboldea.Blogspot.Com/2009/05/Leprosy-of-sin.html (accessed May 2015).

too, was viewed as retribution for sin.[8] In the modern period, such a belief has persisted among some religious groups in relation to HIV-AIDS, especially when it first manifested itself in the early 1980s in the male homosexual community in the United States. American preacher Jerry Falwell insisted that 'AIDS is not just God's punishment for homosexuals, it is God's punishment for the society that tolerates homosexuals.'[9] More generally, it has been observed that stigma attaches to certain groups of physically ill people, as it does to criminals.[10] Stigma is usefully defined by Link and Phelan as involving 'labeling, stereotyping, separation, status loss, and discrimination' in a context where power is exercised.[11] Sick people often report that they find themselves labelled as 'outsiders'.[12] The experience of stigma may well have a further negative effect on health.[13]

What makes the question of blame around illness more complicated today is the increasing realisation that individual choices (to smoke, to eat badly, not to exercise enough, to use alcohol and other drugs to excess, to have unprotected sex) do indeed contribute greatly to poor physical health.[14] Although such behaviours are not generally referred to as 'criminal', those who undertake them may reasonably be held in part 'responsible' for their illness. There is, however, a danger that we will over-blame those who get sick for their plight. It appears that prejudice is particularly strong against those whose illness is severe and deemed to have been behaviourally caused.[15] As Richard Gunderman points out, even among medical professionals, there is an extraordinary tendency to

---

[8] G. FitzGerald, 'The punishment of God: social reactions to syphilis in the works of Hutten, Fracastoro, Clowes and Lowe'. http://velascoberenguer.blogspot.co.nz/2011/05/punishment-of-god-social-reactions-to.html (accessed May 2015)

[9] R. S. McElvaine, *Grand Theft Jesus: The Hijacking of Religion in America* (New York: Random House, 2013), p. 35.

[10] It was Erving Goffman, in his book, *Stigma: Notes on the Management of Spoiled Identity* (New York: Prentice Hall, 1963), who really opened up the topic of stigma for social science research. For an overview of the rich field of research on social stigma since Goffman, see B. G. Link and J. C. Phelan, 'Conceptualizing stigma', *Annual Review of Sociology*, 27 (2001), 363–85.

[11] Link and Phelan, 'Conceptualizing stigma', 363.

[12] Early work on this topic was undertaken by H. S. Becker, *Outsiders: Studies in the Sociology of Deviance* (New York: Free Press, 1963). For a quite recent overview of research in the field since Becker see B. Major and L. T. O'Brien, 'The social psychology of stigma', *Annual Review of Psychology*, 56 (February 2005), 393–421.

[13] Major and O'Brien, 'The social psychology of stigma', 420.

[14] See, for instance, M. Minkler, 'Personal responsibility for health? A review of the arguments and the evidence at century's end', *Health Education and Behavior*, 26 (1999), 121–41 at 121.

[15] C. S. Crandall and D. Moriarty, 'Physical illness stigma and social rejection', *British Journal of Social Psychology*, 34 (1995), 67–83.

blame patients unreasonably, for instance, for their 'failure to respond to therapies which, from the physician's point of view, should have worked'. He cites case notes which state that a woman with breast cancer 'failed the standard breast cancer protocol, subsequently failed our newest investigational protocol, most recently failed autologous bone marrow transplantation, and now presents for palliative care with widely metastatic disease'.[16] Indeed, surgeons conventionally refer to surgical instruments or swabs that they have mistakenly left inside a patient during an operation as having been 'retained' by the patient, as if he or she could be blamed even for that![17]

Crime Seen as Stemming from Disease

Alongside the tendency to view disease as, in some sense, stemming from a sin, or crime, or the inadequacy of the patient, there has been a tendency also to see crime as stemming from some sort of disease. Most notorious was the assertion of late-nineteenth-century psychiatrist Cesare Lombroso, widely accepted at the time, that criminals are distinguished by physical anomalies (which he interestingly named *stigmata*), consisting of abnormal forms or dimensions of the skull and jaw, asymmetries in the face as well as of other parts of the body).[18] In the 1920s, speculative research suggested that much crime might be caused by physical, as well as mental, illness.[19] Modern genetic research, employing rather more reliable scientific principles, examines the extent to which the predisposition to criminality may be genetically determined.[20] There has been discussion, too, about whether people experiencing such degenerative conditions as Huntington's Disease are more prone than others to commit crime.[21]

---

[16] R. Gunderman, 'Illness as failure: blaming patients', *The Hastings Center Report*, 30: 4 (July–August 2000), 7–11 at 8.

[17] A. A. Gawande, D. M. Studdert, E. J. Orav, T. A. Brennan and M. J. Zinner, 'Risk factors for retained instruments and sponges after surgery', *New England Journal of Medicine*, 348 (2003), 229–35.

[18] C. Beccalossi, 'Sexual deviances, disease and crime in Cesare Lombroso and the Italian school of criminal anthropology', in Peckham, *Disease and Crime*, pp. 40–55.

[19] L. L. Stanley, 'Disease and crime', *Journal of the American Institute of Criminal Law & Criminology*, 14: 1 (May 1923), 103–9.

[20] D. W. Denno, 'Revisiting the legal link between genetics and crime', *Law and Contemporary Problems*, 69 (2006), 209–57; N. Rafter, *The Criminal Brain, Understanding Biological Theories of Crime* (New York: New York University Press, 2008).

[21] P. Jensen, K. Fenger, T. Bolwig and S. A. Sorensen, 'Crime in Huntington's disease: a study of registered offences among patients, relatives, and controls', *Journal of Neurology, Neurosurgery, and Psychiatry*, 65: 4 (October 1998), 467–71.

There have, nevertheless, been many critiques, by philosophers from Anthony Flew in the 1950s onwards, of the notion that crime should be regarded as a symptom of disease, in the sense of its deriving from the mental disorder of an individual. In his classic article, Flew asserted that clinicians often tacitly adopt a form of determinism in individual cases, in effect denying that their patients have been able to exercise any free will. He pointed out that such a belief has major implications for social and penal policy.[22] Mariana Valverde explores the related question of the role of free will in cases of alcoholism.[23] On a rather different track is research suggesting that the occurrence of infectious disease may actually contribute to the occurrence of property crimes and violent crimes. In a fascinating article, Shrira, Wisman and Webster argue that '[u]nder persistent disease threat, xenophobia increases and people constrict social interactions to known in-group members.' In such circumstances, they suggest, inhibitions against harming and exploiting out-group members are reduced.[24]

There has been much discussion, too, in a range of disciplines, about forms of correlation other than direct causal linkage, between sickness and crime. So Robert Peckham has drawn attention to the way in which disease and crime were often seen in nineteenth-century Britain as having common origins in derelict and dirty living conditions. 'As the century progressed, disease and crime came to be increasingly located through the visualization of unsettled and unsettling metropolitan places and spaces.'[25] Current research in urban areas of Europe likewise shows a strong correlation between neighbourhood violent crime, poverty and potentially fatal conditions such as coronary heart disease.[26]

Social Roles and Gatekeeping in Relation to Sickness and Crime

It was Talcott Parsons again who first drew attention to the way in which we attach distinct social roles to those in each domain, attributing a 'sick

---

[22] A. G. Flew, 'Crime or disease', *The British Journal of Sociology*, 5: 1 (March 1954), 49–62.

[23] M. Valverde, *Diseases of the Will: Alcohol and the Dilemmas of Freedom* (Cambridge: Cambridge University Press, 1998).

[24] I. Shrira, A. Wisman and G. D. Webster, 'Guns, germs, and stealing: exploring the link between infectious disease and crime', *Evolutionary Psychology*, 11: 1 (2013), 270–87, at 270.

[25] Peckham, 'Pathological properties: scenes of crime, sites of infection', in Peckham, *Disease and Crime*, p. 56.

[26] See, for instance, a study undertaken in Stockholm: K. Sundquist, H. Theobald, M. Yang, X. Li, S-E. Johansson and J. Sundquist, 'Neighborhood violent crime and unemployment increase the risk of coronary heart disease: a multilevel study in an urban setting', *Social Science & Medicine*, 62 (2006), 2061–71.

role' to those who deviate in one direction and a 'criminal role' to those who deviate in the other. In both cases, the role is, to a considerable extent, learned by individuals as they interact with the health system and the judicial system, respectively.[27] The attribution by society of a 'sick role' to the person experiencing illness imposes obligations and controls on those who become ill, just as the attribution of a 'criminal role' does on those convicted of crimes. The person who claims to be sick must be genuinely ill, is obliged to seek treatment, and, most importantly, is obliged to do their best to avoid transmitting the disease.[28] Failure to fulfil this last obligation is blameworthy and may be deemed criminal. Such a failure is, in a sense, at the heart of the issues discussed in this volume.

Both the sick and the criminal are crucially subject to gatekeepers, who define their status and control their actions: medical professionals serve as gatekeepers for the sick; and the police, the judiciary, and even juries serve a similar function in relation to those deemed criminal. In both cases, a significant degree of social control is exercised. (It should be noted that both sets of gatekeepers are concerned equally with admitting and with discharging the individuals in their care.) The two groups of gatekeepers are increasingly in competition over the boundary between their realms:

> Now, the criminal justice system and medical profession compete for this authority – contending that their own definition over actions is the more proper. Behaviors once thought criminal can now be medicalized, ushered into the realm of medicine, and removed from their criminal implication by being redefined as a medical pathology. As the medical field grows and the criminal justice system defends its legitimacy – a contested space is created; actions can now become medicalized or criminalized.[29]

Of course, medical practitioners interact with the penal system in other ways, too: treating prisoners for both physical and mental conditions and advising on whether prisoners have undergone sufficient psychiatric rehabilitation to merit parole.[30] Astonishing as it may seem to people living in other jurisdictions, doctors assist, in some US states, in the administration of lethal injections in judicial executions, despite warnings from the American Medical Association that to do so is unethical.[31]

---

[27] T. Parsons, *The Social System* (Glencoe, IL: Free Press, 1951).

[28] W. Cockerham, *Medical Sociology*, 11th edition (Upper Saddle River, NJ: Prentice Hall, 2010).

[29] http://thesocietypages.org/sociologylens/2011/11/10/illness-or-deviance-a-contested-space-between-criminal-justice-and-medicine/

[30] L. Birmingham, S. Wilson and G. Adshead, 'Prison medicine: ethics and equivalence', *The British Journal of Psychiatry*, 188 (2006), 4–6.

[31] L. Black and R. M. Sade, 'Lethal injection and physicians: state law vs medical ethics', *JAMA*, 298:23 (19 December 2007), 2779–80. See also J. L. Groner, 'The Hippocratic

Medicalisation (and Demedicalisation) of Deviant Behaviour

The boundary between sickness and crime is especially blurred in relation to conditions and behaviours which have an obviously psychological dimension, for instance, actions resulting from psychosis or other major forms of psychiatric disorder, whether long-term or short-term.[32] Moreover, certain behaviours and conditions have oscillated historically between the two categories. Homosexual acts were, for many generations in the West, regarded in some contexts as a crime (and in some religious contexts as a sin) and in others as an illness. Indeed, the first two editions of the *Diagnostic and Statistical Manual of Mental Disorders* (DSM), published from 1952 to 1974, defined homosexuality as a more or less treatable medical condition at a time when, in many of the countries where the manual was used, homosexual acts were also still illegal. Yet homosexuality is now regarded in most Western countries as neither criminal nor a disease, though it is estimated that over seventy countries worldwide have laws prohibiting homosexual acts, and many even prohibit education which treats homosexuality as 'normal'.[33] On another front, there is vigorous debate in many countries about whether it is more appropriate for those addicted to drugs to be treated as criminals or as sick people.[34] The Secretary General of the United Nations Ban Ki-moon took a clear stand on this at the launch of the 2011 World Drug Report, when he declared: 'Drug-dependent people should not be treated with discrimination; they should be treated by medical experts and counsellors. Drug addiction is a disease, not a crime.'[35]

---

paradox: the role of the medical profession in capital punishment in the United States', *Fordham Urban Law Journal*, 35 (2008), 883–917; T. Alper, 'The truth about physician participation in lethal injection executions', *North Carolina Law Review*, 11 (2009), 11–70 and http://bigstory.ap.org/article/oklahoma-execution-renews-debate-doctors-role (accessed 18 May 2015).

[32] J. J. Brent, 'Illness or deviance: a contested space'. http://thesocietypages.org/sociologylens/2011/11/10/illness-or-deviance-a-contested-space-between-criminal-justice-and-medicine/. One of the standard modern texts to treat this topic is P. Conrad and J. Schneider, *Deviance and Medicalization: From Badness to Sickness* (Philadelphia: Temple University Press, 2012).

[33] http://76crimes.com/76-countries-where-homosexuality-is-illegal/ (accessed May 2015).

[34] See, for instance R. McCray, 'Treating addiction as a disease, not a crime', American Civil Liberties Union, Blog of Rights, 23 May 2012. www.aclu.org/blog/criminal-law-reform-prisoners-rights/treating-addiction-disease-not-crime (accessed May 2015).

[35] United Nations, 'UN Secretary General: drug addiction a disease, not a crime', *United Nations, Regional Information Centre for Western Europe*, 23 June 2011. www.unric.org/en/drugs/27033-un-secretary-general-drug-addiction-a-disease-not-a-crime (accessed May 2015).

One might suppose that for a society to reassign a behaviour from the category of 'crime' to the category of 'disease' would be bound to indicate a greater degree of leniency towards it, but that is not necessarily the case. To be deemed 'not guilty by reason of insanity' for the killing of another person will, in many First World nations, result in incarceration in a psychiatric hospital for an indeterminate period, whereas conviction for murder might have resulted in imprisonment for a fixed period.[36] On a very different level, some totalitarian societies, including the former Soviet Union and the current People's Republic of China, have classified various forms of opposition to the government/party line as evidence of mental disorder, rather than as a criminal act – let alone reasonable political behaviour.[37] Such people are thereby prevented from defending their actions in a court of law. To categorise individuals as sick permits the state to control them in ways and to a degree which sending them for criminal trial does not.

Inconsistency in Prosecutions for Spreading Disease

It is worth noting that criminal prosecutions relating to the transmission of infectious diseases are initiated much more often in the individual-to-individual context – as in all the cases referred to in the other chapters of this book – than in relation to actions by corporations, governments or international organisations, which actually damage the health of considerably larger numbers of people. So, though pharmaceutical companies and governments which continued to distribute blood products after they realised that those products could be infected with HIV and Hepatitis C have in some countries been belatedly required to pay civil damages to those infected or their families, the number of criminal prosecutions for these acts has been tiny (see the film *Bad Blood: A Cautionary Tale*).[38] Similarly, Haitians have had the greatest difficulty in obtaining any admission from the United Nations of its responsibility for the cholera epidemic brought

[36] J. Rodriguez, L. LeWinn and M. Perlin, 'The insanity defense under siege: legislative assaults and legal rejoinders', *Rutgers Law Journal*, 14 (1983), 397–430 offered an outstanding early study of this topic and a recent review of theory and practice is to be found in R. Mackay, 'Mental disability at the time of the offence', in L. Gostin, J. McHale, P. Fennell, R. D. Mackay and P. Bartlett (eds.), *Principles of Mental Health Law and Policy* (Oxford: Oxford University Press, 2010), pp. 721–56.

[37] R. Munro, *China's Psychiatric Inquisition: Dissent, Psychiatry and the Law in Post-1949 China* (London: Wildy Simmonds and Hill, 2006).

[38] *Bad Blood: A Cautionary Tale*, 2010. Film directed by Marilyn Ness. http://badblooddocumentary.com/ (accessed May 2015).

to their country by Nepalese troops stationed there under the aegis of the United Nations after the 2010 earthquake and have, to date, received no compensation for it.[39] It has been argued that the prevalence of cholera in Africa should be treated as a crime against humanity, in that failure on the part of First World nations to introduce measures to treat and prevent the disease represents 'one feature of an ongoing policy of genocide.'[40] On the other hand, it should be noted that many Western organisations have recently made large financial and professional contributions to the development of strategies for the prevention and treatment of cholera.[41] On a rather different front, while some governments, both national and local, are seeking to limit the distribution of foods and beverages overloaded with fats and sugars, which undoubtedly contribute greatly to the incidence of heart disease, diabetes and other diet-related diseases, none has taken criminal proceedings against their manufacturers.[42] Writer for the *New York Times* N. Cristof highlighted the anomaly posed by this inaction in the memorable statement: 'Imagine if Al Qaeda had resolved to attack us not with conventional chemical weapons but by slipping large amounts of high fructose corn-syrup into our food supply. That would finally arouse us to action – but in fact it's pretty much what we are doing to ourselves.'[43] Overstated though this statement may be, it highlights the tendency for blame around factors negatively affecting human health to be attached disproportionately to individuals rather than to corporations or governments or economic and social systems.

Having demonstrated something of the diversity and fluidity of relations between our notions of disease and of crime, this chapter now approaches its central topic: the argument that metaphor plays a major part in the association of disease with crime.

---

[39] D. S. Kemp, 'Should the United Nations be liable for the Haiti cholera epidemic?' *Verdict – Legal Analysis and Commentary from Justia*, 21 October 2013. http://verdict.justia .com/2013/10/21/united-nations-liable-haiti-cholera-epidemic; C. Krishnaswami, 'The United Nations' shameful history in Haiti: "Cholera is a crime against humanity!"' *Slate* 19 August 2013. www.slate.com/articles/news_and_politics/foreigners/2013/08/united_ nations_caused_cholera_outbreak_in_haiti_its_response_violates_international.html (accessed May 2015).

[40] L. K. Freeman, 'Cholera in Africa today is a crime against humanity: it is genocide', EIR, 22 July 2011. www.larouchepub.com/eiw/public/2011/eirv38n28-20110722/46-50_3828.pdf (accessed May 2015).

[41] See, for instance, the work of the Taskforce for Global Health. www.taskforce.org/our-work/ projects/coalition-cholera-prevention-and-control-ccpc

[42] See the discussion of this topic in the chapter by Matthew Weait in this volume.

[43] N. Cristof, 'Mike Huckabee lost 110 pounds. Ask him how', *New York Times* (4 February 2006).

Conceptual Metaphors and Public Policy

Since the ground-breaking work of linguist George Lakoff and philosopher Mark Johnson almost thirty-five years ago, it has been widely recognised that the metaphors we employ around any topic not only reflect, but even shape, the way in which we conceptualise, and so behave around, that topic: 'Our ordinary conceptual system, in terms of which we both think and act, is fundamentally metaphorical in nature.'[44] To take a straightforward example, let us look at what a patient experiencing an intractable cancer says: 'There have been times when I felt I was cutting my way through a jungle, other times when it's been quite smooth sailing'. Here, the experience of cancer is what linguists call the 'target domain' of the metaphor and the references to journeys of different kinds represent the 'source domain'. Metaphor links two domains or categories, implying that, while they remain distinct, certain features may be identified as common between the two and that the target domain (in this case, 'cancer') may usefully be seen through the lens of the other domain ('journey'). Strengths of the metaphor include the way in which it captures the potential for the diagnosis to take the patient as readily to a positive outcome as a negative outcome and its emphasis on agency for the traveller. Thinking of CANCER AS A JOURNEY may impact significantly on the attitudes not only of those who experience cancer, but also of the wider public.

It was Donald Schön, also around thirty-five years ago, who argued more specifically that, when a particular metaphor or cluster of metaphors is selected to embody a given social issue, policymakers are inclined to come up with solutions which derive from that original metaphor.[45] He describes these as 'generative metaphors'. Over the period since then, thinkers about issues of public policy such as Anthony Judge have pointed to the importance of metaphors in what Judge terms the 'imaginal framework' through which we view the topic under consideration.[46] Paul H. Thibodeau and Lera Boroditsky have argued more recently that the adoption of a given metaphor to refer to the challenge posed by a social issue will in large part determine not only the policies which officials will

---

[44] G. Lakoff and M. Johnson, *The Metaphors We Live By* (Chicago: Chicago University Press, 1980), p. 3.

[45] D. Schön, 'Generative metaphor: a perspective on problem-setting in social policy', in A. Ortony (ed.), *Metaphor and Thought*, 2nd edition (Cambridge: Cambridge University Press, 1993), pp. 137–63.

[46] A. Judge, 'Enhancing sustainable development strategies through avoidance of military metaphors' (1998). www.laetusinpraesens.org/docs/targets.php

propose to deal with them, but also the attitudes of the public towards those policies.[47] The example they use is directly relevant to the current discussion. Thibodeau and Boroditsky found that, if crime in a given city is referred to as a 'beast' preying on the community, people will tend to support enforcement measures involving detection, capture and prosecution, whereas, if it is presented as a 'virus' infecting the city, they are more inclined to support preventive measures and treat the problem through social reforms.[48] As a number of commentators have suggested, there is a tendency for such metaphors to become literalised or concretised.[49]

Crime as Disease

It turns out that the metaphor of CRIME AS A DISEASE is in widespread use and has been found in many circumstances to be highly productive. It has been most strikingly employed by Gary Slutkin who, on returning to Chicago in 1995 after working for years as an epidemiologist for the World Health Organization on the spread of diseases such as tuberculosis and HIV in Africa, observed similar patterns to be at work in the spread of violence in the city. He argued that it is productive to view crime as if it were an infectious disease and use similar strategies to overcome it. Violent crime, especially, he suggested was 'contagious' and measures should be introduced to limit the 'epidemic'.

> Maps and graphs that chart the spread of violence look almost identical to those that chart infectious diseases with maps showing clusters and graphs showing wave upon wave.... The good news is, once we recognize violence as a contagious process, we can treat it accordingly, using the same methods that successfully contain other epidemic processes – interrupting transmission, and behavior and normative change.[50]

[47] P. H. Thibodeau and L. Boroditsky, 'Metaphors we think with: the role of metaphor in reasoning', PLOS ONE, 6: 2 (2011), 2.

[48] While the CRIME AS BEAST metaphor is not familiar in all countries, it lies behind much discussion of crime in the United States, where the notion of 'keeping the streets safe' is prevalent. Indeed an Act of Congress in 1968 had the title 'Omnibus Crime Control and Safe Streets' Act. For discussion, see J. Simon, 'Governing through metaphors', Brooklyn Law Review, 67 (2001), 1035–70. On the broad topic of metaphors for crime, see S. L. Winter, A Clearing in the Forest: Law, Life, and Mind (Chicago: University of Chicago Press, 2001).

[49] B. F. Bowdle and D. Gentner, 'The career of metaphor', Psychological Review, 112: 1 (2005), 193–216.

[50] G. Slutkin, 'How to reduce crime: treat it like an infectious disease'. http://ideas.time .com/2013/05/30/how-to-reduce-crime-treat-it-like-an-infectious-disease/; see also his TED talk, G. Slutkin, 'Let's treat violence like a contagious disease' (2013). http://on.ted .com/ViolenceEpidemic

He is one of the founders of the organisation Cure Violence, which has worked with city administrations in Chicago, Baltimore, New York, Philadelphia and beyond, appointing selected workers into communities to prevent violence and encourage behaviour change through outreach. Commentators and activists in other countries have used similar metaphors. Writing of the problem of violent crime in Jamaica, social commentator and entrepreneur Henley Morgan wrote an article in the *Jamaica Observer* with the headline: 'Treat the crime epidemic like the disease it is'. He writes of the need to 'understand the pathology of the disease', 'quarantine the constituencies … against spreading the disease to unaffected areas of the population', and concludes that '[i]f we approach fighting crime as if it were a deadly and contagious disease, we will find solving the problem is not beyond us.'[51] Mahatma Gandhi, it should be remembered, declared long ago that: 'All crime is a kind of disease and should be treated as such.'[52]

Reinforcing the CRIME AS DISEASE analogy, we frequently liken detectives to doctors in the way in which they analyse the evidence they find. It is no coincidence that author Sir Arthur Conan Doyle was trained in medicine at the University of Edinburgh and that he modelled the great fictional detective Sherlock Holmes, with his extraordinary powers of observation and deduction, on his medical lecturer Joseph Bell.[53] It should not be surprising that television series such as *Bones*, depicting teams of forensic medicine specialists working at the intersection of detective work and medicine, are so popular. *House* is another program which highlights the pursuit of clues in diagnosis. As Mariana Valverde has shown, public understanding of crime and the legal system is significantly shaped by the grossly simplified representations of detective work and forensic medicine we encounter in films and television series.[54]

Nevertheless, some criminologists have expressed objections to the, sometimes uncritical, ways in which terms such as 'predisposition' and 'rehabilitation', commonly employed in the field of public health, have been borrowed for use in their discipline. Kaye Haw argues that concepts such as 'risk factor' and 'pathway into crime' have moved from being

[51] H. Morgan, 'Treat the crime epidemic like the disease it is', *Jamaica Observer* (7 February 2014). www.jamaicaobserver.com/columns/Treat-the-crime-epidemic-like-the-disease-it-is_15948706 (accessed May 2015)

[52] www.worldofquotes.com/author/Mahatma+Gandhi/7/index.html (accessed May 2015).

[53] For a wonderfully vivid account of one of Bell's demonstrations of his powers, see A. Verghese, 'A Doctor's Touch' (2011). www.ted.com/talks/abraham_verghese_a_doctor_s_touch

[54] M. Valverde, *Law and Order: Images, Meanings, Myths* (New Brunswick: Rutgers University Press, 2006).

useful generative metaphors to the status of professional myth,[55] and Sarah Armstrong asserts that the concept of 'risk management' has undergone a similar shift.[56] She argues, in particular, that the metaphor promotes 'the risk management process as all-seeing, permanent, delivered as an actual edifice, and coordinated into a coherent system of action'.[57] 'Such a frame closes off critical conversations about definitions of problems in the first place ... It also treats human agency as relevant only at the margins.'[58] This critique illustrates the broad argument of Deborah A. Stone on the importance of teasing out the several kinds of causal explanation (mechanical, accidental, intentional, inadvertent) which may be employed around any social problem.[59]

Direction of Meaning Flow in Metaphors

In general, the linkage between two domains through metaphor is perceived as working in one direction only. When a cancer patient refers to his or her experience of the DISEASE AS A JOURNEY, for instance, there is no suggestion that the equation is reversible and that it would be helpful to think of *journeys* as having some of the characteristics of *cancer*, via the metaphor JOURNEY AS DISEASE. Most of the metaphors studied by linguists and philosophers are 'unidirectional'.[60] Nevertheless, it sometimes happens that the flow of metaphorical meaning does actually run in both directions. This occurs especially when the domains on which a metaphor draws are closely adjacent, as with disease and crime. So, alongside statements such as 'violent crime is a cancer on the neighbourhood', where crime (target domain) is viewed through the lens of disease (source domain), we find many instances of metaphors of crime being used to describe or explain disease, as in: 'the HIV virus *lurks* in the ... glands and *insinuates itself* into the blood supply', where the disease (target domain)

---

[55] K. Haw, 'Risk factors and pathways into and out of crime, misleading, misinterpreted or mythic: from generative metaphor to professional myth', *Australian and New Zealand Journal of Criminology*, 39: 3 (2006), 339–53 at 339.

[56] S. Armstrong, 'Managing meaning: the use of metaphor in criminal justice policy' (15 June 2009). http://papers.ssrn.com/sol3/papers.cfm?abstract_id=15083405).

[57] Ibid., 17

[58] Ibid., 18. See also R. Canton, 'Not another medical model: using metaphor and analogy to explore crime and criminal justice', *British Journal of Community Justice*, 8: 1 (2010), 40–57.

[59] D. A. Stone, 'Causal stories and the formation of policy agendas', *Political Science Quarterly*, 104: 2 (Summer 1989), 281–300.

[60] Z. Kövecses, *Metaphor: A Practical Introduction* (New York: Oxford University Press, 2002), p. 25.

is viewed through the lens of crime (source domain).[61] Both viruses and cancers are frequently referred to, even in professional literature, as if they are persons who have malevolent intentions. So, for instance, a report on a research programme at Vanderbilt University on potential vaccines against HIV comments: 'The difficulty in developing a vaccine against the virus that causes AIDS testifies to its *wiliness*. The human immunodeficiency virus mutates rapidly to *evade detection* by the body's immune system.'[62]

While Conan Doyle saw that detectives needed to employ skills akin to those learned by students of medicine, the Vanderbilt report is only one of many reminders that doctors employ skills akin to those of detectives. So we find articles such as Lawrence K. Altman's 'The doctor's world: A correspondent recalls his days as a medical sleuth'[63] and US television's Dr Mehmet Oz bringing together a panel of 'disease detectives' to discuss new ways of diagnosing and treating key diseases.[64] The metaphor DOCTORS AS DETECTIVES is widely accepted and used.

In many cases, research and public education on diseases and their treatments are clearly illuminated by the use of metaphors from the domain 'crime'. So a fascinating article from 2005 in the journal *Nature*, titled 'Cancer: Crime and Punishment',[65] illustrates the way in which human cells use 'exile, execution and lifetime imprisonment' as strategies to prevent mutant cells from turning into fully fledged cancers.

The metaphors which view disease through the lens of criminality are a subset of what Scott Montgomery identifies as the dominant metaphors in the West around disease, the biomilitary (deriving from Pasteur) and the bioinformationist (deriving especially from the discovery of DNA and research in genetics).[66] He shows that these dominant metaphor clusters

---

[61] H. V. Fineberg, 'The social dimensions of AIDS', *Scientific American*, 259: 4 (1988 October), 128–34.

[62] B. Snyder, 'Studies investigate potential HIV vaccines', Reporter: Vanderbilt University Medical Center's Weekly Newspaper (19 June 2009). www.mc.vanderbilt.edu:8080/reporter/index.html?ID=7321

[63] L. K. Altman, 'The doctor's world: a correspondent recalls his days as a medical sleuth', *New York Times* (17 April 2001).

[64] M. Oz, 'Dr Oz's disease detectives, pt 1', The Dr Oz Show, 2012. www.doctoroz.com/videos/dr-oz-s-disease-detectives-pt-1.

[65] N. E. Sharpless and R. A. DePinho, 'Cancer: crime and punishment', *Nature*, 436 (4 August 2005), 636–7.

[66] S. L. Montgomery, 'Illness and image: on the contents of biomedical discourse', *The Scientific Voice* (Chicago: Chicago University Press, 1996), pp. 139–60 at 147. Montgomery traces in some detail the increasing occurrence in Pasteur's writings on microbes through the 1860 and 1870s of terms such as 'invade', 'foreign', 'defeat' and 'overwhelm' and their adoption by biologists and physicians from then on. He also shows how terms such as 'message', 'code',

feature not only in popular discourse but also in technical and professional discourse and that 'they have provided organizing images, even image systems, whose own internal logic later became the guiding basis for inquiry.'[67] The subset of metaphors which represent disease as crime refers to diseases as *attacking*, by *stealth*, and making use of *covert communication systems*. Many of the metaphors used suggest spying, invasion and even terrorism, rather than simple criminality. Montgomery acknowledges that the adoption of such metaphors has shaped professional understanding of, and research in, many fields of medicine in ways which are fruitful.

It may well be, however, that this tendency to view illness through the lens of criminality stems also in part from the etymology of the English words 'health', 'healing' and 'illness'. 'Health' and 'healing' are cognate with both 'whole' and 'holiness', with the implication that the person who lacks 'health' is less than whole and may indeed be 'unholy'. Moreover, the 'ill' of 'illness' is a contraction of the word 'evil', which means that the term 'illness' suggests that an evil has been done – and that, as we have already seen, begs the question of whether it has been committed *to* or *by* the person who is sick.[68] This possibility may start to bring into question the appropriateness of the DISEASE AS CRIME metaphor.

Metaphors of 'Self' and 'Other'

Rather than just a matter of popular belief, the notion that sickness involves some intrusion from the outside has, to a considerable extent, become fixed in the professional conceptualisation of both cancer and diseases of microbial origin. A central feature of the notion of the 'immune system', as it emerged in the late nineteenth century, is the 'self-other' distinction. So, the opening paragraph of a standard text on immunity and immunology states:

> The human organism, from the time of conception, must maintain its integrity in the face of a changing and often threatening environment. Our bodies have many physiological mechanisms that permit us to adjust to basic variables such as temperature, supply of food and water, and physical injury. In addition, we must defend ourselves against invasion and colonization by foreign organisms. This defensive ability is called *immunity*.[69]

'copying' and 'decoding' emerged from genetic and computer research in the 1940s and 1950s, and became indivisibly linked to the military metaphors.

[67] Ibid., 136.

[68] K. M. Boyd, 'Disease, illness, sickness, health, healing and wholeness: exploring some elusive concepts', *Journal of Medical Ethics: Medical Humanities*, 26 (2000), 9–17 at 9.

[69] S. Sell, *Immunology, Immunopathology, and Immunity* (New York: Elsevier, 1989), p. 3.

Yet, as several commentators have pointed out, the self-other distinction is somewhat misleading. In particular, the assumption that 'bacteria', as 'other' to the human organism, are in principle to be feared and, as far as possible, removed, is inaccurate, since the physiology of the body is highly dependent on the presence, especially in the gastro-intestinal system, of large numbers of 'positive' bacteria. To suggest, likewise, that cancer cells originate outside the bodily system is also misleading, given that they are actually mutations of cells internal to that system.[70] The metaphorical leap involved in borrowing the term 'immunity' from legal language is obscured in most textbooks where the concept is presented as if it had literal validity. This is one of a number of areas in which doubt has been raised about the appropriateness of military and criminal metaphors as they are used in relation to sickness.

Military/Criminal Metaphors in Relation to Disease

More broadly, there has been ongoing concern since the 1980s about the implications for social attitudes towards sickness of the widespread use of metaphors with military and criminal connotations to characterise disease. It was novelist and essayist Susan Sontag who raised concerns first in relation to cancer, then to HIV. According to Sontag, the ascribing of military or criminal associations to those diseases tends in the first instance to demoralise the patients. In addition, there is a tendency for the notion of guilt to be somehow transferred from the disease to the patient. 'Ostensibly, the illness is the culprit. But it is also the cancer patient who is made culpable.'[71] This may well indicate, in part, a kind of hangover of earlier assumptions about the origins of disease lying in criminal or sinful actions by the person who gets sick, or those around them. As Sontag also suggested, focus on the 'otherness' of cancer, HIV-AIDS and certain other infectious diseases may engender prejudice against the social other, in the shape of both xenophobia and homophobia. 'This is the language of political paranoia with its characteristic distrust of a pluralistic world',[72] the kind of paranoia which fosters representations of Muslims or Asian immigrants or homosexuals as toxic.

---

[70] E. Cohen, 'Metaphorical immunity: a case of biomedical fiction', *Literature and Medicine*, 22: 2 (Fall 2003), 140–63, 150.

[71] S. Sontag, *Illness as Metaphor and AIDS and Its Metaphors* (New York: Farrar, Straus and Giroux, 1990), p. 57.

[72] Ibid., 106.

A complicating factor in this is that several of the most serious diseases to have surfaced in the world in recent years such as HIV, Severe Acute Respiratory Syndrome (SARS), avian influenza, and now Ebola, emerged first in non-Western countries, with HIV-AIDS and Ebola originating in Africa, and SARS and avian flu in East Asia. Indeed, all of these viruses appear to have been first transmitted to human beings from other animals, thereby doubling their 'otherness'. These facts have made it only too easy for commentators in Europe and the United States to adopt melodramatic metaphors derived not just from the military domain, but from the domains of individual criminality and of terrorism. Referring to the geographical spread of avian flu, two *New York Times* journalists wrote: 'like enemy troops moving into place for an attack, the bird flu known as A (H5N1) has been steadily advancing,'[73] to which other writers added 'the virus lurks' and another still 'it is a serial killer' which 'did not need one of the host's own enzymes to turn traitor and cleave apart the hemagglutinin protein to help the virus infect a cell … the virus toted its own cleaving mechanism into the host on that gene, like a butcher who brings his own knife'.[74]

In reference to public health responses to these threats, Western leaders seem to have thought mostly in terms of defending their own territories and population against 'invasion' by these viruses, rather than seeking to treat them and the people whose lives are devastated by them in Asia and Africa directly. The rhetoric of President George W. Bush in relation to avian flu was particularly remarkable in that it was almost indistinguishable from his rhetoric on international terrorism and 'homelands security', with references to 'insufficient surveillance', the importance of 'stockpiling Tamiflu' (the antiviral medication) not only at the national level, but also at the level of individual households and his promise to give Americans 'the protections they deserve'.[75] It does seem, however, that the response from rich countries to the current Ebola outbreak in 2014 is somewhat more positive, in that it is focusing primarily on the problem as it presents itself in the countries of West Africa.[76] In this context, it is all too easily forgotten

[73] D. Grady and G. Kolata, 'Avian flu: the uncertain threat – Q & A: how serious is the risk?' *New York Times* (28 March 2006).

[74] J. Shreeve, 'Why revive a deadly flu virus?' *New York Times* (29 January 2006), 90: see also M. Hanne, and S. Hawken, 'Metaphors for illness in contemporary media', *Journal of Medical Ethics: Medical Humanities*, 33 (December 2007), 93–9.

[75] T. Wiliams, 'Bush calls for $7.1 billion to prepare for bird flu threat', *New York Times* (1 November 2005).

[76] WHO, 'Statement on the meeting of the international health regulations emergency committee regarding the 2014 Ebola outbreak in West Africa', World Health Organization (8 August 2014). www.who.int/mediacentre/news/statements/2014/ebola-20140808/en/

that, through history, it has been much more often the case that diseases have been transmitted from the first, colonising world to the populations of the third, colonised world, than the reverse.[77]

It is, of course, relevant, too, that diseases, notably anthrax, cholera and typhus, have actually been used as weapons of war[78] and are contemplated as weapons of terrorism.[79] Following the establishment of the Biological and Toxin Weapons Convention in 1972, which has been signed by the governments of 120 countries, to use diseases for military or terrorist purposes is in fact criminal.[80] In this specific sense, therefore, the characterisation of disease as criminal is not wholly metaphorical.

Interestingly, the mirror image of the DISEASE AS TERRORISM metaphor is to be found in the frequent contemporary references to terrorism as a cancer or contagious disease.[81] A vivid example is to be found in the words of President Obama on 20 August 2014, when he spoke of the murder of an American journalist in Syria: 'From governments and peoples across the Middle East, there has to be a common effort to extract this cancer so that it does not spread.'[82]

The Crime of Disease and the Disease of Crime

The widespread use of both the DISEASE AS CRIME metaphor and the CRIME AS DISEASE metaphor derives not just from the general contiguity of the two fields that I referred to at the start of this chapter. More specifically, it springs from the long-established dual conventions whereby we view society as a body and the body as a society. The SOCIETY AS BODY metaphor has been widely used in the West, but with different emphases, for 800 years or more. Whereas, in the Middle Ages, the emphasis was on the detailed anatomy of the 'body politic', with the prince being regarded

---

[77] J. Diamond, *Guns, Germs, and Steel: The Fates of Human Societies* (New York: W.W. Norton and Company, 1997).

[78] F. Frischknecht, 'The history of biological warfare: human experimentation, modern nightmares and lone madmen in the twentieth century', *European Molecular Biology Reports*, 4:Supplement 1 (June 2003), 47–52.

[79] L. Paquette, *Bioterrorism in Medical and Healthcare Administration* (Boca Raton: Florida CRC Press, 2004).

[80] Frischknecht, 'The history of biological warfare'.

[81] I. Shrira, 'Why the fight against terrorism is like the fight against cancer', *Psychology Today* (2 October 2011). www.psychologytoday.com/blog/the-narcissus-in-all-us/201110/why-the-fight-against-terrorism-is-the-fight-against-cancer

[82] Obama, http://blogs.wsj.com/washwire/2014/08/20/obama-transcript-world-appalled-by-foley-murder-isis-cancer-must-be-extracted/.

as 'the head', and every social group corresponding to one or another necessary part of the body, right down to the peasants and craftsmen, who were 'the feet',[83] in the modern era the tendency has been to focus on the question of the 'health' or 'sickness' of the society and, specifically, its vulnerability to some kind of 'infection' from other communities or nations.[84] The BODY AS SOCIETY metaphor has an equally long history, which depends broadly on our identifying the organs as playing different roles in the normal functioning of the body, with, at different times, the heart, the brain and the liver being perceived as 'in charge'.[85] In the modern era, the emphasis has shifted to the processes by which the organs 'communicate' with each other and, as has been seen, the tendency to view the body as subject to 'invasion' and 'colonisation' by outside forces. At a microscopic level, the whole body is depicted as a vast and complex community of citizen cells, not unlike a community of bees or ants (or humans). Discussion of the mechanisms by which the body responds to infection depicts the cells of the body as citizens with specialised roles. For instance, a recent article on the immune system for a general interest magazine refers to the way in which a virus will:

> do its best to infect a host cell and keep out of the way of the immune system, which may, in turn, identify the viral material and sound the alarm. Antiviral elements are then released; uninfected cells are cautioned to bolster their defences against viral intrusion, and cells that have already been infected are coaxed towards committing suicide.[86]

Subsequently, the article refers to 'helper T cells (that mostly help other immune cells by directing them to the right spot and providing guidance and encouragement)'.[87]

The conclusion that follows is that the closeness, in so many ways, of the domains 'crime' and 'disease' and, especially, the widespread use of dual

---

[83] A. Musolff, 'Political metaphor and bodies politic', in U. Okulska and P. Cap (eds.), *Perspectives in Politics and Discourse* (Amsterdam and Philadelphia: John Benjamins Publishing, 2010), pp. 23–41.

[84] D. Skinner and R. Squillacote, 'New bodies: beyond illness, dirt, vermin and other metaphors of terror', in Okulska and Cap, *Perspectives in Politics and Discourse*, pp. 43–60. See also M. Hanne, 'An introduction to the "Warring with Words" project', in M. Hanne, W. D. Crano and J. S. Mio (eds.), *Warring with Words: Narrative and Metaphor in Politics* (New York and London: Psychology Press, 2014), pp. 1–50 at 8–11.

[85] R. Selzer, 'Liver', in *Mortal Lessons: Note on the Art of Surgery* (New York: Houghton Mifflin Harcourt, 1996), pp. 62–77.

[86] M. Broatch, 'A survivor's guide to the immune system', *New Zealand Listener*, 245:3876 (23–29 August 2014), 20–1, 21

[87] Ibid.

direction metaphors between the two domains leads to a worrisome tendency towards a collapse of the conceptual boundary between them. As a result, rather than the one being seen as analogous to the other, they come to be seen as more or less identical. When we are aware that we are using metaphors, we realise that only some of the features of the source domain are transferable to the target domain; however, when the boundary between the domains collapses, we assume that all features are shared between the domains. When, as we saw earlier, the concepts of 'predisposition', 'pathway', 'risk factor' and 'rehabilitation' are employed in an undifferentiated way across both the public health sector and the field of criminology, it becomes very easy to suppose that all the key concepts in the two domains are mutually interchangeable. In the words of Sarah Armstrong: 'The boundary between the literal and the metaphorical can become obscured when a cross-domain mapping occurs between domains that are very near to each other.'[88] While Armstrong's concern, given that she is a criminologist, is with the misleading tendency for offenders to be regarded as patients, the concern of Sontag and her successors, whose preoccupation is with medicine, has been that the patient may too easily be regarded as an offender.

In conclusion, therefore, it is imperative that the issues discussed in the other chapters of this book concerning the criminalisation of people suffering from a potentially terminal illness, who engage in behaviour which may put others at risk of contracting the disease, be viewed against the linguistic and cultural background outlined in this chapter. Although not recommending for a moment, as Susan Sontag did, that we should entirely abandon the use of metaphor in relation to either domain, I do suggest that there is a great need for more critical thinking around just how we refer to the relationship between the two domains, especially in terms of the uncritical use of metaphors derived from the one domain in relationship to the other.

[88] Armstrong, 'Managing meaning', 5.

3

Leprosy and the Law: The 'Criminalisation' of Hansen's Disease in Hawai'i, 1865–1969

KERRI A. INGLIS

On 3 January 1865, the new monarch of the Kingdom of Hawai'i, Lota Kapuāiwa (Kamehameha V), signed into law 'An Act to Prevent the Spread of Leprosy'. Since the first arrival of foreigners in the late eighteenth century, epidemic diseases had brought about devastating effects upon the Hawaiian people, including the traumas of depopulation. As such, leprosy was but one of many epidemics in the islands, but with its prolonged pathology it garnered much of the Board of Health's attention.[1] As the nineteenth century progressed, many had sought to find a cure for leprosy, but had no success beyond producing remedies that gave comfort to those afflicted with the disease.[2] Quarantine was the only viable means available to stop the spread of an infectious disease. The 1865 law provided for the establishment of a leprosy settlement and the authorities chose a remote peninsula on the northern shore of the island of Molokai. Treacherous ocean on all sides and high cliffs at the base surround the Kalaupapa peninsula.

---

[1] Leprosy, also known as Hansen's disease, is relatively slow in its progress, but can be devastating in its pathology and disfiguring in its attack. Although it usually does not cause death itself, leprosy brings death with it. At first attacking the cooler parts of the body (i.e., hands, feet, fingers, face, earlobes), the bacteria damages the peripheral nerve tissue, often destroying skin and mucous membranes. As such, leprosy sufferers are prone to ulcerations as well as to wounds that often lead to infection. As the disease progresses, the inability to move the hands or feet, the unceasing deformity of the feet, exacerbated difficulty in breathing (the bacteria attacks the larynx) and progressive blindness may result. The combinations of nerve damage and diminished immune response often lead to the visible disfigurement to which others in society often react – collapse of the nose, thickening of the skin, loss of eyebrows. Further, the immune system of the leprosy victim is also compromised, leaving the sufferer susceptible to other infectious diseases (Vicki J. Isola, 'Leprosy', *Magill's Medical Guide: Health & Illness* (Pasadena, CA: Salem Press, 1995), 474–7).

[2] See Kerri A. Inglis, ' "Cure the dread disease": Nineteenth Century Attempts to Treat Leprosy in the Hawaiian Islands', *The Hawaiian Journal of History*, 43 (2009): 101–24.

Geographically and culturally, this was to be a land 'set apart'.[3] There was certainly compassion for those with the disease, both within the Native Hawaiian community and from foreigners, and the attempt at quarantine was indeed a rational response to try to control a disease that was dreaded by so many, but the impact of this isolation would have devastating effects upon individuals and their families. Of the approximately five thousand people sent to the Kalaupapa peninsula in the nineteenth century, 98 per cent were Native Hawaiian; another three thousand patients were quarantined in the twentieth century, and with the influx of immigrant labourers to the islands, the percentage of Native Hawaiians at Kalaupapa declined slightly to 90 per cent.[4]

The story of leprosy in Hawai'i is part of a wider history of medical isolation, primarily in the nineteenth and early twentieth centuries, in which racial segregation often overlapped with medical separation. The use of leprosy as a tool for segregation is well documented in medieval European history including how mere accusations of having leprosy were used to remove unwanted individuals from society.[5] Furthermore, creating geographies of exclusion, based on assertions that leprosy was an indigenous disease, is apparent in the histories of infectious diseases (including leprosy) in much of the colonised world. While today evidence for more nuanced understandings of leprosy in the Middle Ages are coming forward, it seems that the 'dark hidden meanings' attributed to leprosy in the early modern era were transferred through European cross-cultural interactions into the colonial world.[6] The overlap of medical isolation with racial segregation in the history of leprosy and colonialism can also be seen in the works on Africa, India, the Philippines, Australia, and the Pacific.[7]

[3] 'An Act to Prevent the Spread of Leprosy,' *Laws of His Majesty Kamehameha V., King of the Hawaiian Islands, Passed by the Legislataive Assembly, at Its Session, 1864–65* (Honolulu, HI: Printed by Order of the Government, 1865), p. 62.

[4] 'Record of Inmates at Kalaupapa,' Series 260, Records Relating to Hansen's Disease, Archives of Hawai'i.

[5] Guenter B. Risse, *Mending Bodies, Saving Souls: A History of Hospitals* (New York: Oxford University Press, 1999), 167–230; Mary Douglas, 'Witchcraft and Leprosy: Two Strategies of Exclusion', *Man*, 26 (1991): 723–36.

[6] Sheldon Watts, *Epidemics and History: Disease, Power and Imperialism* (New Haven: Yale University Press, 1997). See also Luke Demaitre, *Leprosy in Premodern Medicine: A Malady of the Whole Body* (Baltimore: Johns Hopkins University Press, 2007); Carole Rawcliffe, *Leprosy in Medieval England* (Woodbridge: Boydell & Brewer, 2006).

[7] See Megan Vaughan, 'Without the Camp: Institutions and Identities in the Colonial History of Leprosy', in *Curing Their Ills: Colonial Power and African Illness* (Stanford: Stanford University Press, 1991); Eric Silla, *People Are Not the Same: Leprosy and Identity in Twentieth-Century Mali* (Portsmouth, NH: Heinemann, 1998); Jane Buckingham, *Leprosy*

In his analysis of the history of leprosy during the era of British imperialism, Rod Edmond explored the influence Hawai'i's experience with the disease had on British policy. Edmond asserted 'the operation of a health/disease dichotomy was a crucial, but very unstable, marker of difference within and across these defining characteristics of race, gender and class'.[8] It is in a similar context that Alison Bashford situates leprosy in Australia in the nineteenth and twentieth centuries. Demonstrating that 'the control of leprosy became entangled with spatial governance of indigenous people throughout the British Empire, with colonial laws as well as local rule regulating movement, contact and institutionalization', Bashford reveals this control within the social domains of Australia, as well as within the larger context of colonial concerns over 'an imperial danger'.[9] Here, as elsewhere in the colonised world, the management of leprosy in the name of public health was as much about the management of 'race, health and sex … involving boundaries, separation, quarantine, isolation and protection on the one hand, and anxiety about and regulation of contact, contagion, integration and assimilation on the other'.[10] Hawai'i's history with leprosy further illustrates our understandings of these colonial mindsets and concerns over contagion, and here also offers us an opportunity to view personal experiences with the disease from the perspective of those who lived it and have left their mark on the history of disease in Hawai'i.

By analysing public health attitudes and policies in Hawai'i as they pertained to leprosy beginning with the 1865 Act, revisions that took place in the decades following, and the end of the quarantine or isolation (some would say exile) of Hansen's disease patients to Kalaupapa in 1969, the effect of these policies on individuals and families in Hawai'i can be better understood.[11] Privileging Native Hawaiian/patient experiences and responses to the policies, the stigmas attached to the disease, and patients' efforts to bring an end to the isolation policy offer further insight. Indeed

---

in Colonial South India: Medicine and Confinement (London: Palgrave, 2002); Warwick Anderson, *Colonial Pathologies: American Tropical Medicine, Race, and Hygiene in the Philippines* (Durham: Duke University Press, 2006).

[8] Rod Edmond, *Leprosy & Empire: A Medical and Cultural History* (New York: Cambridge University Press, 2006), p. 12.

[9] Alison Bashford, *Imperial Hygiene: A Critical History of Colonialism, Nationalism and Public Health* (New York: Palgrave Macmillan, 2004), pp. 81 and 83.

[10] Ibid., p. 113.

[11] One of the dilemmas in this history is over what to call those 'persons with leprosy' – because of stigma, hurt, and the derogatory nature of the term 'leper' it is not used unless quoting directly from historical sources. Contemporary scholars often use leprosy and Hansen's disease interchangeably in their writings.

it is important to privilege their experiences, as medical anthropologist Arthur Kleinman has stated, 'we, each of us, injure the humanity of our fellow sufferers each time we fail to privilege their voices, their experiences'.[12] As the medicalisation and criminalisation of the disease throughout the 104 years of isolation policy in Hawai'i developed, both served to objectify those with leprosy and perpetuate the stigma attached to the disease. Those with leprosy were criminalised through the arrest and treatment that came with their banishment from Hawaiian society; moreover, medical experiments and notions of 'progress' further objectified these victims of disease.

There are many descriptions from former patients concerning their experiences with leprosy. For many, both the policies and the terminology surrounding the disease left a deep imprint. Naming or labelling of course brings with it implications of identity. What follows is an account from a man who was sent to Kalaupapa in the early 1900s. His narrative, offered through an oral history project decades after he was diagnosed with the disease, describes his experience with contracting Hansen's disease when he was a young boy. Being labelled as one who had contracted leprosy brought with it an immediate shift in his identity:

> My father came to take me home from school. But instead of taking me to the Kalihi Receiving Station immediately like the principal said they should, my parents took me home ... The whole family cried, including my father. The next day my father took me downtown and bought me a new suit. It was my first suit of clothes – they were so nice. I looked good. I had never had clothes like that before because we were poor ... So I wore that suit of clothes to the Kalihi Receiving Station. Even though we were poor, my father said he wanted me to be dressed nicely when I was taken to Kalihi to be declared a leper. They took my picture for the official record of the Board of Health wearing that new suit of clothes. When the picture was taken, my father broke down again and cried. *So, I became a leper.* [emphasis added][13]

This is a profound commentary on the role of identity in this history – that is, this man described a day in his life when *everything* changed – including how he, and others, saw himself. Further, this altering of identity also brought with it layers of criminalisation and objectification, as discussed in the pages that follow. Several laws regarding leprosy were passed from 1865 to 1969, reflecting public health concerns, as well as changes in

---

[12] Arthur Kleinman, *Writing at the Margin: Discourse between Anthropology and Medicine* (Berkeley: University of California Press, 1995), p. 172.
[13] In Emmit Cahill, *Yesterday at Kalaupapa* (Honolulu, HI: Editions, Ltd., 1990), p. 5.

governing authority – taking us from the Kingdom of Hawai'i (established in 1810) to a provisional government in 1893, the Republic of Hawai'i (1894–8) to a US territory (1898–1959), to the State of Hawai'i. Many of these policies encouraged a process that began to alter the way that Native Hawaiians saw themselves, viewed those with leprosy, and reacted to infectious disease – perspectives that differed from their initial cultural reaction, which primarily consisted of acceptance.

The 1865 Act allowed for the selection of a place of quarantine (the Kalaupapa peninsula) and gave both the Board of Health and police officials the authority to arrest those with, or suspected of having, leprosy. By 1870, amendments provided that divorce could be granted to a husband or a wife if contracting leprosy, and no one was allowed to visit or remain at the leprosy settlement without written permission from the Board of Health, and the Board of Health was authorised to make 'Rules and Regulations' as necessary for 'the government and control of the Lepers'.[14] In 1884 the kingdom government re-affirmed the intent of the original Act, asserting that 'the Board of Health is authorized . . . . to send to a place of isolation . . . all such patients as shall be considered incurable or capable of spreading the disease of leprosy'. After the Bayonet Constitution of 1887, laws were passed in 1888 stating that 'No Steam Coasting vessel licensed to carry passengers . . . shall be allowed . . . to carry to or from any port or place in this Kingdom any leper' and further that 'kokua [helpers] . . . may be by such Board declared infected with the disease of leprosy . . . All such kokuas are hereby placed under control of the Board of Health.' Moreover, anyone caught concealing anyone with leprosy or suspected of having leprosy was to be subject to fines. Adding to the regulation of *mea kōkua* (helpers), new rules not only articulated what was expected of *kōkua* in the settlement, but an 1890 law asserted that any helper 'refusing to perform such labor . . . or who shall violate any rule or regulation . . . shall be liable on conviction . . . to expulsion from the settlement'.[15]

After the Kingdom of Hawai'i was illegally overthrown by an elite group of foreign-born businessmen in 1893, the new provisional government sought to tighten the rules and regulations surrounding the leprosy settlement – to protect the islands from becoming known as a 'leprous nation'.[16]

---

[14] 'An Act Relating to Divorce,' *Laws of His Majesty Kamehameha V., King of the Hawaiian Islands, Passed by the Legislative Assembly, At Its Session, 1870* (Honolulu, HI: Printed by Order of the Government, 1870), p. 18.

[15] 'Hansen's Disease, 1867–1941,' Series 334–5, Board of Health, Archives of Hawai'i.

[16] Prince A. Morrow, MD, Leprosy and Hawaiian Annexation, *The North American Review* (1897), 582.

As such, laws were passed stating that any attempt to leave Kalaupapa, including scaling or climbing the cliffs that separated the peninsula from the rest of the island of Molokai, without a permit, was now punishable by fine ($25) or thirty days' imprisonment (with or without labour). More policies concerning the *mea kōkua* were also introduced.[17] In the first few decades of the leprosy settlement, these helpers were the backbone of the community as they cared for their loved ones without regard to any risk that they might also contract the disease.[18]

After annexation by the United States of America, territorial laws re-affirmed that a penal summons was to be issued to any person alleged to be suffering with leprosy; failure to appear would cause the arrest of such person. Perhaps working to overcome stigma, the territory passed a law in 1909 that stipulated that if or when a person was found not to have the disease, the Board was to 'furnish him with a certificate setting forth such fact'. They also passed a law that, if a patient was found to not benefit from further treatment in Honolulu, or if a person had to be arrested, was unwilling to receive treatment, or was unwilling to submit to rules and regulations, he or she was to be removed to Kalaupapa. Moreover, by law, the public was now legally bound to report on others suspected of having the disease.[19]

In an effort to challenge some of the stigma attached to leprosy, the official name of the disease was changed to Hansen's disease in 1949. This also coincided with the decade in which sulfa drugs were introduced to the islands for the successful treatment of the infection.[20] It was not until 1969 that the isolation of those with Hansen's disease sent to Kalaupapa was officially ended, and that policy change was largely due to patient activism.

Disease and Punishment

In the nineteenth century, the only viable response to a contagious disease was to quarantine those who were infectious so as to deter its spread – but

---

[17] 'Hansen's Disease, 1867–1941', Series 334–5, Board of Health, Archives of Hawai'i.
[18] The *mea kōkua* collected water for drinking and bathing, cooked meals, provided shelter and nursed their loved ones until their passing. They received rations from the Board of Health, but their motives were often questioned. See Kerri A. Inglis, *Ma'i Lepera: Disease and Displacement in Nineteenth-Century Hawai'i* (Honolulu, HI: University of Hawai'i Press, 2013), pp. 86–90. Fewer than 5 per cent of the *mea kōkua* who lived in the settlement contracted the disease; Pennie Moblo, 'Ethnic Intercession: Leadership at Kalaupapa Leprosy Colony, 1871–1887', *Pacific Studies*, 22: 2 (June 1999), 28.
[19] 'Hansen's Disease, 1867–1941', Series 334–5, Board of Health, Archives of Hawai'i.
[20] Ibid.

when the quarantine became long-term isolation, as was the case with leprosy, there were also long-term consequences for the affected society. Since leprosy was thought to be highly contagious (especially among Native Hawaiians who had little to no immunity to foreign diseases), government authorities of the Hawaiian Kingdom decided that complete isolation of the afflicted was the best policy to prevent its spread. Intended to stop the 'scourge' and to bring about an end to the 'epidemic', the removal of those with leprosy from their communities to the new settlement resulted instead with the spread of fear, misunderstandings, and stigmatisation. The forcible separation of individuals from family and friends was carried out in an often-harsh manner, re-enforcing the objectification and criminalisation of the afflicted.

As the majority of those affected were Native Hawaiians, many blamed the indigenous people and their culture for leprosy's spread. Indeed, Walter M. Gibson (president of the Board of Health, 1882–7) reported in the bilingual newspaper, *Ka Nūhou*, in 1873:

> It [leprosy] is spreading rapidly ... The chief cause of its increase lies in the native apathy. The healthy associate carelessly with the ... victims. The most awful conditions of the disease neither scare nor disgust ... The horror of this living death has no terror for Hawaiians, and therefore they have need more than any other people of a coercive segregation of those having contagious diseases. Some people consider this enforced isolation as a violence to personal rights. It is so, no doubt, but a violence on behalf of human welfare.[21]

Furthermore, it was variously argued that the disease was spreading because of the 'native diet', Hawaiian living standards, Hawaiian morality, a lack of fear, 'mingling' with immigrant labourers, 'native medicines', caring too much for the afflicted, the weather and more.[22]

Determining how the disease was transmitted was of course also of great concern to government health officials and the public. Here again, Native Hawaiians and their way of life were most often central to any theory – before germ theory was fully accepted, and sometimes even after. The two

---

[21] Walter M. Gibson, 'The Lepers and Their Home on Molokai', *Ka Nuhou* 14 March 1873. Gibson was the editor of the paper.

[22] *Supplement, By Authority. Leprosy in Hawaii, Extracts from Reports of Presidents of the Board of Health, Government Physicians and Others, and from Official Records, in Regard to Leprosy before and after the Passage of the 'Act to Prevent the Spread of Leprosy', Approved January 3rd, 1865. The Laws and Regulations in Regard to Leprosy in the Hawaiian Kingdom.* In *MMHC, Box 27: Leprosy. File 289 (1)*, Honolulu, HI: Daily Bulletin Steam Printing Office (1886).

most publicly sensationalised theories were that the disease was sexually transmitted and possibly the fourth stage of syphilis, and that the disease was transmitted through the digestive tract.[23] Throughout the nineteenth century native Hawaiians were subjected to condemnations over their sexuality and suffered from venereal diseases such as syphilis after the initial arrival of Captain Cook and his crew in 1778.[24] That they used their fingers to eat the dietary staple, *poi*, from the same bowl was sometimes used to blame Hawaiians for their own demise.[25] Theories that the disease was hereditary mixed with miasma theory and thoughts on contagion; assumptions about race combined with attitudes about 'civilisation', and the reason for medical quarantine soon overlapped with ethnic divides.

Throughout the 1800s, several foreign diseases were introduced to Hawai'i (venereal diseases, tuberculosis, cholera, influenza, measles, smallpox, whooping cough) and the outbreaks sometimes hit more than once. Indeed for some of these epidemics quarantines were put into place (e.g., smallpox, 1853) and ships known to have sickness on board were denied entry or kept in quarantine until it was thought that the infection had run its course – but these were short-term measures. Leprosy presented a different scenario; isolation was long term; fear and stigma were perpetuated; those who contracted leprosy were in essence criminalised.

The criminalisation of leprosy in Hawai'i began with the 1865 Act itself. The experience of large numbers of people being arrested by police, on the authority of the Board of Health, for having this disease was unique to leprosy in the context of infectious diseases in the islands. The Act stated that 'any person alleged to be a leper' was 'to be arrested and delivered to the Board of Health' and that the 'Marshal of the Hawaiian Islands and his deputies, and ... the police officers [were to] assist in securing the conveyance of any person so arrested' to such a place as the Board may direct, 'to assist in removing such person to a place of treatment, or isolation'.[26] Officials travelled to the various districts across the islands, rounded up those suspected of having leprosy and sent them to the Honolulu receiving

---

[23] The connection with syphilis was promoted by a small but vocal group of physicians in Hawai'i, see Inglis, *Ma'i Lepera*, p. 81; the digestive tract theory was advanced by A. Mouritz, *Path of the Destroyer* (Honolulu, TH: Honolulu Star-Bulletin, Ltd., 1916).

[24] O. A. Bushnell, *The Gifts of Civilization: Germs and Genocide in Hawai'i* (Honolulu, HI: University of Hawai'i Press, 1993), pp. 24–6.

[25] Ronald F. Chapman, 'Leprosy in Hawaii: Scare Advertising at the Turn of the Century', *Hawaiian Journal of History*, 13 (1979), 124.

[26] 'An Act to Prevent the Spread of Leprosy, 1865, Section 3', in *Leprosy in Hawaii: Extracts from Reports of Presidents of the Board of Health, Government Physicians and Others, And from Official Records* (Honolulu, HI: Printed by Order of the Government, 1886), p. 9.

station for further investigation or confirmation that they had the disease. Some were released and returned to their home islands if found not to be leprous, but most were generally sent on to Kalaupapa.

As those suspected of having leprosy were usually sent to Honolulu first, the Marshal would often hold them in the Oʻahu Prison until the medical board could examine them.[27] The notion that prison was an appropriate response to a medical condition continued throughout the nineteenth century, as at various times, persons suspected of the disease were held in prisons in Honolulu, Lahaina, and Hilo.[28] To the viewing public there was little difference in the placement of a person with leprosy versus a common thief. There may, however, have been some benefit from their time in the prison. In her report to her brother the king, regarding a visit to the leprosy settlement in July 1884, Princess Liliʻuokalani remarked on the supplies provided to the leprosy patients and made a comparison with what was provided to the inmates of the Oʻahu jail; Honolulu prisoners were receiving more in food and shelter than the patients on the peninsula.[29]

There were many who expressed their concern and the need for greater compassion. In 1882, the president of the Board of Health, W. N. Armstrong, commented in his yearly report:

> When a leper is seized and taken to Molokai, it is a sentence of death. He has committed no crime. He has met with a great misfortune. He is driven out of society, that others may live. Without intending to act harshly, the Government has not been careful enough of his feelings … The policy of the government should be to treat him so that he may enjoy life while he has it.[30]

And Dr. N. B. Emerson agreed, after a visit to the settlement in March 1882, that 'the necessity for isolation is a sad fact' but also admonished that 'courage is needed in a nation, as in a patient, to nerve it to the dread ordeal of a painful surgical operation.'[31] Regardless of these calls for compassion and courage, for the most part, most Native Hawaiians perceived the actions of the Board of Health as harsh and uncaring.

---

[27] Series 334–5, Board of Health, Incoming Letters, July–September, 1873, Archives of Hawaiʻi.

[28] Inglis, *Maʻi Lepera*, p. 63.

[29] Liliʻuokalani, *Report of Her Majesty Queen Kapiolani's Visit to Molokai, by H.R.H. Princess Liliuokalani, July, 1884, Appendix to the Report on Leprosy of the President of the Board of Health to the Legislative Assembly of 1886* (Honolulu, HI: P. C. Advertiser Steam Printing Office, 1886).

[30] *Supplement* (1886), 116.

[31] Ibid., 129.

Personal accounts by leprosy patients who were arrested and sent to Kalaupapa are rare in the Board of Health archives. More often these stories are found in the Hawaiian language newspapers wherein vivid descriptions of their experiences are provided. In most accounts, Board of Health authorities and those acting on their behalf were seen as having little compassion for those being arrested. One description of an arrest comes from a man by the name of W. Kahalelaau, who describes the ordeal that he and his daughter experienced in 1869.[32] The authorities came in the night, and even though his daughter was too ill to walk on her own and he was unable to carry her, the officers insisted on taking them. The captain of the boat that was to take them stated: 'if she is unable, she should be tied onto a horse and brought; if she dies right on the road, bury her there.'[33] The girl survived as the family came together to carry her on their shoulders in a box and transported her safely to the harbour. Kahalelaau finishes his letter by questioning the motives of the authorities, suspecting that they are simply trying to 'sweep away' the Hawaiians by unfairly carrying out the quarantine law and disempowering the indigenous people.[34]

Patients' experiences of being arrested and transported to the leprosy settlement attested to their experiences of being criminalised. In an August 1872 letter, written by a woman named Kaiwi, it was reported how those suspected of having leprosy were held in the Lahaina prison where they awaited transport. Many family members were also present, waiting on the wharf to see them off or even try to go with them. She stated that the 'number of those people who have leprosy has increased in the prison here in Lahaina. Not only here in Lahaina but on Lanai, according to some people – men, women, and children.'[35] As researchers Silva and Fernandez observe, Kaiwi's letter 'illustrates how the government used the language and tools of policing and punishment for the patients. The patients were imprisoned in a jail rather than quarantined in a hospital or clinic.'[36] This government 'language' is further reinforced by the designation of the

---

[32] W. Kahalelaau, 'Ka hana pono ole i na mai lepera i lawe ia mai' [Not doing right to those transported with leprosy], *Ka Nupepa Kuokoa*, 24 April 1869; an analysis of which is found in Noenoe K. Silva and Pualeilani Fernandez, 'Mai Ka 'Āina O Ka 'Eha'eha Mai: Testimonies of Hansen's Disease Patients in Hawai'i, 1866–1897', *The Hawaiian Journal of History*, 40 (2006), 80–3.

[33] Silva and Fernandez, 'Mai Ka 'Āina O Ka 'Eha'eha Mai', 81.

[34] Ibid., 82.

[35] Kaiwi, 'Na Mai Pake i Lawe ia ma Kalawao' [Transporting those with leprosy to Kalawao], *Ka Nupepa Kuokoa*, 31 August 1872. Also found in Silva and Fernandez, 'Mai Ka 'Āina O Ka 'Eha'eha Mai', 83.

[36] Silva and Fernandez, 'Mai Ka 'Āina O Ka 'Eha'eha Mai', 84.

settlement in Board of Health literature as a 'natural prison'. Indeed, in the 1865 Act, the Kalaupapa peninsula was referred to as a 'natural prison' by authorities referencing the two thousand foot cliffs at its base and ocean surrounding all sides.[37]

While the Board of Health had begun this endeavour with the idea that those with leprosy would be sent to the Kalaupapa settlement to establish a colony and fend for themselves, they could not. Most were too ill to plant and harvest food, collect water, or build shelters. They needed the *mea kōkua* to come with them and care for them. Thus the Board of Health determined that a resident superintendent was necessary, not to offer medical care to the patients, but to manage and police the new community as an agent of the Board. The resident superintendents served under the main superintendent, Rudolph Meyer, a German immigrant who married into a Hawaiian family and resided above the leprosy settlement on Molokai's topside. The first resident superintendents were Euro-Americans, non-Hawaiian speaking, non-patients, but after some patient resistance, 'a more normal village environment was realized under the leadership of part-Hawaiian patient resident-superintendents'.[38] They remained subordinate to Meyer, however, because 'natives were not trusted with financial affairs'.[39] It might also be argued that residing topside as the ultimate superintendent, Meyer functioned much like a natural panoptic, surveying his charges within the settlement.[40]

The isolation of the settlement was geographical in nature, and at times cultural as well. Not surprisingly, the justification for what many viewed as banishment was an on-going topic in the Board of Health discussions. Indeed, in his 1870 report to the Hawaiian Legislature, then president of the Board of Health, F. W. Hutchison, admitted that 'the forcible separation of individuals from their friends and the world, although necessary for the welfare of society at large, must appear harsh to many of those afflicted', but little would change for at least another thirty years.[41] There were both real and imagined concerns for those involved, including the inner conflict over the (in)humanity of the situation. In the early decades of the settlement, patients were often subject to the random decisions and powers of the resident superintendents. For example, on one occasion in 1878, it

---

[37] 'An Act to Prevent the Spread of Leprosy', p. 63.
[38] Moblo, 'Ethnic intersection', 28.
[39] Ibid.
[40] See Michel Foucault, *Discipline & Punish: The Birth of the Prison* (New York: Random House, 1991), pp. 195–228.
[41] *Supplement* (1886), 135.

was reported that some patients had been restricted 'with ball and chain, for no other offense than running or attempting to run away', and others had been held 'with irons for small offenses or breaches of the peace'. At other times the resident superintendents were punishing other patients by 'enforcing labor and imposing fines and penalties for non compliances'.[42]

As the number of patients in the settlement continued to climb year after year, reaching a peak of approximately 1,200 in 1890,[43] the motivation to find a cure also intensified. Research was being done in Hawai'i (as it was elsewhere) in hopes of finding a cure for leprosy, and the use of human subjects in medical research was not unusual during this time. Further adding to the racial overtones surrounding leprosy in the islands, as well as reinforcing the criminalisation connotations, all of the research done by foreign-born physicians in Hawai'i at one point or another used Native Hawaiians as their test subjects. Furthermore, the most well-known leprosy research investigation in the island kingdom, meant to determine the mode of transmission of the disease, was done on a Native Hawaiian man by the name of Keanu who was a convicted murderer. Set for execution, Keanu was given over to Dr. Eduard Arning so that Arning could experimentally inoculate him with leprosy instead.[44] Research experiments on Native Hawaiians did not begin nor end with Arning. Other physicians had inoculated non-leprous *mea kōkua*, and some had worked directly with their Native Hawaiian patients.[45] Whether it was Arning or the others, the common factors in their research were twofold: leprosy and Native Hawaiians.

Other political implications are also apparent in this history. During the years of significant political events in Hawai'i (1887 Bayonet Constitution, 1893 overthrow of the monarchy, 1898 occupation by the United States) there were dramatic increases in the numbers of Native Hawaiians sent to the leprosy settlement on the Kalaupapa peninsula.[46] It was during these moments that the laws pertaining to the arrest and

---

[42] Ibid., 86.
[43] Although death was prevalent in the settlement there were generally more admissions than losses each year; see Inglis, *Ma'i Lepera*, p. 74.
[44] Edward Arning, 'Copies of Report of Dr. Edward Arning to the Board of Health, and of Correspondence Arising Therefrom' (Honolulu, HI: Daily Bulletin Steam Printing Office, 1886); A. A. St. M. Mouritz, *The Path of the Destroyer*; A. A. St. M. Mouritz, 'Human Inoculation Experiments in Hawaii Including Notes on Those of Arning and of Fitch', *International Journal of Leprosy*, 19: 2 (1951): 203–15; O. A. Bushnell, 'Dr. Edward Arning: The First Microbiologist in Hawaii', *Hawaiian Journal of History*, 1 (1967), 3–30.
[45] Mouritz, 'Human Inoculation Experiments...', 203–4.
[46] Inglis, *Ma'i Lepera*, p. 74.

confinement of those with leprosy became much stricter – in policy and in their application. For example, as of 1894 the foreign-led government punished those who were willing to 'mingle' with the ill, the *mea kōkua*. If they did not have official permission from the Board of Health to be in the settlement, they were not just removed, but were subject to arrest and jail time for trespassing. In an editorial found in the Hawaiian language newspaper, *Ka Makaainana*, 31 December 1894, it was reported with some distress that nine *mea kōkua* had been captured and tried in front of a judge on Molokai on 21 December, for their intrusion. They were punished for their offence. On 28 December, two more *mea kōkua* were tried and punished for the same.

During this same decade bounty hunters were going after individuals and groups suspected of having leprosy. In a famous incident on Kaua'i (beginning in 1893) provisional government officials arrived to take into custody a group of Hawaiians (about thirty people, in families) who had self-isolated themselves. The officials came with guns and cannons and were especially fixated on one man, Ko'olau, and his family. In the ensuing altercation wherein Ko'olau was fired at, Ko'olau shot back and killed the deputy sheriff who had come after him. Ko'olau was thus deemed an outlaw and authorities continued to hunt for him, though without success. Ko'olau survived for about three years, with his wife and child, in a secluded valley. His wife, Pi'ilani, buried her child and then her husband in that valley before returning to her community – not knowing if she too was now considered an outlaw. She was not arrested, but was able to tell their story of love and survival.[47]

Ko'olau had originally agreed to go to the leprosy settlement, if his wife could go with him as his *mea kōkua*, but the laws had changed and his request was rejected, so Ko'olau refused to be separated from his family. Indeed, when Pi'ilani told of the events surrounding her family's time in hiding from the authorities, she emphasized leprosy as *ma'i ho'oka'awale 'ohana* (the disease that separates family). She did not fear contracting the disease, but rather the possible forced separation of their family. As she stated, for many the leprosy settlement had come to be known by that time as 'the grave where one is buried alive'.[48]

It was during this time that a shift in identity among Native Hawaiians emerged, from the perspective of both those who had contracted the

[47] Frances N. Frazier (trans.), *The True Story of Kaluaikoolau, as Told by His Wife, Piilani* (Lihue, HI: Kauai Historical Society, 2001).
[48] Ibid., p. 8.

disease and those who observed others with it. That is, Hawaiians were now using the foreign concept of 'leper' to identify someone with the disease (including oneself) as one who was (to be) cast away from society, and removed for a life/death sentence at Kalaupapa. An example of this comes from Kaʻehu, a well-known chanter and hula master, who composed a chant that reflected his own experiences with leprosy. In this very personal composition, he stated 'Seeing me they drew away. They moved to sit elsewhere, whispering, and a friend pointed a finger: "He is a leper." I bowed my head, I knew it was true. In my heart I hugged my shame.'[49]

When the islands became a territory of the United States (1900–59) the leprosy situation remained central. For the patients on the peninsula, the main concern was over who would be running the settlement itself. A committee of patients wrote a letter and voiced their concerns to *Ka Nupepa Kuokoa*; it was published on 24 October 1902. Robert W. Wilcox, the first delegate to the US Congress from the Territory of Hawaiʻi, had proposed to place the settlement under the jurisdiction of the federal government and the committee feared that being placed under 'the rule of strangers' would make their lives even more difficult. Significant to this discussion is that the editors of the paper chose to situate the letter in the centre of the page, and encircled it with a linked chain – metaphorically signifying their literal imprisonment in Kalaupapa.[50]

Once again, soon after the United States took full control of the Hawaiian Islands, new laws were enacted and meticulous efforts were made to observe more strictly the isolation policies. A new leprosy hospital was established on Oʻahu and renewed efforts were made at finding a cure, in this colonising venture.[51] Previous policies were re-affirmed: people were expected to report others suspected of having the disease or else face a $100 fine, and those found to have leprosy were to 'remain in the custody of the board and its agent until lawfully discharged' and were to be 'cared for as well as circumstances [would] permit.'[52] The new law also stated that a patient could be removed from the Honolulu hospital and

[49] Kaʻehu, 'Song of the Chanter Kaʻehu', in Mary K. Pukui and Alfons L. Korn (eds.), *The Echo of Our Song: Chants & Poems of the Hawaiians* (Honolulu, HI: University of Hawaiʻi Press, 1973), p. 127.
[50] 'He Leo Uwalo i Ka Lahui Hawaii Mai Kalaupapa Molokai Mai' [A voice calling out to the Hawaiian nation from Kalaupapa], *Ka Nupepa Kuokoa*, 24 October 1902.
[51] See Michelle T. Moran, *Colonizing Leprosy: Imperialism and the Politics of Public Health in the United States* (North Carolina: University of North Carolina Press, 2007).
[52] Act 81: 'An Act Providing for the Care and Medical Treatment of Persons Afflicted with Leprosy', *Laws of the Territory of Hawaii*, 14 April 1909, Session Laws, Archives of Hawaiʻi.

sent to Kalaupapa if they were 'unwilling to receive such treatment or to submit to [the] rules and regulations'.[53]

There were also new laws put into place that were meant to protect the patients. A person taken into custody was to be examined as soon as possible by at least two physicians – one appointed by the Board of Health, and one chosen by the patient.[54] A third physician would be called upon if necessary. All had to be licensed to practice medicine in the Territory. Patients could choose to be treated by their own physician, in Honolulu, if that was possible. If found not to have the disease, a patient was to be given a certificate stating that s/he was not leprous.[55] It also became policy that no pictures were to be taken of patients without written permission from the Board.[56]

In the early 1900s, the Kalaupapa settlement had become much more institutionalised and regulated by the Territory of Hawai'i government. *Kōkua* were now hired by the newly formed Board of Hospitals and Settlements, and although they were often related to patients, that was not always the case, thus creating more of a separation between the patients and those who were caring for them. Since the 1890s, some *mea kōkua* had also been hired to be police officers within the settlement. A visitors' compound was established so that those family members who wished to could visit their loved one living in Kalaupapa. Physical barriers separated the well from the sick as one might expect. The visitors' house where they would meet had not just a table down the centre of the room to maintain the divide between the patients and their guests, but also a chain-link fence from floor to ceiling.

Sulfone therapy – halting the progress of the bacillus that causes Hansen's disease – was introduced in the 1940s.[57] With this treatment came patient demands for release from Kalaupapa. Unsure of the complete success of the drugs, settlement authorities allowed patients to be 'paroled' for short periods of time.[58] Referred to as 'inmates' in the record books,[59]

---

[53] Act 81, 1909.

[54] Act 122: *Laws of the Territory of Hawaii*, 30 April 1907, Session Laws, Archives of Hawai'i.

[55] Act 81, 1909.

[56] Act 78: *Laws of the Territory of Hawaii*, 21 April 1923, Session Laws, Archives of Hawai'i.

[57] Zachary Gussow, *Leprosy, Racism, and Public Health: Social Policy in Chronic Disease Control* (Boulder, CO: Westview Press, 1989), p. 7; drug resistance would present the need for newer drugs in the decades that followed.

[58] Olivia Breitha, in *Simple Courage: An Historical Portrait for the Age of AIDS*, produced, written and directed by Stephanie J. Castillo (Honolulu, HI: 'Olena Media, 1992).

[59] It was not uncommon during this era for patients of a medical institution to be referred to as inmates.

their clothes were fumigated before they could leave the settlement (the smell indicating to all who they came in contact with, where they were from), and they of course had to be checked regularly to see if the disease had returned. In his recent autobiography, Makia Malo, a former patient, says of those times:

> The doctors would take snips from us now and then and if the test came back negative one, two, three times, you were 'deactivated' and you could leave the settlement.[60]

A series of oral histories recorded in the late 1970s reveals how public health policies throughout the twentieth century affected the patients, while expressions of criminalisation permeated their lives. One man, born in 1929 and at Kalaupapa since 1944, stated, 'back in the 1950s I was declared negative and paroled'. He further commented that, 'inside, we were once prisoners, but now we are free'.[61] A woman, at Kalaupapa since 1936, explained:

> But for us lepers, when you ran away [from Honolulu], they would put you into isolation – solitary confinement, like they call it in prisons. Or, you had another choice. You could volunteer to be sent to Kalaupapa. When people were sent to Kalaupapa, we thought it was to die. It was final.[62]

Richard Marks, a patient at Kalaupapa since the 1940s, says of those days:

> People were still making you feel like you were paying a debt to society or that you were serving time and were to blame for what happened to you. Along with that was the attitude that since we were responsible for getting the disease, we shouldn't complain about how others are making decisions about us. Their attitudes and feelings took precedence.[63]

Sometimes, more drastic medical measures were taken when patients wished to leave the settlement; sterilisation policies of the twentieth century served to treat the 'patients' as criminals, assaulting their bodies beyond

---

[60] Makia Malo, *My Name Is Makia: A Memoir of Kalaupapa* (Honolulu, HI: Watermark Publishing, 2011), p. 53. To test if the disease was present, snips of skin were taken from the patient and observed under a microscope.

[61] T. Gugelyk and M. Bloombaum, *Ma'i Ho'oka'awale: The Separating Sickness* (Honolulu, HI: Social Science Research Institute, University of Hawai'i, 1979), p. 50. Many of these oral histories were given anonymously, the patient being identified only by age, ethnicity and number of years at Kalaupapa.

[62] Gugelyk and Bloombaum, *The Separating Sickness*, p. 58.

[63] Quoted in Stephanie J. Castillo, *Father Damien of Moloka'i: Simple Courage for the Age of AIDS*, 4th Draft Script (Honolulu, 13 June 1991), p. 12.

what Hansen's disease had already accomplished.[64] A man at Kalaupapa since 1921 explained that as the authorities did not want the patients to have children, 'They had a sterilization programme inside Kalaupapa.' He revealed that:

> they would ask us if we wanted to be sterilized. The doctor asked me back in 1941; he asked me if I wanted that operation. I said, 'Doctor, if you want me to be sterilized, it's all right with me. It's up to you doctor.' So he did. I think today you call it vasectomy? I don't know what they did with the women, but they did something.[65]

According to this patient, the Board of Hospitals and Settlement of the Territory of Hawai'i tried to make a law that would force all leprosy patients at Kalaupapa to be sterilised. The sterilisation programme began in 1938, but patients had a 'choice' in the matter. He further described their 'choice':

> they have taken everything out of us. They took us away from our fami-lies, they sent us here against our will, and even that wasn't enough ... in 1938 they tried to promote that sterilization policy on us. Any patient who wanted to go to Honolulu for a visit had to submit. Now you know, we missed Honolulu very much. Especially those patients who had children and family there. Those patients who were negative were given a condition for permission to visit Honolulu. The Board of Health didn't want patients to have children. They felt children would get leprosy. So to prevent lep-rosy spreading from parents to children, they wanted us to submit to being made sterile.[66]

Some were so desperate to get back to Honolulu and visit their families that they submitted to the procedure. The sexualisation of leprosy (e.g., some theorising that it was the fourth stage of syphilis) had projected deep anxieties about the disease into Hawaiian society. Another male patient explained:

> I wanted to go to Honolulu to visit my son. I could go on only one con-dition, to be made sterile. My son was only two and one-half years old. I had never seen him from the day he was born at Kalaupapa. They took him straight out ... I got word he was sick. So I asked the administrators if I could go out and visit him. They said you can see him, but only if you are

---

[64] Medical records for the time period in which these sterilisations occurred remain protected under US HIPPA Privacy Rule, and thus any information we currently have on these pro-cedures comes only from those patients who were willing to share their experiences in oral histories.

[65] Gugelyk and Bloombau, *The Separating Sickness*, p. 38.

[66] Ibid., p. 39.

made sterile. They cut off my balls. You had no choice. That's the only way
you could go, so I *submitted* and I went; I *saw my only son.*[67]

Perhaps the most compelling example of the objectifying of patients comes
from Henry Nalaielua's story of "progress" found in his autobiography, *No
Footprints in the Sand*. Born on 3 November 1925, along the Hamakua Coast
of the island of Hawai'i, Henry Nalaielua was sent to Kalaupapa at age fifteen,
after spending five years in Kalihi Hospital. He became an artist and musi-
cian, and a compelling storyteller. In sharing his experiences, he describes
the scene wherein he as a young boy was made to undress in a cubicle, and
then as the patients were called out one by one, they were to stand on a raised,
circular table, as physicians examined them using pointing sticks. The entire
exercise was meant to allow the attending physicians to see if the disease had
'progressed'.[68] For Henry, and no doubt for the others too, it was a moment that
he found degrading, humiliating and, as he says, caused him to 'feel shame'.

Another good example, or metaphor, of the distinction that the medical
and political policies surrounding leprosy in twentieth-century Hawai'i
instilled between patients and others, or those with and those without
this disease, was the 'visitors' house'. There was a visitors' house at both
Kalaupapa and the Kalihi Hospital in Honolulu. Former patient, Olivia
Breitha, described it as follows:

> One area of the [visitors'] quarters was called the 'caller house' and this was
> where patients and visitors met. This place had a concrete floor and win-
> dows for protection from the wind and rain. There was a six-foot chain link
> fence between the patient and his or her visitor, which made it so difficult to
> see each other. I called it the 'dog kennel'....
>   When Mr. Judd came [late 1940s], the first thing that came down was the
> railing in his office ...[69]

Even when the physical barriers came down, Olivia relates that the emotional and social barriers still remained and were never really forgotten.

End of Isolation

By 1949, in an attempt to lessen the stigma of the disease, leprosy officially became known as 'Hansen's disease' in Hawai'i. Sulfa drugs, penicillin, anti-anaemic medications, vitamins, sedatives and analgesics were all

---

[67] Ibid., p. 40.
[68] Henry Nalaielua with Sally-Jo Bowman, *No Footprints in the Sand: A Memoir of Kalaupapa*
(Honolulu, HI: Watermark Publishing, 2006), pp. 18–19.
[69] Olivia Breitha, *Olivia: My Life in Exile?* Lawrence Judd, former Governor of Hawai'i, was
the superintendent of the Kalaupapa settlement in the 1940s.

being used in the daily treatment of Hansen's and the Department of Health was also making efforts to reduce the stigma surrounding the disease.[70] Even with an official name change, educating the public and public understanding are two different things, as the following letter to the editor in a local newspaper illustrates. A physician had proposed a plan to set up a leprosarium in five separated counties, including a treatment centre at Hale Mohalu on O'ahu. In response to this suggestion, a Mrs. Weltmir wrote to the *Honolulu Advertiser* voicing her opposition on the grounds that it would cost the Territory too much money, but even more so that:

> ... five hospitals means 5 danger zones ... Suppose one or more patients escape from the local leprosarium – think of the potential danger existing while police and others search for the missing patient.... And occasionally patients from the proposed sanitarium could and would escape ... do you want your children to sit in a crowded movie house while some 'escapee' sits next to them?[71]

It is interesting to note that in the same year that Hale Mohalu was established, amidst such public discomfort, Governor Ingram M. Stainback responded by calling for the eventual abandonment of Kalaupapa, as he recognised that leprosy was 'not highly contagious' and that 'isolation of persons having the disease amounts to enforced and inhumane incarceration'.[72] Stainback felt that compulsive segregation was 'unnecessary' and a 'useless cruelty imposed upon patients and their relatives and friends'.[73] The recent success in treatments had given the authorities hope that Hansen's disease could be eliminated, and as such, isolation settlements should be abandoned and replaced by more 'humane and modern treatment' for those who might still contract the disease. Stainback stated that the 'present method of isolation, which might well be termed banishment and little short of legal death', was nothing short of a crime against innocent victims of disease, and that it defeated its own purpose by frequently causing those afflicted and their relatives, to conceal afflictions instead of seeking early medical aid and cure.[74]

---

[70] H. A. Kluegel, 'A Brief Summary of the Report for the Year Ended June 30, 1942', *Board of Hospitals and Settlement, Territory of Hawaii* (Honolulu, HI: 1942), p. 3 in Series 260, Department of Health, Archives of Hawai'i.

[71] Mrs. Weltmir, 'Keep Kalaupapa Where It Is,' *Honolulu Advertiser*, 27 June 1949, 12.

[72] '"Inhumane Incarceration" Is Termed Blot Against Hawai'i, *Honolulu Advertiser*, 18 February 1949, 11.

[73] 'Inhumane Incarceration', 11.

[74] Ibid., 11. It is also possible that with concerns about obtaining statehood, politicians were looking to remove any possible negative implications from the record, and did not want Hawai'i's treatment of Hansen's disease patients to appear too archaic.

It would eventually take patient advocacy – specifically breaking the law – some twenty years later, to bring about an end to the isolation policy in 1969. There were 183 patients living at Kalaupapa (137 inactive cases and 46 in treatment) in 1968; another 124 inactive cases had left the settlement to return to their home communities.[75] In an effort to overcome the ignorance and stigma that still existed, patients spoke out. Appearing on the cover of *Beacon: Magazine of Hawaii* in February 1968, Kalaupapa patient Richard Marks stated 'I am a Leper'. In his writings to the chief officer over the Hansen's Disease Program at the Hawaii Department of Health, the editor of the article that featured Richard also referred to him as a 'leper' stating:

> I know it is against the law for me to call Richard a leper. I know that your office 'recommends' that we all use the word Hansen's disease. Richard defies the edict for different reasons than I. He feels, with some basis I think, that the word can be banished only when the attitude [is] banished. ... If the words 'leper' and 'leprosy' will jolt the public into facing facts and doing something about them, we think they're well used.[76]

In the article Richard expressed his frustrations with the politics of being released: 'the minute you ask permission to go home you get the run-around' but then once release has been granted, 'they expect you to turn right around and dash back here before you contaminate the general public'.[77] He also spoke of restrictions on the patients, medications and the fumigation process, comparisons with the leprosarium in Carville and the future of Kalaupapa. His deepest concerns were clearly with the prevailing stigmatisation of leprosy:

> I call myself a leper because I still feel we are actually treated like lepers! No two ways about it. Of course we're much better treated today than in the old days, better medication, better living conditions – but the public attitude toward us and the State's treatment of us in regard to rigid rules is still like that of the oldtime outcast leper. And changing the name from leper to Hansonian or Hansonite or victim of Hansen's Disease doesn't change a thing really.[78]

The editor ended his article with the charge that 'the general public is guilty of intolerance, ignorance, and discrimination against the leper', asking

---

[75] Bob Maxwell, 'Isle of Exile', *Beacon: Magazine of Hawaii*, February 1968, 14.
[76] Ibid., 20.
[77] Ibid., 17.
[78] Ibid., 17.

'how open any of them would be to the return of the cured patient to the house next door'.[79]

For his candid observations, the January 1969 cover of the *Beacon* declared Richard Marks their 'Man of the Year'. Indeed his leadership and advocacy for the patients of Kalaupapa remained a force to be reckoned until his death in 2008.

Conclusion

In the past few decades, many former patients have also shared their experiences with leprosy and of life in Kalaupapa. They have spoken in public forums, visited schools, been featured in documentaries, and published their stories – all in an effort to advocate for change and educate the public.[80] Some patients established their own tour companies in Kalaupapa – Richard Mark's 'Damien Tours' has been the most successful and long-lasting. Often leading the tours himself, Marks would share his experiences along with the history of the leprosy settlement, breaking down barriers with every story offered.[81] His family continues to offer tours six days a week, year round, to visitors who come from all parts of the world in order to learn more of Kalaupapa's history.

Another patient, Bernard Punikaia, was also a strong advocate for the rights of his fellow patients, both in Hawai'i and internationally. He called his efforts a 'quest for dignity' and the expression 'was adopted for a 1997 exhibition about the accomplishments of Hansen's disease patients around the world that was unveiled at the United Nations and traveled to several countries'.[82] As Olivia Breitha had shared, even though physical barriers had been removed and the isolation policy officially came to an end in 1969, emotional barriers and stigma remained. Indeed, the scars of both the disease and the forced isolation of the 1865 Act still remain in Hawai'i today.

Beginning in the nineteenth century, persons with leprosy were separated physically, culturally and emotionally by the Molokai settlement,

---

[79] Ibid., 21.
[80] See Richard Marks and Olivia Breitha, in *Simple Courage: An Historical Portrait for the Age of AIDS*, produced, written and directed by Stephanie J. Castillo (Honolulu, HI: 'Olena Media, 1992); Bernard Punikaia, 'Leadership', Gugelyk and Bloombaum, *The Separating Sickness*, pp. 100–118.
[81] The author experienced the tour several times from 1999 to 2005, escorting university students and other groups to the peninsula.
[82] 'Activist Fought for Leprosy Patients', *Star-Bulletin*, 27 February 2009.

isolated and imprisoned for life/death. Cultural and personal identities were altered and sometimes lost. Further, a greater process of cultural colonisation of the Hawaiian people was at work. Under the rubric of the 1865 Act and subsequent policy revisions, the formation of a leprosy settlement at Kalaupapa and segregation of those afflicted by the disease was a diverse array of ideological and administrative mechanisms by which an emerging system of knowledge and power extended itself into and over Native Hawaiians.[83] Policies surrounding leprosy in Hawai'i served as an instrument of colonisation and blurred the distinction between medical isolation and racial segregation.

Moreover, leprosy represented not one, but a variety of meanings and metaphors. Were those persons who contracted leprosy in Hawai'i, from 1865 to 1969, patients or prisoners? They received medical treatment; thus they can be perceived as patients, but the objectification and often criminalisation that was embedded in that treatment denoted their position in society as akin to being prisoners. As the mode of transmission was not well understood in the nineteenth century, leprosy's contagiousness provided the opportunity for accusations and exclusion from society. That is, Native Hawaiians were viewed as the source of the disease, with the potential to bring harm to Euro-American society, which justified constructing them as 'targets for strategies of rejection' and banishment.[84] Leprosy in Hawai'i also served as a metaphor for social disorder, one that needed to be re-ordered and controlled by a paternalistic foreign-influenced Board of Health in the 1800s, and a US territorial government in the 1900s. The power of treatment was not given to physicians, but to lawmakers, allowing concerns over public fears and stigma to over-shadow medical understandings at any given time.[85] Concerned not only with the nature of leprosy and its potential spread, the authorities also feared international perceptions of disease in Hawai'i and the economic ramifications of those perceptions. Thus the arguments for isolation continued despite the acknowledgement of the harshness with which it was often being carried out. Banishment to the 'natural

---

[83] David Arnold, *Colonizing the Body* (Berkeley: University of California Press, 1993).

[84] Douglas, 'Witchcraft and Leprosy', 724.

[85] Furthermore, Michel Foucault's work asserts that in the nineteenth century in the West, the body – observed in clinics, prisons and hospitals – could become the object of and the instrument for the exercise of power. See also L. A. Rhodes, 'Studying Biomedicine as a Cultural System', in C. F. Sargent and T. M. Johnson (eds.), *Medical Anthropology: Contemporary Theory and Method* (New York: Greenwood Press, 1996), pp. 168–9.

prison' of Kalaupapa peninsula was justified lest 'our Hawaiian people . . . become a nation of lepers'.[86]

Throughout the history of Hansen's disease in Hawai'i (1865–1969) all of the patients sent to Kalaupapa experienced the isolation of the leprosy settlement in one form or another, whether it was physical, cultural, social, emotional, or all combined. Their lives were set apart from the rest of the islands and the rest of the world; public health policies further served to overlay their lives with connotations of criminality. Yet despite the challenges, patients found ways to exist with, and sometimes resist, the disease and its accompanying ramifications – often advocating for change and acknowledgment of their rights. After medical advancements brought an end to the need for a life of quarantine, it was patients who brought about an end to the isolation in their quest to overcome the fear and stigma that had been constructed through leprosy's relationship with the law.

[86] *Supplement* (1886), 76.

4

The Impact of Criminalising Disease Transmission on the Healthcare Professional-Patient Relationship

CERI EVANS

The potential criminalisation of those who recklessly transmit HIV and Herpes Simplex Virus[1] (HSV) has had a profound effect on the staff offering diagnosis, treatment, care and support to those with sexually transmitted infections (STIs) in England and Wales. Sexual healthcare professionals are trained to offer a supportive, non-judgemental service to their patients. Whilst it is not 'anti-patient' to inform them of the potential legal consequences of transmitting the disease they have – it is part of the information they need to receive – many healthcare professionals disagree with this use of the criminal law and feel uncomfortable with having to discuss it with their clients. They know also that they may be called upon to give evidence in court about the advice they give. They feel that the quality of the service they provide may be compromised by the issue of criminalisation and that having to raise this topic may damage the rapport between staff and patients.[2]

The two main sexual health and HIV organisations in the United Kingdom, British HIV Association (BHIVA) and British Association of Sexual Health and HIV (BASHH), believe that this use of the criminal law is 'unhelpful and potentially harmful to public health'.[3] BASHH and BHIVA support the United Nations AIDS Program (UNAIDS) recommendations to limit the use of criminal law in this area[4] and the Oslo declaration that a

[1] *R v Dica* [2004] EWCA Crim 1103; *R v Konzani* [2005] EWCA Crim 706; *R v Golding* [2014] EWCA Crim 889.
[2] C. Dodds, M. Weait, A. Bourne, A. S. Egede, K. Jessup and P. Weatherburn, *Keeping Confidence: HIV and the Criminal Law from Service Provider Perspectives* (London: Sigma Research, LSHTM, 2013), Section 4, 'Responsibility and Public Health' p. 4
[3] M. Phillips and M. Poulton, *HIV Transmission, the Law and the Work of the Clinical Team* (BHIVA/BASHH, 2013), p. 2. www.bhiva.org
[4] UNAIDS/UNDP, *Policy Brief: Criminalization of HIV Transmission* (Geneva, July 2008).

'non-punitive, non-criminal HIV prevention approach' is desirable.[5] This is because, although there may be a place within law for the punishment of those who 'maliciously' transmit HIV to others, in the main, it is likely that a punitive approach to criminalising HIV transmission will drive those who have (or suspect they might have) HIV underground. This will certainly not lessen the transmission of HIV if people avoid testing, engaging with healthcare professionals or become too scared to inform partners. To use the law to punish transmission of HIV and other sexually transmitted infections 'do[es] not change behaviour rooted in complex social issues, especially behaviour that is based on desire and impacted by HIV-related stigma'.[6] A more pragmatic option than the use of the criminal law might be 'measures that create an environment that enables people to seek testing, support and timely treatment, and to disclose safely their HIV status'.[7]

I have been a Sexual Health Adviser since 1991, working for different National Health Service (NHS) sexual health clinics in London and this chapter is written from the perspective of a practitioner. Over the years, I have been involved in many of the organisations that shape the way we think about sexual health and HIV, and have had the opportunity not only to attend, but also to speak at conferences on topics such as partner notification (discussed in the sections that follow) and criminalisation. Of course, what has most informed and educated me has been the daily work with the patients who attend sexual health clinics and the colleagues with whom I have worked. There have been significant changes during my career. For example, when I first started working as a Sexual Health Adviser, HIV results took two weeks to come back and there was very little in the way of treatment. The main roles of those working with people with HIV were to counsel, to offer support and to ease pain. The change in prognosis and treatment options has been immense in the past twenty-four years, but, having seen, listened to and advised hundreds of people with HIV over that time, it seems that the one thing that has not changed is the stigma that attaches to the disease. In 2009,

[5] *Oslo Declaration on HIV Criminalisation*, 13 February 2012.
[6] *Oslo Declaration*, para. 8, which cites, E. J. Bernard and R. Bennett-Carlson, *Criminalisation of HIV Non-disclosure, Exposure and Transmission: Background and Current Landscape* (Geneva: UNAIDS, February 2012)
[7] *Oslo Declaration*, para. 2, which cites, among other documents: UNAIDS/UNDP, *Policy Brief: Criminalization of HIV Transmission* (Geneva: UNAIDS, 2008); Open Society Institute, *Ten Reasons to Oppose the Criminalization of HIV Exposure or Transmission* (New York: Open Society Institute, 2008).

the HIV Stigma Index undertook a qualitative study that looked at the experiences of 867 people living with HIV in the United Kingdom. It reported that:

> stigma relating to HIV still remains a significant challenge in the UK because it has an impact on the accessibility and orientation of services (not only health, but also legal, care and support services) as well as on the self-esteem and general quality of life of people living with HIV.[8]

This is particularly noticeable in the more marginalised groups – the study looked at a subset of 276 respondents who described themselves as migrants. They reported that:

> Felt stigma was common. Over half of the survey participants reported feeling ashamed because they were living with HIV … Depression was also reported. Nearly half the number of men and a third of the women reported that they felt suicidal.[9]

The criminal law has developed quickly and in an *ad hoc* manner which has required rapid adaptation by healthcare professionals. The first prosecution in England and Wales for the reckless transmission of HIV was brought in 2003.[10] The law was developed through an unanticipated Court of Appeal judgment that overturned a nineteenth-century decision. There had been no prior consultation or discussion of the issue – indeed the government had recently decided *not* to follow a Law Commission recommendation that reckless transmission should be an offence.[11] At first the decision applied only to HIV; however, a recent decision[12] has extended the offence to the transmission of genital herpes, and theoretically to all other STIs particularly hepatitis B and C. Although the legal issues are similar, the characteristics of the illnesses and the populations affected raise different concerns for healthcare practitioners. This has necessitated changes in practice and guidance from the professional bodies and, therefore, perhaps, a change in the nature of the role of healthcare professionals.

[8] *Give Stigma the Index Finger! Initial Findings from the People Living with HIV Stigma Index in the UK* (2009). www.stigmaindex.org/united-kingdom (accessed 14 June 2015), p. 2.

[9] M. J. Chinouya, A. Hildreth, D. Goodall and D. Inegbenebor, *Migrants and HIV Stigma: Findings from the Stigma Index Study (UK)*, www.stigmaindex.org/united-kingdom (accessed 14 June 2015), p. 6.

[10] *R v Dica* [2004] EWCA Crim 1103.

[11] Home Office, *Violence: Reforming the Offences against the Person Act 1861* (1998).

[12] *R v Golding* [2014] EWCA Crim 889.

Treating Those with HIV

Just as there are difficulties for healthcare professionals understanding the law, so there have been problems for lawyers in understanding the rapidly changing medical issues around this disease, in particular, issues around the risk of transmission. Lawyers – for the prosecution and defence – will need to take into account what the defendant knew about his or her HIV status and the risks of transmitting the virus to another. This section examines the current state of knowledge and practice.

HIV emerged into the public consciousness in the early 1980s. The virus is passed on through infected bodily fluids such as semen, blood, vaginal fluids and breast milk. The most common ways HIV is transmitted are through sex without a condom and through sharing infected needles, syringes or other injecting drug equipment. HIV is often difficult to detect without specific testing, as people with HIV can be well and healthy for many years. If HIV is not diagnosed, it can cause damage to the immune system, and the person may become ill from very serious infections and cancers. At this stage, a diagnosis of Acquired Immune Deficiency Syndrome (AIDS) may be given. AIDS is not considered a disease, but a syndrome – a collection of different signs and symptoms, all caused by the same virus, HIV.[13] From an illness that was regarded as a death sentence in the 1980s, it can now be reasonably well managed through drug regimes. The vast majority of people diagnosed with HIV and on treatment comply with the medication regime prescribed for them: in 2013, 98 per cent of the 5,970 people aged 15 or above who were newly diagnosed were linked to HIV care within 3 months of diagnosis and 90 per cent of adults seen for HIV care were prescribed antiretroviral treatment compared with 69 per cent in 2004. The aim of antiretroviral treatment is to keep the viral load (the amount of HIV in the blood) as low as possible;[14] 90 percent of all adults receiving antiretroviral treatment were virally suppressed.[15]

In 2013, there were an estimated 107,800 people living with HIV in the United Kingdom. This has altered over the past thirty years, although gay, bisexual and other men who have sex with men continue to be the

---

[13] 'Stages of HIV Infection' at www.aidsmap.com (accessed June 2015).

[14] World Health Organisation, 'Consolidated Guidelines on the Use of Antiretroviral Drugs for Treatment and Preventing HIV Infection: Recommendations for Public Health Approach' (WHO, 30 June 2013).

[15] Z. Yin, A. E. Brown, G. Hughes et al., *HIV in the United Kingdom 2014 Report* (London: Public Health England, 2014), p. 5.

group most affected. In 2013, of the 6,000 new diagnoses, 3,250 were of gay men; 2,490 were of heterosexual men and women. Two-thirds of all heterosexual people living with HIV in the United Kingdom are black Africans (approximately 38,700). The number of new HIV infections in 2013 acquired through injecting drug use remains low at 130.[16]

Although men who have sex with men, particularly in towns and cities, tend to have good knowledge of HIV and the importance of regular HIV testing, healthcare practitioners often still struggle with accessing those who are at a high risk of HIV. We estimate that over 7,000 men who have sex with men and 13,000 black African heterosexuals remain unaware of their HIV infection.[17] This may be because they fear the consequences of being found to be HIV positive – stigma, rejection or potentially the concern that their lifestyle, drug use or immigration status may be used against them. Others may not realise that they have been at risk of contracting HIV and decline the offer of testing when they attend their General Practitioner (GP) or other healthcare services.

As with any life-changing or life-threatening diagnosis, receiving a positive HIV result is likely to be a difficult and harrowing experience. It is rarely possible to predict how such a result will be received and there can be as many reactions as there are individuals. People may be shocked, traumatised, angry, distressed, confused or disbelieving. Others who may have been expecting a positive result may be calm, disappointed, sad, accepting or relieved that they can now get the care and treatment they may need. There is a great deal of information that needs to be communicated to the patient along with the diagnosis: what clinic appointments they might need to attend; what blood tests are necessary and how often; when treatment might start; how often they have to take it and what the side effects might be; who they should tell about their diagnosis – their family, friends, employers, GP or dentist. It requires skill from the healthcare professional to determine the best time and manner to do this and to monitor how, if at all, such information is being taken in by the patient.

This advice is usually offered though one-to-one counselling and advice, leaflets, websites and support groups. Different people will require different ways of managing their questions and worries, and healthcare professionals should be able to tailor advice and information to each individual. For example, some people may need a lot of initial face-to-face

---

[16] Ibid., p. 14.
[17] Ibid., p. 6.

support, while others prefer to do their own research via the internet and get support through anonymous chat rooms. We need to ensure that information is provided in other languages or that interpreters are used. Of course, not all patients can read, which requires even greater care in giving explanations. If a patient is not fluent in English or competent in reading or comprehension, understanding complex issues of criminalisation may cause even more anxiety and tension between the healthcare professional and the patient.

Good practice suggests that HIV transmission and the legal implications should be discussed with all people with HIV. Healthcare professionals in settings where HIV and STIs are diagnosed may disagree with such a law personally and professionally, or may agree that reckless transmission should be treated with legal consequences. However, all must agree that personal feelings should not encroach on their professional work. Responses from participants interviewed for *Keeping Confidence*,[18] a qualitative study on HIV and the criminal law from a Service Provider Perspective, suggested that specific training for staff around the law is uncommon in many services and in some instances, that staff's 'understanding of the law was guided more by common sense and a sense of morality as it related to reckless behaviour, rather than being based upon a firm understanding of the law as it stands'.[19]

As healthcare professionals, we have to weigh up when the legal situation can be most usefully imparted to our patients. In *Keeping Confidence*,[20] clinicians were asked about their practices in raising the topic of criminalisation with newly diagnosed HIV positive patients. It seemed common to have a routine set of information to give to the patients, and in all the clinics where the research was undertaken, information on potential criminal liability was provided by staff.[21] It seems that responsibility for raising this issue frequently falls to healthcare staff as community-based service providers (HIV charities, social care services and other local organisations supporting people diagnosed with HIV) interviewed for the study said it would be 'unusual' for them to discuss HIV and the law with a newly diagnosed service user at an early stage for 'fear of overloading patients with too much information or causing unnecessary alarm'.[22] Some of the

---

[18] Dodds et al., *Keeping Confidence*.
[19] Ibid., p. 2.
[20] Ibid.
[21] Ibid., p. 2.
[22] Dodds et al., *Keeping Confidence*, p. 1.

participants did describe circumstances, presumably unprotected sex, 'where behaviour that might put people at risk of HIV acquisition might prompt a professional to raise the topic.'[23]

There appears to be a wide variety of practice among healthcare professionals but we should try to tailor it to the patient's response. Issues such as prognosis or treatment regimens may be deferred to a subsequent meeting if the patient appears distressed, but the question of the potential criminal liability in some cases may need to be raised immediately. This may be particularly important if, for example, the individual has given a history of unprotected sex with casual or regular partners and the possibility that this might continue post diagnosis. This requires some difficult judgement calls. If patients are highly distressed, they are unlikely to retain what is said to them. Phillips and Schembri[24] questioned newly diagnosed HIV patients in a large Manchester clinic about HIV transmission and criminalisation. 'Many'[25] respondents had no recollection of such a discussion taking place despite the study having been conducted in a clinic where this issue was discussed (and this discussion documented in the patients' clinic notes). Some stated they had 'no idea'[26] of what the law was; others appeared to have belief in their knowledge but in fact had an incomplete understanding. This potentially could put some individuals at risk of prosecution. This was of concern to the researchers who concluded: 'It is possible that the data are being given at a point where there is an information overload, and that understanding of the law should be treated more as a process than an event.'[27]

Often patients will bring up the issue of their current partner or concerns about their future sexual activity when they are given their positive HIV result. This enables the healthcare professional to answer their questions and also include the legal aspect. We would always encourage people to contact previous sexual partners who may have been at risk – patients may fear prosecution if they have had unprotected sex prior to their positive HIV result. Interestingly, from a legal point of view patients are not obliged to inform previous sexual partners of the fact that they had undiagnosed HIV when they had sex, so if patients refuse to inform

---

[23] Ibid., p. 2.
[24] M. D. Phillips and G. Schembri, 'Narratives of HIV: measuring understanding of HIV and the law in HIV positive patients', *Journal of Family Planning and Reproductive Health Care*, online, 14 January 2015, doi:10.1136/jfprhc-2013–100789.
[25] Ibid., p. 3
[26] Ibid., p. 2
[27] Ibid., p. 4

previous sexual partners or decline Provider Referral,[28] there is little that can be done about this, except for the ongoing discussion and support. The National AIDS Trust Report[29] recommends that it is important to keep HIV partner notification as an ethical, voluntary process rather than a coercive one involving the law.

Of course, any conversation about criminalisation of transmission is possible only if the patient attends their appointments following their positive HIV result. There are a small number of patients who become 'lost to follow up' from clinics. It is thought (through the HIV and AIDS Reporting System or HARS) that most patients who 'vanish' from the clinic that they were diagnosed in eventually present at other clinics for their HIV care and therefore will be linked back into healthcare and conversations about their ongoing sexual health and safer sex. There will, however, be some patients who, for whatever reason – shock or inability to cope with the diagnosis or due to shame and stigma – may leave the clinic after their HIV test result and not return. Although all clinics carry out diligent follow-up, we often find that false contact details have been given and that we are not able to recall the patient for further care and support around their HIV. Criminalisation may not have been discussed in this initial consultation, and patients may leave without the knowledge to protect themselves and others. This may also be seen as a reason to discuss criminalisation sooner rather than later.

It is seen as good practice to inform a person with HIV about the issues of criminalisation, even though HIV is very difficult to transmit if a condom is used correctly during vaginal or anal sex. Condoms used 100 per cent of the time, though not necessarily 100 per cent perfectly (i.e., with usual rates of breakage and slippage) provide protection of 80–5 per cent against HIV (uncertainty range: 76–93 per cent). In other words, for every 100 cases of HIV infection that would happen without condom use, about 15 (range: 7–24) would happen when condoms are used consistently.[30] 'Patients treated successfully so that their viral load

---

[28] This involves the patient providing the name and contact details of previous sexual partners. The healthcare professional contacts the former partner/s to advise that they may have been at risk of being in contact with HIV – or any other sexually transmitted infection – without revealing the name of the index patient. Information on whether the former partner has taken a test and any result is not passed onto the index patient, as this would compromise the confidentiality of the contact.

[29] National Aids Trust, *HIV Partner Notification: A Missed Opportunity?* (London, 2012).

[30] Aidsmap, 'Do Condoms Work?' www.aidsmap.com/Do-condoms-work/page/1746203/ (accessed June 2015).

is undetectable can almost eliminate their risk of passing on infection through sexual contact.[31] The phrase 'almost eliminate' can cause confusion and anxiety for patients, healthcare practitioners and lawyers alike. However, if a patient adheres to their antiretroviral treatment and their viral load is fully suppressed, there is increasing evidence that effective antiretroviral treatment considerably reduces the risk of sexual transmission of HIV and that this reduction is comparable to that seen with consistent condom use.[32] The Crown Prosecution Service has cautiously taken note of this and states in its guidance that 'It may be argued that taking medication may, in some circumstances, be as effective a safeguard as, for example, the use of a condom in reducing risk and therefore negating recklessness. Prosecutors should take great care with such cases however, as medical opinion on the reduction of the risk of infection is not settled, and evidence of the actual taking of medication in accordance with medical instructions may not be as clear-cut as evidence of the use of other safeguards such as condoms.'[33] This is further supported by BASHH Guidelines stating that if the viral load is undetectable in a person with HIV, post-exposure prophylaxis (PEP) for an HIV negative person (male or female) is recommended only if the negative person has had unprotected receptive anal sex with an HIV positive person.[34] The CPS also states that:

> Evidence that the suspect took appropriate safeguards to prevent the transmission of their infection throughout the entire period of sexual activity, and evidence that those safeguards satisfy medical experts as reasonable in light of the nature of the infection, will mean that it will be highly unlikely that the prosecution will be able to demonstrate that the suspect was reckless.[35]

[31] A. E. Brown, A. Nardone and V. C. Delpech, 'WHO "Treatment as Prevention" guidelines are unlikely to decrease HIV transmission in the UK unless undiagnosed HIV infections are reduced', *AIDS*, 28: 2 (2014), 281–3.
[32] G. P. Garnett and B. Gazzard, 'Risk of HIV transmission in discordant couples', *Lancet*, 372 (2008), 270–1.
[33] Crown Prosecution Service (CPS), 'Intentional or Reckless Transmission of Infection'. www.cps.gov.uk/legal/h_to_k/intentional_or_reckless_sexual_transmission_of_infection_guidance/ (accessed June 2015).
[34] BASHH, 'UK Guideline for the Use of Post-exposure Prophylaxis for HIV Following Sexual Exposure' (2011). www.bashh.org. Post-exposure prophylaxis (PEP) is a month-long course of HIV drugs that someone takes very soon after sex which had a risk of HIV transmission. The drugs are the same ones taken by people with HIV. The sooner PEP is started, the more likely it is to work; within twenty-four hours is best, but no later than seventy-two hours (three days). After seventy-two hours PEP is unlikely to work (tht.og.uk)
[35] CPS, 'Intentional or Reckless Sexual Transmission of Infection'.

Therefore, when discussing transmission of HIV, we are able to discuss with patients that the consistent and correct usage of condoms or in some cases use of antiretroviral treatment leading to undetectable viral load (even without disclosure of HIV status) or disclosure of HIV status if there is a breakage of the condom (to allow sexual partners to access post-exposure prophylaxis) is likely to be seen in court as a reasonable defence against recklessness.

Patients often, understanding on one level the importance of condom use/treatment adherence or informing partners to protect sexual contacts from contracting HIV may find it difficult to put theory into practice. This may be due to a number of reasons that we, as professionals, hear on a regular basis. For example, patients may feel ashamed, embarrassed or stigmatised by their HIV diagnosis, or fear that they might be vilified or rejected if they tell people or insist on using condoms. This may lead them to close their mind to the possibility of infecting others. Others may feel that they are feeling so well and healthy that it is difficult to remember they have HIV and to take necessary precautions. Some may find that alcohol and drug use make it difficult to bring up the issue of safer sex, and others may be diagnosed with HIV whilst in a long-term relationship where condoms have not been used, and cannot find a way of raising the issue. Some patients may fear domestic violence if they disclose their status, or being deported, or imprisoned or of having their children 'taken away' by Social Services. For the vast majority of these scenarios there will be ways of supporting or solving the issue if the person with HIV is willing and able to work with healthcare providers. Where emotional support is necessary for embarrassment or shame, peer educators, support groups or counselling may help. For more practical problems such as drug and alcohol use, domestic violence or immigration issues, referrals can be made to relevant agencies.

Staff may sigh with relief once the potentially tricky area of criminalisation has been navigated for the first time, but it is likely that they will need to have the conversation with their clinic clients on a regular basis. This is because improvements in medical treatment mean that people with HIV are now expected to live normal lives. For most people that means having a sex life which may change over the years depending on their relationships and health. Criminalisation does not go away nor should be considered 'dealt with' just because it has been discussed once. It is important to recognise that once people are diagnosed HIV positive, although their medical issues should take precedence in their appointment with their clinician/healthcare professional, a regular discussion about their sexual practice is also of utmost importance. Patients who are well and healthy may now be attending their HIV clinics only once or twice a year, so there are fewer opportunities to ensure that they are making informed decisions about the sexual life they have. In a busy and under-funded National Health Service, it may be felt by healthcare professionals that there is not enough time in appointments to do anything except present facts around prosecution so that the patient does not get distressed. However, this can lead to an assumption that the patient has understood the agenda of the professional which may not be the case.[36] Patients should have the opening offered to them on each visit to discuss – in a sensitive and appropriate manner – their sexual history since their last attendance. This also gives an opportunity for discussion around safer sex and risk assessment and allows both the professional and the patient to discuss any areas of concern or worry as a routine part of the appointment. Referral can be made if necessary to sexual health advisers or similarly experienced professionals for lengthier and more in-depth discussion. If this is seen as a normalised part of each appointment, patients will hopefully cease to see such discussion as intrusive and threatening.

The Crown Prosecution Service recognises that 'people who are informed that they have an infection which may possibly be life-shortening are likely to be in a state of shock at that time, and any further information that is given at the same time may be unlikely to have registered fully with the suspect' and that 'Prosecutors will need to be aware that proof of knowledge is likely to be difficult.'[37] If 'shock of diagnosis' was used as a defence for reckless transmission, the defence might seek evidence that, for example, the patient left the clinic in great distress and that the issue of transmission or criminalisation had not been discussed (this has not been tested in court at the time of writing).[38] Healthcare professionals should be aware that the court can issue a summons for patient notes to be produced, or that they may be released by the consent of the patient themselves. Therefore clear and explicit documentation in the patient's notes (whether electronic or paper) is vital. Healthcare professionals would be derelict in their duty if they were not to document thoroughly and clearly all consultations and discussions with patients, either face to face, or via letter, e-mail or telephone calls as per professional guidance.[39] Healthcare

---

[36] Phillips and G. Schembri, 'Narratives of HIV'.
[37] CPS, 'Intentional or Reckless Sexual Transmission of Infection'.
[38] Ibid.
[39] General Medical Council, *Good Medical Practice* (London: GMC, 2013), paras. 19–21.

professionals should ensure that documentation in notes includes not only the advice and information relayed to the patient in the session, but also any concerns they may have about how the patient reacted to what he or she was told, or whether the patient seems to be coping mentally or emotionally with the diagnosis and associated issues. Although this would normally be considered routine good practice, with criminalisation issues, it has become even more important that healthcare professionals are aware of the importance of their documented notes. If healthcare professionals do not advise patients to protect others from infection or break a patient's confidentiality without authorisation or due reason, they may be liable to pay compensation. This has been imposed outside the United Kingdom and it is thought that courts in the United Kingdom would take a similar approach.[40]

Most healthcare professionals will have come across situations where a person with HIV is apprehensive about telling a sexual partner with whom they have had unprotected sex after their positive HIV diagnosis. However, with careful support and counselling, most people will feel an obligation to inform and will carry out the action, or allow the healthcare professional to carry out Provider Referral. Conversely, if this does not happen, and there is felt to be a serious risk to another person of becoming infected with HIV, then the patient may be advised that if he or she does not tell the sexual partner then the partner may be informed by a healthcare professional. Obviously this is possible only if the service has the name and some contact details of the person presumed to be at risk. A decision to break the confidentiality of a patient particularly where there is no 'duty' of disclosure is a difficult decision, and it is vitally important that no healthcare professional make a decision to inform sexual contacts (whether a patient of the service or not) without discussing fully with senior members of staff and taking legal advice if necessary. Actions such as this may cause a crisis of confidence for patients with their healthcare providers, as they may feel betrayed or unsupported. It may also cause healthcare professionals to feel 'torn between duties to service users and to the broader health of the public'[41] or to a specific individual.

In many healthcare settings, discussions with patients around safer sex, sexual health and criminalisation and other less 'medical' issues have often

---

[40] A. Grubb and D. Pearl, 'HIV transmission: doctor's liability to future partner', *Medical Law Review*, 40 (1990), 250–6 and J. Chalmers, 'Criminalisation of HIV transmission: can doctors be responsible for the onwards transmission of HIV?' *International Journal of STD and AIDS*, 15: 12 (2004), 782–8.

[41] Dodds et al., *Keeping Confidence*, p. 3.

been left to sexual health advisers and nurses. The different groups have
their own similar professional codes and duties which may influence how
they make their decisions. It is the job of medical professional bodies to
issue guidance to their members to help to protect patients and to improve
medical education and practice across the United Kingdom.[42]

Guidance for doctors on sexually transmitted infections is offered by the
General Medical Council (GMC). The Nursing and Midwifery Council
and the Society of Sexual Health Advisers also publish codes of professional conduct which covers confidentiality.[43]

The GMC guidance reiterates the need to explain to patients how they
can protect others from infection and the importance of informing sexual
contacts about the risk of transmission.[44] Guidance from the GMC also
states:

> Disclosure of personal information about a patient without consent may
> be justified in the public interest if failure to disclose may expose oth-
> ers to a risk of death or serious harm. You should still seek the patient's
> consent to disclosure if practicable and consider any reasons given for
> refusal [...] If a patient's refusal to consent to disclosure leaves others
> exposed to a risk so serious that it outweighs the patient's and the public
> interest in maintaining confidentiality, or if it is not practicable or safe to
> seek the patient's consent, you should disclose information promptly to
> an appropriate person or authority. You should inform the patient before
> disclosing the information, if practicable and safe, even if you intend to
> disclose without their consent.[45]

All professional groups working in this field should ensure that they are
up to date with current advice from their professional bodies. It is vital
that people with any sexually transmitted infection are advised clearly that
they should inform their partners.[46] From a practical point of view, if the
sexual contact(s) of the patient with HIV is also a patient of the clinical

---

[42] A full discussion of the legal responsibility of professionals is too complex to go into detail
here. Useful explanations and algorithms can be found in Phillips and Poulton, *HIV
Transmission*.

[43] Nursing and Midwifery Council, *The Code: Professional Standards of Practice and Behaviour
for Nurses and Midwives* (London, 2015); Society of Sexual Health Advisers, *Code of
Professional Conduct*. www.ssha.info/about/code-of-professional-conduct/ (accessed June
2015).

[44] General Medical Council, *Confidentiality: Disclosing Information about Serious
Communicable Diseases* (London: GMC, 2009), para. 9.

[45] General Medical Council, *Confidentiality* (London: GMC, 2009), paras 53 and 55.

[46] Clinical Effectiveness Group of British Association for Sexual Health and HIV, *National
Guideline for the Management of Anogenital Herpes* (2014).

service and the index patient cannot be persuaded to inform them them-selves or allow Provider Referral, it is considered 'likely that the courts would recognise a duty by a doctor to disclose the HIV diagnosis to the sexual contact in such a case. A failure to disclose might therefore be a breach of duty owed to the sexual contact resulting in liability in damages if the contact became HIV positive as a result.'[47] If the sexual contact(s) is not a patient of the healthcare professional it is 'thought that there is a *power* to disclose, but no *legal obligation* to do so'.[48]

As the face of HIV is changing, with patients perhaps having only to attend to see their physician once or twice a year, all staff seeing patients with HIV need to take on the responsibility of these discussions (or ensure referrals to relevant professionals) to ensure that patients get the best holis-tic care for their medical and psychosocial needs to be met. It is therefore advisable that all services that deal with people with HIV have a clear and robust set of guidelines and access to training around criminalisation, as it is likely that this is an issue that will continue to affect both patients and staff for the foreseeable future.

This is not the only situation in which healthcare professionals face such dilemmas. There are increasing responsibilities on those working in the health service to monitor and potentially report to other authorities (e.g., the police, government bodies) if there are concerns around issues such as child protection, female genital mutilation, terrorism or abuse to vul-nerable adults. For healthcare professionals, this can sometimes feel dan-gerously close to losing the relationship with the patient by 'informing' on them, even if the individual (or contact of the individual) is at a high risk of harm. Particularly in sexual health and HIV services, the long-held belief in the right of confidentiality is held in high regard and previously protected by *National Health Service (Venereal Diseases) Regulations* 1974 which stated that information shared at a sexual health clinic is stored within the clinic's medical records only, and not shared with the wider NHS, or even within the same hospital, without the patient's consent. However, at the time of writing, these regulations have been dropped and the Department of Health is still consulting on what laws or regulations might replace them.

Owing to the nature of their work and the circumstances in which people with HIV were treated when the illness first emerged, those work-ing in this field often have had a different relationship with their patients

---

[47] Phillips and Poulton, *HIV Transmission*, p. 9.
[48] Ibid. (emphasis in the original).

to other healthcare professionals and see themselves as having a particular role. It has been difficult for healthcare professionals working within sexual health and HIV, as there has often been a tradition in the past of 'protecting' people with HIV, by allowing those with HIV to believe that only those who work within these specialist clinic services understand HIV enough to deal with it. Now, as HIV testing is becoming more normalised and treatment has become so accessible and effective, healthcare professionals are encouraging those with HIV to register with general practitioners, to be open about their diagnosis and to live full and active lives. However, a special relationship still exists for many of those with HIV and their clinicians, nurses and health advisers, and for some HIV positive people, clinic staff may be the only people who are aware of their status. It may then feel like a betrayal for those patients and staff to acknowledge that issues of criminalisation, safer sex and partner notification may need to be discussed. This is why it is so important, as mentioned previously, that such sensitive topics are dealt with in an empathic and non-judgemental manner by healthcare professionals so that patients still feel supported.

Herpes

Until 2010 in England and Wales, prosecutions for recklessly transmitting sexual offences under Section 20 were restricted to HIV. However, in August 2011, David Golding[49] was convicted of causing grievous bodily harm after recklessly infecting his girlfriend of the time with type 2 HSV. This case was significant because it lowered the threshold for the seriousness of the conditions that the law included and this has made a further impact on sexual health services that were already dealing with the many issues that had come out of the criminalisation of HIV transmission.

Despite herpes being a common, non-dangerous and non-life-threatening infection, it is still a diagnosis that can cause a lot of distress for patients, usually because of the negative connotations around the virus. Misinformation (particularly with easy access to internet searches) is rife, which often leads to stigma – a situation that the spectre of criminalisation has done nothing to avert. The *Golding* case attracted a lot of publicity when Golding's ex-partner sold her story to the media and was quoted under headlines such as 'My callous lover gave me herpes so that no one else would want me.'[50] (Golding 'strenuously denied

---

[49] M. Weait, 'Pass on herpes, go to jail?' *The Guardian*, 19 August 2011.
[50] A. Dolan, 'My callous lover gave me herpes so that no one else would want me', *Daily Mail* (London), 18 August 2011.

the victim's accusation that he had transmitted the disease in a bid to ensure that she would not attract other partners. He maintained that he had been in fear of the relationship ending at the time and recognised that his behaviour was unacceptable.')[51] There was much press coverage vilifying Golding for his actions and reporting the view of the expert prosecution witness Dr Mohanty, who stated that that herpes is 'devastating' and 'incurable'.[52] The opinions of Dr Mohanty on the seriousness of herpes was refuted by the Herpes Virus Association in a press release following the court case in 2011: 'Genital herpes is not serious, is not life threatening and normally has minimal implications for the infected person's health so it fails to meet the CPS criteria'[53] (of grievous bodily harm), and Dr Keith Radcliffe et al. in a letter to *The Times* stated that 'We challenge this view of herpes, as more than 70 per cent of the adult population has one or both types of herpes simplex, mostly without symptoms. It is seldom serious and circumstances when it may be life- threatening are statistically negligible.'[54]

Golding had been given a provisional diagnosis of herpes from a sexual health clinic in 2008, although what actual information and advice he was given, particularly on the issue of asymptomatic transmission, was disputed as there was no specific advice documented in his sexual health clinic notes or his GP notes. Golding pleaded guilty on the basis that he knew that he had herpes when he had sex with his then partner. The court, having received expert medical evidence, concluded:

> in the absence of concrete evidence as to the advice given to the appellant on his infectiousness ... there is nothing to detract from the effect of the appellant's admission by his [guilty] plea that he knew that there was a risk and went ahead anyway.[55]

Although at the time of writing, there has only been one conviction for criminal transmission of herpes in the United Kingdom, it is interesting to contemplate the potential implications that this holds for those working in sexual health, and anywhere that people may be seen with sexually transmitted infections. It suggests that the law may assume that even where there

---

51 *R v Golding* [2014] EWCA Crim 889, para. 78.
52 Ibid., para. 59.
53 Herpes Virus Association Press Release. 'Having genital herpes is not a crime – why Northampton Crown Court is wrong', 10 August 2011, hva.org.uk
54 Keith Radcliffe, Peter Greenhouse, Marion Nicholson, Nick Partridge, Deborah Jack, Phil Hammond, et al., 'Sexual diseases and criminal law', *The Times*, 25 August 2011.
55 *R v Golding* [2014] EWCA Crim 889, paras 82, 83.

is no, or unclear, documentation, 'best practice' will have been followed. Clarke et al. state: 'If conviction is based on what the defendant foresaw then what a patient with herpes is told, and what they understand, is crucial. In the Golding case it was not possible to tell from the medical notes what he had been told. A court may fall back on what it expects to have been done.'[56] This effectively puts the onus on the defendant to establish that they had not been given the correct information about disclosure or transmission.

There are two types of herpes that can affect the genitals: HSV type 1 (HSV-1) the usual cause of oro-labial herpes (the 'cold sore') and now the most common cause of genital herpes in the United Kingdom; and HSV type 2 (HSV-2), historically the most common cause of genital herpes in the United Kingdom, and the virus type that is more likely to cause recurrent ano-genital symptoms such as small blisters or ulcers.[57] Herpes raises different medical issues to HIV and there are more evidential difficulties in any prosecution. It is a much more common infection: around one in five people with herpes will have no symptoms; three in five will have mild symptoms so are unlikely to be diagnosed; and one in five will have obvious symptoms and will be diagnosed.[58] With herpes, the transmission issue is very different from HIV, and it is much less clear as to how transmission can be prevented. Herpes is much more common than HIV; by the age of fifteen, around 25 per cent of UK population have HSV-1 rising to around 50 per cent, by age thirty. Around 25 per cent of the sexually active UK population have HSV-2 and it is much more infectious than HIV. It is contracted by direct skin contact with the affected part, when the virus is active but not necessarily symptomatic – hence the possibility of herpes being passed on where there are no visible symptoms. It does not require genital penetration, just skin-to-skin contact or oral-genital contact. Even if no further outbreaks occur, patients potentially can pass on herpes through asymptomatic shedding of the virus. This occurs most commonly in patients with genital HSV-2 in the first year after infection and in individuals with frequent symptomatic recurrences. Asymptomatic shedding is an important cause of transmission but is reduced by all antiviral therapies and for many patients it will decline with time.[59] Transmission is not

---

[56] E. Clarke, J. Green and R. Patel, 'Sex post Golding: Time for a debate on whether the criminal law is the best way to deal with infectious diseases', *British Medical Journal*, 349 (2014), doi: http://dx.doi.org/10.1136/bmj.g4457 (Published 14 July 2014), p. 1.

[57] Clinical Effectiveness Group of British Association for Sexual Health and HIV (BASHH), *National Guideline for the Management of Anogenital Herpes*, (2014), p. 2

[58] Herpes Virus Association, *HVA.org.uk*

[59] Ibid.

totally prevented by condom use. Male condoms, when used consistently and correctly, might reduce the risk of genital herpes transmission. A 50 per cent reduction in the rate of transmission is seen in those using condoms for at least 25–60 per cent of the time.[60]

As healthcare professionals we have often found dealing with herpes and the criminalisation of transmission particularly challenging. We frequently have only one opportunity to engage with the patient in person when they attend with symptoms, and the debate has been whether it is necessary to initiate the discussion in that initial, and perhaps only, session. Patients often return to the clinic only after their first outbreak if they have further episodes that require treatment. Subsequent outbreaks (if any) are usually much less painful than the initial one and patients often manage it without medical intervention. The 'median recurrence rate after a symptomatic first episode is 0.34 recurrences/month for HSV-2 and is four times more frequent than the recurrence rate for HSV-1 and recurrence rates decline over time in most individuals, although this pattern is variable.'[61] Because of this general lessening of symptoms over time with the consequence of patients being less likely to re-attend, we have far less opportunity to engage with them than with those who have HIV. Herpes, by its very nature, does not require regular visits to the clinic for treatment, interventions or discussion, and we are much more likely to have ongoing opportunities to revisit information with those with HIV and to ensure that it has been understood and acted upon.

Following *Golding*, it is not just our clinical duty to ensure patients are given accurate, clear and easily understandable information about herpes and transmission, it is now potentially legally important. The legal responsibilities and requirements for those in relationships where one person has herpes and the other does not are currently unclear. Although, as with HIV, there is no legal requirement for those diagnosed with herpes to disclose to sexual partners, BASHH guidelines advise that disclosure is advised in all relationships since this is associated with lower transmission risks and may be a protection against legal action. The guidelines also advise that discussions around disclosure and transmission should be documented.[62] Healthcare professionals are all too aware that there

---

[60] E. T. Martin, E. Krantz, S. L. Gottlieb et al. 'A pooled analysis of the effect of condoms in preventing HSV-2 acquisition', *Archives of Internal Medicine*, 169 (2009), 1233–40; BASHH, *National Guideline for the Management of Anogenital Herpes*.

[61] Clinical Effectiveness Group of British Association for Sexual Health and HIV (BASHH), *National Guideline for the Management of Anogenital Herpes* (2014), p. 2.

[62] Ibid., p. 7.

may be a wide gap between the information we have given patients and what they understand. Green et al. suggest that when we are discussing herpes transmission with our patients and discussing partner notification and, now, criminalisation, 'careful counselling and support are needed'.[63] Clarke et al. conducted a 'mystery shopper' survey in UK genitourinary medicine clinics. The results suggest that what people are told about herpes by professionals is sometimes muddled, confusing and incomplete and the risks of transmission while asymptomatic were not always clearly set out.[64] It is well accepted, as discussed, that patients in a state of distress and perhaps pain may find it difficult to take in important information about transmission. People who will not or cannot tell their partners about their infection need careful and accurate information on reducing the risk of transmission as far as possible. Telling a partner is not easy, and infected people are likely to fear rejection. They may fear that their partner will tell others. They may, in some cases, fear physical violence.[65] Staff may feel, as with HIV criminalisation, that they need more focused and specific training around all aspects of herpes.

Conclusion

It is important for healthcare professionals to keep all these issues in perspective. Concern for the liability of healthcare professionals should not encourage us to overstate what are reasonable precautions – for example, advising people with HIV to never have sex unless they inform people of their HIV status in advance. Equally, concern about distressing the patient by discussing criminalisation should not allow us to understate reasonable precautions. It is eminently possible that we will see more and more convictions for 'recklessly' transmitting sexually transmitted infections, but we should not let this stop us from offering the best possible service to our patients and ensuring all staff are adequately trained and supported. It is possible that the law will change over the next few years and it should be a core responsibility of all those working in HIV and

---

[63] J. Green, S. Ferrier, A. Kocsis, J. Shadrick, O. C. Ukoumunne, S. Murphy et al., 'Determinants of disclosure of genital herpes to partners', *Sexually Tranmsmitted Infections* 79 (2003), 42–4.

[64] L. Munday, E. Foley, T. Lamb, J. Green, C. Evans and S. E. Barton, 'HSV-1 counselling what actually happens in consulting rooms? A qualitative evaluation of practice using mystery shopping in English level 3 GUM clinics', *Sexually Transmitted Infections* 88: Supplement 1 (2012), A4.

[65] Clarke et al., 'Sex post Golding'.

Sexual Health Services to safeguard both staff and patients as they work and live through these potentially confusing times. In the responses taken from the 'Keeping Confidence' study, it was recognised that many of the staff interviewed identified the lack of practical information available as a major issue. However, the report found that most of these information needs could be met by existing resources (these are named in the resource list in the document). The report concluded that the key challenge was the effective dissemination of this existing information to healthcare staff – an important point for all of us working and offering training in this field.[66] Finally, and very importantly, healthcare professionals should recognise that we work in a field that can challenge us medically, legally, ethically and morally on a daily basis. Our jobs in HIV and sexual health are exciting, life affirming and often exhausting and we should be proud to have an integral role in peoples' lives but these legal developments have opened up a new frontier in our work that may have ramifications in the future. We must be prepared – for ourselves and our patients – to ensure we are well informed and adequately trained.

---

[66] Dodds et al., *Keeping Confidence.*

5

Criminal Law and Contagious
Diseases – A Nordic Perspective

ASLAK SYSE

Introduction

In Norway, as in several other European Countries, there has been an on-going discussion during the past 10–15 years, as to whether or not it should (still) be considered a criminal offence to transmit a contagious disease to another person. The contentious issue primarily arises when a person transmits a serious and intractable infection, such as HIV, knowing that he (or she) is a carrier, and that the other person may be infected through intercourse or other intimate sexual interaction. This discussion has rarely been carried out in the public domain. More often than not, it has been of interest just to organisations, groups and individuals who in some way or other are stakeholders in the field, either themselves being infected, or working with infectious diseases or belonging to groups at risk, for example, due to their sexual orientation. In Norway, as in many other countries, the incidence of those recently infected with HIV is far higher among men having sex with men, than in any other group.[1]

The Penal Codes of all Nordic countries have historically contained clauses that make the transmission of serious contagious diseases a potential criminal offence. The understanding of the Penal Code in Denmark has changed recently. Denmark has decided on decriminalisation when HIV is transmitted from one person to another.[2] The other Nordic countries, including Norway, are upholding their traditional legal positions. In

---

[1] The Norwegian Institute of Public Health: In 2013, there were 233 newly diagnosed HIV cases in Norway, compared to 242 in 2012. The estimated number for 2014 is 250. The decline is mainly seen among heterosexuals. Among men who have sex with men (MSM), the HIV figures remain high. See: www.fhi.no/artikler/?id=109595.

[2] In November 2011, Denmark repealed Section 252, part 2, of the Danish Criminal Code, with the result that no diseases currently are covered by the penal provision on exposure to infection.

Norway, Section 155 in the 1902 Penal Code (with the last amendment from 2003) reads:

> Any person who, having sufficient cause to believe that he is a bearer of a generally contagious disease, willfully or negligently infects or exposes another person to the risk of infection shall be liable to imprisonment for a term not exceeding six years if the offence is committed willfully and to imprisonment for a term not exceeding three years if the offense is committed negligently. Any person who aids and abets such an offense shall be liable to the same penalty. If the aggrieved person is one of the offender's next-of-kin, a public prosecution shall be instituted only at the request of the aggrieved person unless it is required in the public interest.

Whenever the Norwegian Parliament has considered this issue, the members have, until now, more or less unanimously stuck to criminalisation as a preventive measure for combating the spreading of contagious diseases. When adopting the specific sections into the new 2005 Penal Code, which was amended in 2009, the two leading opposition parties in the Parliament – now constituting the Norwegian government – asked for a Law Commission to give recommendations in this field due to uncertainty as to whether or not penal sanctions were effective remedies in combating HIV infections. They also asked the ministry to come back to the Parliament with an updated report.[3] Once this had been agreed to, the new Sections 237 and 238 were adopted unanimously.

The government then, on 3 December 2010, appointed such a Law Commission. Altogether, twelve members were appointed by the government, and I was appointed as Chair. I have headed similar broadly composed Law Commissions in the fields of family law, disability law and medical law. I found this topic to be challenging and of great, general interest.[4]

The Commission was composed of experts in different fields: medicine, medical ethics, social sciences, legal reasoning and included stakeholders working specifically with HIV and AIDS at national and international level. The Commission also included an HIV positive member working with HIV and AIDS information to homosexuals, and an outspoken proponent

---

[3] Innst. O. nr. 73 (2008–9), see Proposal No. 5.

[4] Although I did not have any recent experience with contagious diseases, I had worked as a medical doctor for twenty years, two of which were in Zimbabwe – a country struggling to contain the several tropical, infectious diseases. In addition, the country faces a great HIV/AIDS problem. However, for the past twenty years I have been working as an academic lawyer not dealing with such issues.

of removing Section 155 of the 1902 Norwegian Penal Code: what activists referred to as the 'HIV-paragraph'.

The core mandate of the Commission was to review the current legislation combating the spreading of serious infections and to recommend any changes deemed necessary. The Commission had several other legal questions to answer. Among others, these questions included, what kind of regulations would be best suited to protect society from serious contagious diseases spreading through the air, for example, legionella from cooling towers, from drinking water and from the food supply.[5] These issues are outside the scope of this chapter, and will therefore not be discussed any further.

As mentioned, these issues had not been generally known or discussed. It was therefore a great learning experience to chair this Commission, where many participants had in-depth and personal knowledge and experience in this field. They brought qualified points of view from different perspectives into the Commission's deliberations. This chapter is an attempt to summarise my views, formed through the almost two years I chaired the Commission. In the white paper, NOU 2012: 17 *Om kjærlighet og kjøletårn*,[6] we did our best to draft good and enforceable Norwegian legislation. The white paper (NOU) was handed over to the Minister of Health and Social Affairs in October 2012.

The 2005 Penal Code went into force 1. October 2015 without any alterations of the 2009 amendments of the new Sections 237 and 238. There are just minor distinctions between the Section 155 amended into the 1902 Penal Code in 1984 when compared to the new sections in the 2005 Penal Code, now in force. Therefore, there are no reasons for clarifying these differences.

Collecting and Sorting Out Information

The first and foremost prerequisite to enable meaningful discussions among a diverse group of experts, who do not know each other beforehand,

---

[5] Norway has had some experience with the spreading of serious infections such as *E. coli* in meat, and at least one drinking water scandal in a major city where some 5,000 people were infected with the parasite *Giardia lamblia*.

[6] NOU (Official Norwegian Reports), and the title 'Om kjærlighet og kjøletårn' may be translated: 'On love and cooling towers'. 'Love' refers to spreading by intimate contact whilst 'Cooling towers' refers to general spreading through the air. The subtitle in Norwegian: 'Strafferettslige spørsmål ved alvorlige smittsomme sykdommer' would read in English: 'Criminal Law and Serious Contagious Diseases'. The full text (in Norwegian) may be found at www.regjeringen .no/pages/38086281/PDFS/NOU201220120017000DDDPDFS.pdf – There is a summary in English. This chapter is partly based on the summary which was drafted by me as chairperson in collaboration with the secretary of the Commission, Ms. Kirsten Been Dahl.

is to establish a common knowledge base. We spent half of our two-year timetable founding such a common basis in the fields of medicine, medical ethics, social science and legal reasoning; accepting and rejecting arguments that might be relevant for the discussions to come.

In all European countries that prosecute the transmission of infection, or exposure to the risk of infection, the criminal law approach is perceived as only a minor part of society's efforts to combat the transmission of serious communicable diseases. Penal sanctions are reserved for cases of reckless and unacceptable behaviour and are recognised as having a punitive character. In some jurisdictions, such as the Nordic countries, the penal provisions are also considered to help promoting attitudes and behaviour that reduce the overall risk of infection in society.

The countries' legislation differs somewhat, but it is all – at least to some extent – based on international recommendations. The laws authorise certain interventions in respect of individuals and the general public in situations where this is deemed necessary in the interests of public health. Coercive interventions will largely be relevant to combat serious contagious diseases, and are seldom applied.

Sexually transmitted diseases are covered to a varying degree by the communicable disease control legislation and systems for reporting communicable diseases. The national health authorities generally ensure extensive communicable disease control efforts based on information, cooperation and voluntary measures. In Norway, there are a few provisions providing for coercive treatment.[7] These provisions are seldom used and have for the last 15–20 years in practice been applied only to treat patients with multi-resistant tuberculosis who do not understand their risk of transmitting this disease and, therefore, are refusing to take medication.

We invited representatives from various non-governmental organisations (NGOs) in Norway working in the field to establish what kind of legislation they would find suitable and their views of criminalisation.

These deliberations did not take place in a vacuum. There is an on-going international debate in this field, partly driven by United Nations AIDS Program (UNAIDS), and partly driven by certain internationally recognised scholars. In my opinion, many of them seem to function mainly as advocates for a decriminalisation policy.

To my surprise there was little research-based knowledge providing guidance in the criminalisation versus decriminalisation question. What were presented as general 'facts' often turned out to be just key persons'

[7] Infectious Disease Control Act from 1984, chapter 5.

personal beliefs, or results from studies that were biased or not representative for other reasons. The Commission in the end concluded that there
were no research-based studies that provided real guidance that would
help answering the key question we were facing – whether criminalisation
is a measure which helps prevent the spread of serious diseases, or whether
it is a measure that makes some vulnerable groups even worse off, without
having any real effect on the transmission rate.

A good example may be the UNAIDS' final report from May
2013,[8] finishing with nine full pages of references. The medical and
social scientists in our Commission read – and re-read – many seemingly well-documented international papers without finding any real
fact-based or study results contained in the extensive notes that vali-
dated their seemingly 'crystal clear' conclusions. One important issue for
UNAIDS is to combat some draconic legislation in certain African and
Arabian countries. To recommend a general and full decriminalisation,
except in extreme cases of intentional spreading, appears to be an important instrument in this respect.

Such political views are held by many European ministries, supporting
financially the international work within the HIV/AIDS field. It may be
the reason for the structure and scale of the international organisations
set up to address these issues. International agencies working on HIV/
AIDS issues are big businesses, partly living their own lives, and organising worldwide conferences.[9] Such observations were in some way confirmed during our discussions in Geneva with World Health Organization
(WHO), UNAIDS and United Nations Development Programme (UNDP)
to get a better understanding of this international work.[10]

The Commission visited five countries during the initial phase of its
work, namely, Denmark, Sweden, the Netherlands, the United Kingdom
and Switzerland. Usually a Law Commission in a Nordic Country should

---

[8] *Ending Overly-Broad Criminalisation of HIV Non-disclosure, Exposure and Transmission:*
     Critical Scientific, Medical and Legal Considerations
[9] In addition to these meetings, Members of the Commission participated in UNAIDS' *Expert*
     Meeting on the Scientific, Medical, Legal and Human Rights Aspects of the Criminalisation
     of HIV Non-disclosure, Exposure and Transmission in Geneva, August and September 2011;
     FEMP 2011 – The Future of European Prevention among MSM in Stockholm November
     2011; *The High Level Policy Consultation on the Science and Law of Criminalisation of HIV*
     Non-disclosure, Exposure and Transmission arranged by UNAIDS and the Norwegian
     Ministry of Foreign Affairs in Oslo14 and 15 February 2012 and *The XIX International*
     AIDS Conference, 22–27 July 2012 in Washington DC.
[10] The UNAIDS building in Geneva is bigger and better looking than the building of World
     Health Organisation, or at least that's how it was four years ago when I last visited the sites.

be familiar with the legal situation in the other Nordic countries. Therefore we also called for information on the legislation and practices in Iceland and Finland. The non-Nordic countries were chosen because we expected that there would be some interesting differences in their legislation and attitudes towards the actual issues. In the five chosen countries, we met with the relevant governmental bodies, the prosecution lawyers, academic scholars with an interest in the field and relevant NGOs working with contagious diseases or representing the HIV community, or both.[11]

During its second year, the Commission gathered for a series of two- or three-day meetings, considering the core legal issues, working on the white paper and the legal provisions we would recommend the government to propose to Parliament. We held a public hearing to get input from different stakeholders, and the voices of these stakeholders, individuals and groups in favour of decriminalisation were embedded in a separate chapter in the report.

Relevant International Law and Scientific Evidence

Owing to binding sections in human rights' conventions – so-called hard law – a Commission such as ours had to consider what would be required by the Norwegian government to comply with our international obligations. Other relevant legal sources, such as recommendations and guidelines, are often referred to as 'soft law' – although they will in many ways be more relevant than the limited weight that is attached to them in purely legal terms.

The issue of the underlying 'hard law' was for obvious reasons addressed early in the Commission's work. The various human rights instruments contain fundamental standards with regard to such issues as the individual's freedom and participation in society (civil and political rights), but impose requirements to the effect that the state must ensure that the basic needs of individuals are met to a reasonable degree (economic, social and cultural rights).[12]

---

[11] In the United Kingdom, for example, in addition to the relevant governmental bodies, we met with the Terrence Higgins Trust and National Aids Trust, and Professor Matthew Weait (Professor of Law and Policy), Birkbeck University of London.

[12] There are several UN and Council of Europe conventions on human rights. The most important of these have been incorporated into Norwegian law through a specific Human Rights Act. In the event of conflicting provisions, the Human Rights provisions shall take precedence over other Norwegian legislation. This was recently more firmly established in the written Norwegian Constitution, by an amendment of May 2014.

Many declarations and statements from UNAIDS and other organisations working with HIV have a global objective and do not necessarily
reflect the great cultural differences between regions and states. To a large
extent, therefore, the states will be able to take account of national cultural
values and attitudes among the population when they consider the soft
law recommendations, as long as their interpretation is consistent with the
binding convention texts, such as the European Convention on Human
Rights (ECHR) and the jurisprudence of the European Court of Human
Rights (ECtHR).[13]

The Commission quite quickly concluded that there is no 'hard law' of
direct relevance to the question whether it is consistent with the human
rights instruments to apply criminal penalties to the transmission of infection, or to the exposure of another person to the risk of infection. Neither
the conventions ratified by Norway nor the comments of the treaty bodies or the ECtHR judgments address this issue directly. Moreover, nothing on this topic can be inferred with any certainty from the conventions.
The same applies to European Economic Area law. The statements dealing
with this issue are clearly 'soft law'.

UNAIDS has, for example, communicated clear recommendations
that the application of criminal sanctions in this field should be limited
to cases where infection has been transmitted, and where such transmission has been committed with purposeful intent. In the international
guidelines on HIV/AIDS and human rights, issued in 2006, the UN High
Commissioner for Human Rights (OHCHR) and UNAIDS are less clear
on this point, even though the guidelines could possibly be interpreted in
the same direction. Moreover, these agencies recommend that no special
penal provisions and no special statutory regulation of HIV transmission
should be adopted, but that general penal provisions should be applied
to the transmission of infection with purposeful intent. In the material
found by the Commission, only the UN Special Rapporteur on the Right
to Health states that the criminalisation of infection transmission and
exposure is directly contrary to the human rights instruments.[14] There
does not, however, appear to be a basis for such a statement in the sources

---

[13] Very few cases relating to HIV have been presented to the ECtHR. The latest was
I.B. v. Greece, see Judgement 3 October 2013, where the dismissal of a HIV positive
employee in response to pressure from other employees in the company, was considered a
breach of Article 8 (right to respect for private and family life) taken together with Article
14 (prohibition of discrimination). A similar decision was taken by the Supreme Court of
Norway, in the well-known *Henki Case* in 1988.

[14] 64 A/HRC/14/20. – See Section IV on HIV transmission.

of law. The Commission emphasised that any penal provisions and criminal prosecution must be in accordance with the general human rights standards in criminal law, including when infection transmission or exposure is concerned. This entails the requirement of a fair trial and that penal provisions must be sufficiently clear to make the legal position foreseeable. The human rights instruments also lay down certain requirements regarding the execution of sentence and dictate that legislation should avoid disproportionality between blameworthiness and the actual sanctions.

To move from law to science, there appears to be little evidence to support the theories about the impact of criminal legislation on infection transmission and exposure on which the recommendations of UNAIDS are based. The points of view are formulated with a global objective, which is particularly surprising given the wide divergence of the underlying cultural context among the member countries.[15] The Commission, therefore, found that these recommendations would be of little value for our final conclusions. One of the members of the Commission was working in the Norwegian Ministry of Foreign Affairs, especially with questions related to HIV programs and combatting contagious diseases, and even she had to acknowledge that the UNAIDS' recommendations were relevant documents though not too valuable when deciding the Norwegian policy in this field.

The Legal Situation in Some European Countries

We got, through visits, international contacts and from published material[16] a fairly good insight into the legal situation of several European Countries. We also noted dissimilar laws and jurisprudence in the different

---

[15] Some UNAIDS work in the field is particularly focused on high-income and secular countries like Norway, but here, too, significant variations will be seen among countries when it comes to legal traditions, the application of criminal law and the level of penalties, as well as cultural factors related to confidence in the legal system and a sense of responsibility in human interaction. We, nevertheless, took all published material, and especially UNAIDS' recommendations, into account in our deliberations.

[16] The Global Network of People living with HIV (GNP+) has published 'The Global Criminalisation Scan' with information about the legal situation concerning Criminal Law and Contagious diseases for many countries in all parts of the world (www.gnpplus.net/criminalisation/). Information on the legal situation regarding Criminal Law and Contagious diseases for many countries may be found here: NAM: HIV & the criminal law, London, 2010; Criminal transmission of HIV (www.avert.org/criminaltransmission.htm); Working paper: Criminalisation of HIV Non-Disclosure, Exposure and Transmission: Background and Current Landscape. Prepared as background for the Expert Meeting on the scientific, medical, legal and human rights aspects of the criminalisation of HIV non-disclosure, exposure and transmission 31 August–2 September 2011, Joint United Nations Programme on HIV/AIDS, Geneva, Switzerland. Information on the

states/provinces/territories in the United States, Canada and Australia, and that the national debates in this field appeared to be quite similar to the debate taking place within European countries and in international fora.

With regard to countries in Africa or Asia, many of the legal traditions, legal systems and actual circumstances differ substantially from the situation in the Nordic countries, and hardly add anything to the question of how to address the legal questions in Norway. At the same time, some members of the Commission were arguing that the Nordic countries may be looked upon as model countries, and, therefore, should avoid any criminalisation since the legal situation in many African countries is unacceptable, prosecuting more women than men and applying draconian penal sanctions against homosexual persons and persons with HIV infection.

If we look at other countries' legislation and practice, we can find examples of both specific HIV laws that impose penalties for infection transmission and exposure, and of provisions in the general Penal Code that specifically cover the transmission of HIV infection and exposure to the risk of HIV infection. We did not find any penal provisions on infection transmission and exposure to be included in more general public health or communicable disease control legislation.

All of the countries where the Commission received sufficient information, with the exception of Iceland, have experience of convictions in this field, and most of the countries have reported convictions for both infection transmission and exposure.[17]

In some countries, for example, in Sweden and England, different penal provisions apply depending on the degree of culpability and, in relevant cases, depending on whether the case involves infection transmission or exposure. In several countries, particularly those which apply general penal provisions governing bodily harm as is the case in Sweden, the transmission of infection will be punishable as a completed violation, while exposing another person to the risk of infection is punishable as an attempted violation.

In some countries, such as the Netherlands, the situation at present is that there is no legal basis for instituting criminal proceedings, at least not

legal situation regarding European countries, United States and Canada, may be found here: High Income Countries Issue Brief: Laws and practices relating to criminalisation of people living with HIV and populations vulnerable to HIV, for the High Income Countries Dialogue of the Global Commission on HIV and the Law, 17 September 2011, Oakland, CA. Information on the legal situation regarding the Nordic countries may be found here: HIV-Norden: Q&A: HIV and the criminal code in Nordic countries, Oslo, 2010.

[17] The collected information primarily relates to the spreading of HIV.

in cases where infection transmission or exposure has taken place in connection with consensual sexual activity between peers. This is the result of two Supreme Court decisions.[18] In Sweden, criticism has been raised about the uncertainty as to how the legal provisions should be applied. There seem to be differences between district courts as to how cases will be concluded in terms of the degree of culpability and thus which penal provision should be applied.[19]

The acts resulting in conviction in the countries studied by the Commission were mainly unprotected sexual activity without notifying the aggrieved person. This applied to the Nordic countries as well. The state of the law as regards the use of condoms appeared to be unclear in some countries, but the Commission did not find any convictions in cases where a condom was used during the entire act of intercourse.

The legal significance attributed to information regarding infection status, and to the consent of the person exposed to the risk of infection, varies from one country to another. In some countries, the consent of a sexual partner being aware of the concrete risk of infection exempts the potential perpetrator from punishment.[20]

The penalty level varied significantly in cases regarding infection transmission and exposure, even *within* the individual countries, for example, in Sweden.[21] This reflects, at least to some extent, the different circumstances of the cases, such as the number of victims, whether infection was transmitted (and, if so, to how many people), the number of times the aggrieved person(s) was/were exposed to the risk of infection, the degree of risk of infection in each individual case and finally whether the convicted person failed to inform, or indeed misinformed, the aggrieved person about his or her infection status. The degree of culpability will also be of significance for the sentence imposed, and is decisive in some countries regarding which penal provision is applied.

---

[18] The Dutch Supreme Court verdicts are respectively from 18 January 2005 (Case No. 02659/03 IV/SB) and from 2007. In the last verdict the Court stated that in 'normal circumstances of two consenting adults deciding to have sex out of their free choice' there is no place for criminalisation/criminal law regardless of whether HIV transmission occurred or not. The Supreme Court exempted willful or intentional transmission, for example, if a person forcibly injected another with HIV infected blood which was the case in 2008.

[19] Peter Gröön og Madeleine Leijonhufvud: *Hiv och straffansvar – en ouppklarad problematik* (HIV and penal sanctions – an unresolved dilemma, Svensk Juristtidning (*The Swedish Law Review*), 2009, pp. 609.

[20] This was the case in the Netherlands and Denmark, even before the decriminalisation.

[21] See note 19.

On the basis of the information available, the total number of criminal prosecutions in all the countries appeared to be very limited in relation to the number of persons diagnosed with HIV each year.[22] This may in part be explained by the fact that a significant percentage of patients are infected abroad, as is the case for Norway. Nonetheless, the number of prosecuted cases seems to be significantly lower than the number of persons infected in the countries in question. Such cases will seldom come to the attention of the police or prosecution authorities unless the aggrieved person reports the offence. There seems to be a general trend, arising from the necessary relationship of trust between health personnel and patients, for health authorities *not* to report cases of infection transmission or exposure to the police.

Analyses that have been carried out indicate that the incidence of criminal prosecution in relation to the number of HIV positive persons in the country is somewhat higher in Northern European, and particularly Scandinavian, countries than in other countries in Europe and large parts of the rest of the world. One theory held, among others by Professor Matthew Weait as well, is that this is due to a high degree of confidence in the legal system coupled with a sense of mutual responsibility between individuals in these countries.[23] Though the Commission did not do any structured research in this field, the available anecdotal evidence from Norway appears to support this theory. Whenever I asked colleagues at the Law Faculty – and I have held several presentations on this topic – a vast majority, men and women alike, when asked, found it most blameworthy not to disclose being infected before trying to make love to a known or unknown partner, and argued that this should still be a punishable offence. The same applied to more public presentations.

The Norwegian Law – From a Normative Perspective

The core mandate given to the Commission was to recommend whether or not the transmission of infection, or the exposure of another person to the risk of infection, should (still) be a criminal offence and, if so, under what circumstances.

---

[22] The numbers in Norway seem to be representative; out of 250 new cases of HIV-transmissions, 1–2 cases are brought before the courts. The crucial factor seems to be whether or not the aggrieved person(s) will file a complaint against the perpetrator.

[23] Matthew Weait, 'Punitive Economies: The Criminalization of HIV Transmission and Exposure in Europe' (Paper Presented at *The Future of European Prevention among MSM* (FEMP 2011), 11 November 2011). http://birkbeck.academia.edu/MatthewWeait/Papers/1141693/Punitive_Economies_the_Criminalization_of_HIV_Transmission_and_Exposure_in_Europe

The principal reason to criminalise any action, according to the preparatory documents for the 2005 Norwegian Penal Code, is the *harm* principle.[24] This differs from that of the United Kingdom which has no such overarching philosophy. Therefore, a criminal sanction should be applied only if the behaviour causes harm, or the risk of harm, to interests that should be protected by society. Even if a type of behaviour, such as the transmission of infection, has harmful consequences, a closer assessment must nonetheless be undertaken to decide whether or not a criminal penalty should be applied.

There is no definitive or general answer to the question of whether or not the transmission of infection in general is of such a nature and such seriousness as to justify the application of a criminal sanction. The assessment must at least take into account certain assumptions regarding the nature of the disease in question, the mode of transmission, the parties' individual situations and other circumstances that may be relevant. Penal provisions must, however, never be regarded as the key component in combating the spread of HIV. In Norway, the Infectious Disease Control Act from 1984 and the Public Health Act from 2011 are the main legal tools in safeguarding public health, supported by non-judicial instruments. These instruments are of far greater importance than penal provisions in protecting the population against serious communicable diseases. However, the Nordic countries have a tradition whereby infection transmission and exposure may be prosecuted, on the basis of penal provisions in general criminal legislation, intended to protect both public health and individuals.

The Infectious Disease Control Act does not provide for any suitable means for dealing with infected persons who, after repeated requests and counselling, do not comply with the recommendations on matters such as 'safer sex' and other proper behaviour for preventing transmission to other persons. The Commission did not find it appropriate to supplement the Infectious Disease Control Act with administrative penal-like sanctions for persons who fail to follow the advice given, thereby not seeing relevant forms of sanction as an alternative to the criminalisation of reckless and improper behaviour.

In the Commission's view, any criminal regulation of – direct or indirect – person-to-person transmission of infection, for example, in

---

[24] See the governmental proposal for the Parliament on the new Criminal Code in 'Ot. prp. nr. 90 (2003–2004) Om lov om straff (straffeloven)', which may be translated as 'On a new Penal Code'.

connection with sexual activity, should be limited to diseases of a serious nature. A *serious* disease should normally significantly reduce the long-term quality and/or expectancy of life of the infected individual. HIV infection fulfils such a criterion. The seriousness of the harm caused will also have a bearing on the assessment of responsibility for prevention and the moral blameworthiness of the person who exposes another person to the risk of infection, as well as on the limitations which society should place on individuals' general freedom of action.

There are sound reasons to regard HIV as a serious infectious disease, even with the recognition of modern medical treatment. HIV causes bodily harm, and thus necessitates a life-long treatment with drugs that have potentially harmful side effects. A well-medicated person with HIV still suffers from a chronic infection which in many cases has implications for the length of life, and there may be side effects of the medication 'cocktail'.[25] There is little doubt whether HIV poses a threat to *public health*, though advances in medicine have significantly reduced the impact of the disease on the individual.

The Commission did not, however, attribute importance solely to the public health argument. The members held different views regarding the impact on the public health of actual penal sanctions. There is, as already pointed out, limited documentation of the effect of criminal regulation, both regarding its contribution to infection prevention, as well as on unintended consequences alleged to have the opposite effect.

People in favour of decriminalisation often use the expression 'it takes two to tango'. However, eleven out of twelve Commission members found that the *infected party* has a special responsibility for preventing onward transmission of a serious disease. An infected person, being aware of his or her infection status and having received infection control counselling, should take steps to ensure adequate protection against further transmission. This is a responsible and proper way of conduct to prevent doing harm to other citizens. At the same time everyone, including those who are not infected or do not know that they are infected, undeniably have a shared responsibility for avoiding the transmission of infection, based on a general knowledge of communicable diseases and modes of transmission. This applies in particular to diseases against which protection may be assured by simple means, such as by using a condom.

---

[25] Professor, Doctor of Medicine, Stig Froeland, member of the Commission, wrote an extensive Appendix to the Report, titled 'HIV/AIDS – Medical Aspects'.

The circumstances in a number of the Norwegian cases prosecuted for transmission of infection are such that the infected party had acted in a blameworthy way, making a criminal sanction both right and reasonable. This is particularly the case where the infected person deliberately has given erroneous or misleading information about his or her infection status, perhaps over a long period of time, thereby giving the other party no incentive to ensure protection against infection. This increases the subjective blameworthiness of the infected person, and thus the justification for a penal sanction.

In Norway, there had been no general public reaction to the present penal provision; both the statutory decision to increase the penalty in 2003 and the new penal provisions in 2009 were adopted unanimously by the Parliament. Furthermore, none of the court rulings implies that the actual penal provisions seem to be discriminatory or unreasonable. There are a majority of lay judges in all criminal cases and the lay judges, when dissenting, go for the harder punishments. Thus, the criminal regulation seems to be in accordance with the general sense of justice within the Norwegian society. The same applies to Sweden and Finland. Denmark, on the contrary, is a more liberal country like the Netherlands, where the state seems to be more reluctant to act like a 'Nanny' towards her citizens. Transmission of HIV infection has in both countries, as previously mentioned, been decriminalised in practice.

The Proposals of the Commission

The majority of the Commission – eleven out of twelve members – concluded that under Norwegian law, the transmission of infection to another person should remain a criminal offence. They argued in addition that there should be *specific* penal provisions that govern the transmission of infection, instead of applying the general penal provisions relating to bodily harm. This will make it easier to pay attention to foreseeability and to have consistent court rulings. General penal provisions protecting life and/or health will lead to greater legal uncertainty. Besides, specific provisions make it possible to regulate the importance of consent from the other person, the standard of guilt and the effect of practicing 'safer sex' and so on adapted to just these types of cases.

Moreover, it was the majority's assessment that the continuity of specific provisions in the Penal Code would not have much bearing on the degree of stigmatisation experienced by the infected person, that is, whether prosecution proceedings are instituted under the general penal provisions governing bodily harm and the like, or under a specific penal provision governing the transmission of infection and exposure of another person to the risk of infection, but without stating any specific diseases. The persons who are arguing for the use of general penal provisions are, at least in Norway, the ones who really argue for a full decriminalisation. The dissenting member of the Commission held this view, which was explicitly formulated in chapter 10 of the report.

Having concluded that such provisions were appropriate, the Commission had to conclude on more detailed issues. Some key issues addressed were what modes of transmission and which diseases should be covered by penal sanctions, and whether only the transmission of infection should be regulated by criminal law, or whether or not the exposure of another person to the risk of infection should be included. Standards of guilt and how much importance should be ascribed to the use of infection control measures and other factors that affect the risk of infection were further key issues addressed by the Commission. Another important issue was the implications of an informed consent from the person exposed to the risk of infection.

Of the Commission's majority of eleven out of twelve members who considered that a separate penal provision relating to the transmission of infection should be maintained, a majority of nine members also found that *improperly* to expose another person to the risk of infection should be punishable, even if no disease is transmitted. The risk of infection and transmission of infection arise from the same type of acts, whether a transmission takes place or not. Only by ensuring that the penal provision also covers *reckless* exposure of another person to the risk of infection will the law promote a change in behaviour and thereby contribute to infection control.

Two members found that only an actual *transmission* of infection should be liable to a penalty. A core part of their argument was that the general risk of HIV infection is low, particularly when persons receive medical treatment. They argued that, even if it is difficult to determine the infection risk in individual cases, a penal provision that covers *any* act that exposes another person to the risk of infection would be too broad. It might include cases where the risk of infection is close to theoretical. The minority did not fear that such a decriminalisation of infection exposure would lead to more infected persons having unprotected sex. At the same time, such a regulation would send a signal to everyone in the population that they have an independent responsibility for their own health. The majority found these arguments valid, emphasising that if there were no risk of infecting another person, or transmission was prevented by using a condom, the penal provision would not be applicable.

The Commission, thereafter, drafted a Bill based on the abovementioned considerations from the majority, with dissenting votes given by the two minority parties. As mentioned, the majority (nine out of twelve members) argued that the Penal Code should cover both transmission of infection and exposure of another person to the risk of infection, but should not be applicable to each and every case of infection exposure. The Commission therefore recommended – and proposed in the specific section – that it was a prerequisite for prosecution that the perpetrator exposes *two or more* persons to the risk of infection, or exposes another person to such a risk on *repeated occasions* or through *reckless behaviour*. Examples given for what should be entitled as 'reckless behaviour' include that the infected person is older or in other relevant aspects is not on an equal footing; that he or she is preventing the other from using a condom or is lying about his or her health. A single 'slip-up', for instance, in the form of unprotected sex between equals, should not be punishable unless the perpetrator behaves recklessly in another manner. After one incident, the infected person should have time to reflect on the matter and good reasons to implement infection control measures on the next occasion and to disclose information about his or her status. If the first instance of intercourse would be punishable, the law gives no incentive for informing the other person since a criminal offence has already been executed.

A further key component of the Commission's recommendation was to limit criminalisation to communicable diseases that cause significant harm to body or health. An assessment must be made on a general basis of whether a disease has such consequences. In the present situation, HIV will be such a disease until a curative treatment is present, as now is the case for syphilis which is easily treated by antibiotics over a short-time period. Ebola virus transmission would at least be of the same serious nature. This is a disease where the infected person for the time being has no control over further transmission of the disease, and therefore cannot be held responsible for further transmission.[26]

In the Commission's recommended draft, the mental standard of guilt is determined to be intent or gross negligence. In the Commission's opinion,

---

[26] Until recently, the belief has been that a person may contract Ebola just through contact with the blood or bodily fluids of an infected animal such as a monkey or fruit bat, so there would be – with yesterday's knowledge – no perpetrator to bring to court. New medical knowledge may result in a change here.

the direct or indirect person-to-person transmission of infection should not be punishable when only simple negligence has been shown. A person, who is not likely to know that he or she is infected and may transmit the disease, will therefore not be punishable.

The recommendation also contains a provision addressing whether or not consent from the contracting partner should exempt a person from liability in the case of infection transmitted by sexual activity. In order for consent to have such an *exempting* effect, the proposed regulation says that the consent must be given in the presence of health care personnel in connection with infection control counselling. These formal requirements are intended to ensure that the consent given is informed and well-considered, and that the relevant facts relating to the granting of consent are established and that the consent is given after proper infection control counselling. There is no requirement of a special connection between the parties, such as marriage or long-term relationship, as is the case under the provision adopted in the 2005 Penal Code. Such consent should be written into the health journal of the actual infected person, thereby ensuring that there is a written record.

Furthermore, the draft statute contains a provision to the effect that no penalty is applicable when proper infection control measures have been observed. This means, for example, that sexual activity with proper use of condoms should not be punishable, even though the use of a condom does not assure full protection against infection transmission, even when used consistently.[27] This exemption applies regardless of any disclosure of infection status or any consent that may have been given by the partner. This is a codification of the actual Nordic jurisprudence.

The exemption from a criminal penalty does not cover medical treatment that reduces the risk of infection. As regards HIV, it is noted that even if effective treatment reduces the risk of infection to a high degree, there is not enough scientific documentation to determine precisely the magnitude of the risk of infection, particularly as far as individual cases are concerned. The degree of risk of infection may vary even in the case of patients under effective treatment, and is contingent on a number of circumstances beyond the control of the parties, and especially the infected person's partner. The non-infected person's susceptibility to infection also varies. Moreover, by using protection against infection, such as a condom, the infected person can actively implement measures to protect his or her

---

[27] See note 25.

partner. This decriminalisation may be regarded as a reward for proper behaviour.

The importance of medical treatment that mitigates the risk of infection must – in the light of continued medical development and new scientific findings – be considered under the question of whether there is a real risk of infection in a legal sense, an approach already adopted in the preparatory works relating to Sections 237 and 238 of the 2005 Penal Code, now entered into force. The probability that the risk of infection is reduced may also, depending on the circumstances, be given weight when sentencing, as shown by examples in case law under Section 155 of the 1902 Penal Code. In light of the above, the draft statute constitutes a certain degree of decriminalisation in relation to both the 1902 Penal Code and the 2005 Penal Code.

Behaviour covered by the majority's formulation of the penal provisions corresponds largely with jurisprudence under Section 155 of the 1902 Penal Code. There is no jurisprudence under the actual sections in the 2005 Penal Code. The amendments proposed by the Commission clarify the state of the law and render it more predictable. It is primarily behaviour that is acceptable or appropriate in the context of infection control that eventually will be decriminalised. The Commission has endeavoured to formulate the penal provisions in such a way that they encourage proper behaviour.

Still, the scope of the Law, due to the proposed wording, would be 'too wide' and cover situations where there are no good reasons for interfering in people's lives with criminal sanctions. The full Commission, therefore, explicitly stressed that the prosecution authorities should take care before prosecuting in certain situations, even when the wording of the law would indicate prosecution was possible. These situations include mother-child transmission in connection with pregnancy, childbirth and breastfeeding, cases where both parties are already infected, infection in connection with drug users' sharing of injection equipment and in connection with sex work, particularly if the sex worker is pressured to engage in unprotected sex.

To conclude this section on the Commission's recommendations, it is worth mentioning the proposed sentencing if a perpetrator is found guilty. The *maximum penalties* in the draft statute are differentiated according to the degree of culpability and whether the violation is aggravated, an aspect that is specially regulated in a separate paragraph. When determining whether the transmission of infection is *aggravated*, particular importance should be ascribed to whether the infection has caused loss of life, has been transmitted to two or more persons, or has been transmitted through particularly reckless behaviour. The maximum penalty for *intentional* violation should be a term of imprisonment not exceeding three years, while the maximum penalty for *grossly negligent* violation should be a term of imprisonment not exceeding one year. In its comments, the Commission recommends somewhat milder sanctions, under certain circumstances, than those found in current jurisprudence related to Section 155 of the 1902 Penal Code. In simple cases without transmission, the punishment should more often than not be a fine or a suspended sentence. In the case of *aggravated violation*, the maximum penalty is a term of imprisonment not exceeding six years for both intentional and grossly negligent violations. This corresponds to the maximum penalties in Section 237 and 238 of the 2005 Penal Code.

The Commission points to several factors to which weight should be given when sentencing. In addition to objective factors related to the act(s) that expose(s) another person to the risk of infection and the perpetrator's individual circumstances, consideration may, depending on the circumstances, be given to the aggrieved person's own behaviour, such as whether the latter was aware of the real risk of infection and nonetheless exposed himself or herself to it, but did not give a consent that, according to the mentioned prerequisites, would *exempt* the perpetrator from a criminal sanction.

Criminalisation Is Not the Most Efficient Tool for Combating Infectious Diseases like HIV

The Commission spent some time examining the relationship between communicable disease control legislation and criminal regulation. The Commission did not propose any changes in this relationship, or any amendments to the Communicable Disease Control Act. Nevertheless, the Commission drew attention to the potential for improvements in the application of the Communicable Disease Control Act. The Commission proposed that guidelines should be prepared addressing several of the matters raised by the Commission, thereby promoting better, more uniform application of the Act. The Commission also recommended strengthening sexual education, particularly at lower secondary school level, with special focus on sexual health and sexually transmitted diseases. Moreover, it pointed out that assistance and infection control should be interpreted broadly for infected persons, and not simply consist of health services relating to the communicable disease. It is important to provide psychosocial support and other assistance to infected persons in order to avoid them infecting other persons, and to non-infected persons who are at risk of being infected. Such assistance includes treatment for mental disorders and/or substance abuse.

The Commission also addressed the topic of infection control assistance for immigrants, including asylum seekers, and proposed certain measures that might help to improve follow-up in this field. The incidence of HIV and certain other serious communicable diseases is higher in some immigrant communities, for example, coming from areas where HIV infections are endemic, than among the general population.[28] Immigrants should, therefore, be given general information on communicable diseases and infection control in a variety of contexts. Work in this field presents special challenges, not only due to language and cultural differences.

The Commission also proposed a new provision to the Criminal Procedure Act authorising the examination of suspects in sexual offence cases to ascertain their infection status for clarifying as quickly as possible whether the aggrieved person may have been exposed to a risk of infection. The aggrieved person has been subjected to considerable strain in connection with the actual offence and should not be exposed to an additional burden to have to wait for a long time for such clarification. Under the Commission's draft section a physical examination of the suspect may be carried out without any requirement of specific reasons for believing that the suspect is infected, if there are sufficient grounds for suspecting that the person concerned has committed a sexual offence and the examination, for example, taking a blood test, does not constitute a disproportionate intervention. The purpose is to ascertain whether the aggrieved person has been exposed to a risk of infection with a sexually transmitted disease, and the proposed provision will strengthen the aggrieved person's position in cases relating to sexual offences.

What Has Happened to the Proposals of the Commission

The responsibility for the topics and proposals lie partly with the Ministry of Justice and for a minor part with the Ministry of Health. The Commission was appointed in cooperation by the two ministries. The recommendations of the Commission were, as mentioned, published in an Official White Paper in October 2012. As is customary in Norway for

---

[28] Norwegian Institute of Public Health, see www.fhi.no/artikler/?id=109595.

reports of this nature, the report was immediately distributed to relevant parties for a public hearing that took place during winter in 2013.

In June 2013, one of the amendments proposed by the Commission was passed by the Parliament. The Parliament concluded, precisely as proposed by the Commission, that medically assisted reproduction may be offered irrespective of whether it is the man or the woman who is the carrier of a serious infection like HIV. This is now Norwegian Law.

The main question is still unanswered by the Ministry of Justice: whether or not some behaviour connected to transmission of HIV should still be punishable, as is the case to-day after the 2005 Penal Code was enforced 1. October 2015. During the Ministry's enforcement process, no particular attention was drawn to the two actual sections. This implies that there has been no decriminalisation until now, but that the current legal situation continues. There have been criminal proceedings in some few, serious cases during the past two years.[29]

The consequence of no amendments will be a continuation of the legal situation which makes it illegal to expose another person to a serious contagious disease, irrespective of whether or not transmission takes place.

The proposals of the Commission's majority represent partly a decriminalisation and partly make more ordinary offences less punitive. The majority of the Commission advocated continued prosecution and imprisonment of persons with the most blameworthy and reckless behaviour who do not appropriately take into account the partners' risk of acquiring a serious disease.

Such recklessness will in Norwegian Law be deemed as intentional, and the Commission recommends no reduction of the maximum penalty in such cases. We have seen some quite appalling cases in Norway, and three of the cases were appealed to the Norwegian Supreme Court.[30] In one of the cases, the Supreme Court asked for an assessment of whether or not there should be an increase in the maximum sentence to be applicable for such cases.[31] The Parliament answered in 2003 with an increase in the maximum penalty from three to six years' imprisonment. As mentioned, this was a unanimous decision.

---

[29] In August 2014, for example, a thirty-year-old man was imprisoned for rape and for wilfully exposing another person to the risk of HIV infection. He has previously been convicted for transmitting HIV infection to two other men and for exposing another nine people to the risk of HIV infection.

[30] Norwegian Supreme Court, published (in Norwegian) i 'Norsk Retstidende' (Rt.) for 2000 p. 195, for 2002 p. 606 and for 2006 p. 1246.

[31] Norwegian Supreme Court, published Rt. 2000 p. 195.

The new government after the elections of 2013 and the new Minister of Justice and his ministry have the responsibility of following up on these challenging questions. There have been no leaks from the on-going discussions within the ministry. However, when reviewing the new, conservative government's political platform, there is reason to believe that other legal questions are being given a higher priority. Although Denmark has recently changed the style of reasoning in this field, the three other Nordic countries – Sweden, Finland and Iceland – seem to have no plans for changing their actual regulation, this being not too different from the current legislation in Norway.

However, there is in Norway, as in most European Countries, an effective and on-going lobbying of the government and the political parties from several stakeholders, among them the one dissenting member of the Law Commission. They organise meetings and publish articles arguing for a total decriminalisation in this field in Norway. On the contrary, the Norwegian Institute of Public Health more or less supports all the recommendations from the Commission. At present (January 2016), it is not easy to predict what the Parliament will decide. The government has not given clues to what they will suggest. And the debate keeps rolling in the newspapers and on webpages.

These broad questions open up issues for all kinds of expertise, just as we were staffed in this Law Commission. However, and in the end, these questions have to be 'solved' through moral and political deliberations, and where the experts' contributions, are just contributions. There are no clear-cut answers – either on moral or political grounds – to such questions. What seems to be the 'right' solution today may be deemed erroneous tomorrow. I have presented what seems to be right one for the time being in Norway, based on the factual, historical and cultural situation in the country, within a Nordic context and from a Nordic perspective.

6

Criminal HIV Exposure Statutes and Public Health in the United States

LESLIE E. WOLF

This chapter explores the role of criminal law and HIV transmission in the United States. It focuses on the HIV-specific criminal statutes that states have adopted, their historical context, their content and how they may conflict with public health prevention efforts. It concludes with a description of the changing policy environment that holds promise for change that would avoid some of the problems associated with the current criminal HIV exposure laws.[1]

Origins of the HIV/AIDS Epidemic

In 1981, the US Centers for Disease Control and Prevention (CDC) reported that five homosexual men in Los Angeles had contracted *Pneumocystis pneumonia*.[2] This report was the first to identify the opportunistic infections that were the hallmarks of the new disease that would become known as Acquired Immune Deficiency Syndrome (AIDS).[3] Although the disease was initially reported among homosexual men, by 1983, AIDS cases had been reported among infants, female sexual partners

---

[1] The term HIV exposure laws will be used throughout this chapter. As will be described in more detail, in the United States, transmission is typically not required for prosecution under criminal HIV laws, although some statutes increase penalties when there is transmission.

[2] CDC, 'Pneumocystis pneumonia – Los Angeles', *Morbidity and Mortality Weekly Report*, 30 (1981), 250–2. *See also* J. W. Curran, 'Reflections on AIDS: lessons for the future', *Journal of Urban Health: Bulletin of the New York Academy of Medicine*, 83 (2006), 1–2.

[3] Curran, 'Reflections on AIDS', p. 1.

of males with AIDS and people who had received blood transfusions or other blood products.[4]

Through field investigations and disease surveillance, the CDC was able to identify the primary mechanisms through which the disease was transmitted – sexual contact and exposure to blood and blood products – before the etiologic agent for AIDS, the human immunodeficiency virus (HIV) was identified. On the basis of this information, the US Public Health Service issued AIDS prevention recommendations in 1983.[5] These recommendations included avoiding sexual contact with persons known or suspected to have AIDS, limiting the number of sexual partners and, for people at high risk of AIDS, to avoid donating plasma or blood. Reflecting on those original recommendations in 2011, Drs. James Curran and Harold Jaffe, who were involved in developing them, concluded 'even in retrospect, the recommendations appear to have been essentially correct'.[6]

The continuing impact of this early work is reflected in our current understanding of the disease. HIV is transmitted through the exchange of bodily fluids, including blood, semen, breast milk and vaginal and rectal fluids. In the United States, HIV is primarily transmitted through vaginal or anal sexual contact and through sharing of drug injection equipments.[7] Mothers can transmit HIV to their infants during pregnancy and labour or by breastfeeding after birth,[8] and this risk has been substantially reduced through the use of highly active antiretroviral treatment (HAART).[9] Similarly, the risks of transmission through blood transfusion, blood products or organ or tissue transplants are low since the advent of HIV testing in 1985.[10] Contact with saliva, oral sex, deep

---

[4] J. W. Curran and H. W. Jaffe, 'AIDS: the early years and CDC's response', *Morbidity and Mortality Weekly Reports Supplements*, 60 (2011), 64–9; U.S. Department of Health and Human Services, 'A Timeline of AIDS', aids.gov/hiv-aids-basics/hiv-aids-101/aids-timeline; K. M. De Cock, H. W. Jaffe and J. W. Curran, 'Reflections on 30 years of AIDS', *Emerging Infectious Diseases*, 17 (2011), 1044–8.

[5] Curran and Jaffe, 'AIDS the early years', p. 66.

[6] Ibid., p. 66.

[7] US Department of Health and Human Services, Centers for Disease Control and Prevention (CDC), 'HIV/AIDS basics, HIV transmission', cdc.gov/hiv/basics/transmission.html.

[8] CDC, 'HIV transmission'.

[9] US Department of Health and Human Services, Centers for Disease Control and Prevention (CDC), 'HIV among pregnant women, infants, and children – pregnant women, gender, risk', cdc.gov/hiv/risk/gender/pregnantwomen/facts.

[10] CDC, 'HIV transmission'.

kissing or biting rarely transmit HIV;[11] documented cases of such transmission usually also involve some blood contact.[12]

Prevention measures can significantly reduce the risk of HIV transmission. Recent evidence has shown, for example, that consistent use of condoms can reduce the risk of transmission by 80 per cent.[13] Consistent use of HAART can reduce the risk of transmission of HIV by as much as 96 per cent.[14] Combined use of condoms and HAART can reduce risk of transmission by as much as 99.2 per cent.[15] Recent studies have also demonstrated that HIV negative individuals who take antiretroviral drugs prophylactically (referred to as pre-exposure prophylaxis or PrEP) can significantly reduce their risk of infection; this approach has been documented for men who have sex with men, heterosexual HIV-discordant couples and injection drug users.[16] This approach is similar to that used so successfully in reducing mother-to-child HIV transmission.

Response to the HIV/AIDS Epidemic

When the disease seemed to affect only homosexuals, the public paid little heed to it. By the end of 1982, the general public became fearful when it became apparent that AIDS could spread beyond the gay community.[17] These fears were not surprising. AIDS was a new disease that affected

[11] Ibid. That saliva is unlikely to transmit HIV has been known since early in the AIDS epidemic. See, for example, N. M. Flynn, S. M. Pollet, J. R. Van Horne et al., 'Absence of HIV antibody among dental professionals exposed to infected patients', *Western Journal of Medicine*, 146 (1987), 439–42 (concluding that their study of HIV antibodies among dental professionals 'also provides further evidence that casual contact with the saliva of HIV-infected persons, such as may occur within households, in the workplace or in public places, is extremely unlikely to result in transmission of the virus to uninfected persons').

[12] CDC, 'HIV transmission'; S. K. Chan, L. R. Thornton, K. J. Chronister, et al., 'Likely female-to-female sexual transmission of HIV – Texas, 2012', *Morbidity and Mortality Weekly Report*, 63 (2014), 209–12, at pp. 209–10

[13] S. C. Weller and K. Davis-Beaty, 'Condom effectiveness in reducing heterosexual HIV transmission (review)', *The Cochrane Collaboration*, 1 (2002): Art. No.: CD003255, p. 1

[14] M. S. Cohen, Y. Q. Chen, M. McCauley, et al., 'HPTN 052 study team, prevention of HIV-1 infection with early antiretroviral therapy', *New England Journal of Medicine*, 365 (2011), 493–505, at p. 503.

[15] P. Patel, C. B. Borkowf, J. T. Brooks et al., 'Estimating per-act HIV transmission risk: a systematic review', *AIDS*, 28 (2014), 1509–19, at p. 1514.

[16] US Department of Health and Human Services, Public Health Service, 'Preexposure prophylaxis for the prevention of HIV infection in the United States – 2014: a clinical practice guideline', cdc.gov/hiv/pdf/prepguidelines2014.pdf, p. 12

[17] Curran and Jaffe, 'The early years', p. 65.

young, previously healthy individuals and had a high fatality rate.[18] Despite government recommendations that emphasised its spread through sexual contact or contact with blood or blood products, the public feared that AIDS could be transmitted through casual contact with AIDS patients or even through insects.[19] Public fears resulted in discrimination against people with AIDS. People diagnosed with AIDS risked losing their jobs, housing and even medical care.[20] Children were kept from public schools.[21] Police wore rubber gloves when arresting people in some communities, and emergency responders refused to perform mouth-to-mouth resuscitation on those suspected of being homosexual.[22]

These fears put pressure on public officials to take action to protect the public. The Reagan administration had been criticised for failing to respond more aggressively to the AIDS epidemic.[23] Indeed, President Reagan did not mention AIDS publicly until September 1985.[24] That the epidemic was first identified among homosexuals and intravenous drug users (IDUs) may partially explain the slow response; the conservative, 'family-values'-oriented administration did not condone the 'homosexual lifestyle' or drug use.[25] It is also important to understand the limits of federal powers in the US system. The US Constitution divides power between the federal government and the states. The federal government has those

[18] Ibid., p. 64.

[19] Ibid., p. 65.

[20] A. M. Brandt, 'AIDS: from social history to social policy', Law, Medicine & Health Care, 14 (1986), 231–42, at p. 234.

[21] Brandt, 'AIDS,' at p. 234 citing 'The fear of AIDS', Newsweek 23 September 1985, 106: 18–25, See also 'History of AIDS up to 1986', avert.org/history-aids-1986.htm.

[22] Brandt, 'AIDS', at p. 234, citing L. Eisenberg, 'The genesis of fear: AIDS and the public's response to science', Law, Medicine & Health Care, 14 (1986), 243–9; R. Bazell, 'The history of an epidemic', The New Republic, 189 (1983), 14–18; and R. Goldstein, 'The uses of AIDS', Village Voice, 5 November 1985, 25–7.

[23] See, for example, H. Plante, 'Reagan's legacy', San Francisco AIDS Foundation, sfaf. org/hiv-info-/hot-topics/from-the-experts/2011-02-reagans-legacy.html; P. S. Arno and K. Feiden, 'Ignoring the epidemic: how the Reagan administration failed on AIDS', Health Policy Advisory Center Bulletin, 17 (December 1986), 7–11, at p. 10 (discussing, among other things, inadequate funding of research and education efforts and citing the National Academy of Sciences conclusion that federal efforts on AIDS were 'dangerously inadequate').

[24] AIDS Timeline 1985. See Arno and Feiden, 'Ignoring the epidemic', for a discussion of the Reagan administration's response to the epidemic.

[25] Arno and Feiden, 'Ignoring the epidemic', p. 9. Randy Shilts chronicled the early AIDS epidemic and the Reagan administration's failure to respond to it in his book And the Band Played On: Politics, People, and the AIDS Epidemic, which came out of his reporting of the epidemic for the San Francisco Chronicle.

powers enumerated in the Constitution – primarily the authority to tax and spend and to regulate interstate commerce. The remaining powers, including the 'police powers' to promote the general health, safety and welfare of the community, are reserved to the states.[26] Thus, the federal government can allocate funds (e.g., for research, education and treatment), provide guidance and education (e.g., through PHS recommendations) and approve or disapprove investigational drugs through the Food and Drug Administration Act. It can also enact laws that affect the military and activities that occur on federal lands. States retain most of the authority with respect to HIV/AIDS, and they adopted numerous statutes addressing a range of topics in the early years of the epidemic.[27]

The first HIV-specific criminal exposure laws were adopted by three states in 1986, one year after the HIV antibody test became available.[28] Although the federal government could not compel states to adopt such statutes, it explicitly encouraged them to do so through its policies. In 1988, President Ronald Reagan's HIV advisory commission recommended adoption of criminal statutes regarding knowing exposure to HIV.[29] Criminal statutes were seen as a way of deterring 'HIV-infected individuals from engaging in high-risk behaviours, thus protecting society against the spread of disease'.[30] Congress added teeth to the Presidential Commission's recommendation in the 1990 Ryan White Comprehensive AIDS Resources Emergency Act, which required every state to certify that its criminal laws were 'adequate to prosecute any HIV-infected individual' who knowingly exposed another person to HIV as a condition of receiving funding under the Act.[31] Because the Act provided substantial funding

---

[26] L. O. Gostin, 'Public health law in a new century: part II: public health powers and limits', *Journal of the American Medical Association*, 283 (2000), 2979–84.

[27] See L. O. Gostin, 'Public health strategies for confronting AIDS: legislative and regulatory policy in the United States', *Journal of the American Medical Association*, 261 (1989), 1621–30 (describing substantial legislative and regulatory activity on a number of issues, including HIV testing, antidiscrimination, confidentiality and criminalisation of HIV exposure).

[28] J. S. Lehman, M. H. Carr, A. J. Nichol et al., 'Prevalence and public health implications of state laws that criminalize potential HIV exposure in the United States', *AIDS Behavior*, 18 (2014), 997–1006, at p. 999

[29] Presidential Commission on the Human Immunodeficiency Virus, 'Report of the presidential commission on the human immunodeficiency virus epidemic' (1988) archive.org/details/reportofpresiden00pres, pp. 130–1

[30] Ibid., p. 130.

[31] Ryan White Act, Pub. L. No. 101–381, 104 Stat. 576, § 301(a). The Ryan White Act provides funding to cities, states and other public and private non-profit entities to provide coordinated services to people living with HIV. It is considered a funder of 'last resort'; that is, when there is no other funder to provide the services. Services funded include: emergency

for services that states were struggling to provide, there was a significant incentive for states to comply. Because the Act did not specify criteria for determining the adequacy of state laws, it was up to the states to determine whether they needed to adopt new laws, to amend existing public health laws or could rely on existing criminal laws. The certification requirement was removed in the 2000 reauthorisation of the Ryan White Act, presumably because all states had made their certification.[32]

It is not clear how important the federal government's endorsement of HIV exposure laws were in state adoption of these laws. Between 1986 and 1990, when the Ryan White Act was adopted, twenty-two states adopted HIV-specific statutes. By 2000, when the certification requirement was removed, an additional nine states had adopted new laws and eleven states had amended their existing laws.[33] In this period, many states adopted tougher laws, probably in response to well-publicised cases of multiple partner exposure, such as the Nushawn Williams case.[34] Since 2000, only four additional states have adopted new laws, the most recent in 2011, and five states have amended their existing laws.[35] Federal support for state criminal HIV exposure laws has waned since 2010, as described in the pages that follow.

State Criminal HIV Exposure Statutes

Because the Ryan White Act did not require states to enact specific types of criminal laws to meet its certification requirement, states had various options available to them.[36] One option was to look to existing sexually transmitted infection statutes.[37] Public health statutes criminalising

---

assistance in metropolitan areas most affected by the HIV/AIDS epidemic (Part A); funding to states to provide health care, prescription drugs and support services (Part B); funding to provide comprehensive primary health services (Part C), funding to provide family-centred services for children, youth and women (Part D), plus funding for special programmes. US Department of Health and Human Services, Health Resources and Services Administration, 'About the Ryan White HIV/AIDS programs', hab.hrs.gov/abouthab/aboutprogram.html; the Henry J. Kaiser Family Foundation, 'Financing HIV/AIDS care: a quilt with Many Holes', kff.org/hivaids/issue-brief/financing-hivaids-care-a-quilt-with-many.

[32] L. E. Wolf and R. Vezina, 'Crime and punishment: is there a role for criminal law in HIV prevention policy?', *Whittier Law Review*, 25 (2004), 821–86, at p. 883

[33] Lehman et al., 'Prevalence', pp. 999–1000

[34] S. F. Morin, 'Early detection of HIV: assessing the legislative context', *AIDS*, 25 (2000), S144–50, at p. S148

[35] Lehman et al., 'Prevalence', pp. 999–1000; Iowa Code § 709D.1 (2014).

[36] Wolf and Vezina, 'Crime and punishment', pp. 844–59

[37] Ibid., pp. 857–8

exposure to sexually transmitted infections (primarily syphilis and gonorrhoea) date back to the late nineteenth and early twentieth centuries.[38] These statutes typically imposed minimal criminal penalties (small fines and short imprisonment (maximum one year)) for intentionally or knowingly exposing an individual to one of the listed sexually transmitted infections. Although these criminal laws were rarely enforced, they provided a realistic threat of coercion to use in conjunction with other public health efforts, such as screening and partner notification, to reduce sexually transmitted infections.[39] While, in comparison to the HIV-specific criminal exposure statutes, which can impose long prison sentences,[40] these statutes seem relatively benign, it is important to remember that, at the time these statutes were adopted, there were no cures for syphilis and gonorrhoea. Similar to HIV, public fears and misunderstandings about the diseases were significant.[41] Thus, like the later HIV-related exposure statutes discussed later on, they may not accurately reflect the risk of disease transmission nor be effective means for preventing transmission. However, these statutes did not always automatically apply to HIV. For example, a New York court held that its existing statute did not apply to HIV because HIV was treated differently from other sexually transmitted infections in other public health laws, such as those concerning testing and partner notification.[42] Accordingly, amendments to these statutes may have been necessary to include HIV within their scope.

In addition, states could rely on general criminal laws, such as those criminalising assault, reckless endangerment and attempted murder.[43]

---

[38] Brandt, 'AIDS', pp. 231–3; S. V. Kenney, 'Criminalizing HIV transmission: lessons from history and a model for the future', *Journal of Contemporary Health Law and Policy*, 8 (1992), 245–73, at pp. 255–6.

[39] Brandt, 'AIDS', pp. 231–3; Kenney, 'Criminalizing HIV transmission', pp. 255–6

[40] In my work with Richard Vezina, we found a range of maximum sentences from three years to life for sexual exposure without transmission (two statutes had different penalties for transmission), with a mean maximum sentence of approximately twelve years.

[41] Brandt, 'AIDS', p. 232.

[42] *Plaza v. Estate of Wisser*, 211 A.D.2d 111 (1995), pp. 119–20. It is important to note that New York did not amend its existing sexually transmitted infection statute nor did it adopt an HIV-specific statute. Rather, it continues to rely on general criminal statutes. Lehman et al., 'Prevalence', p. 1005.

[43] Wolf and Vezina, 'Crime and punishment', pp. 858–9. Comparing our original assessment to the more recent Lehman analysis, Massachusetts, New Hampshire, Texas, and Oregon are states that still have no HIV-specific or sexually transmitted exposure laws, but rather would rely on general criminal laws to prosecute HIV exposure.

While prosecutors complained about the challenges of convicting some-one of HIV exposure under general criminal laws,[44] there have been successful prosecutions under general criminal laws.[45] For example, New York successfully prosecuted Nushawn Williams, who was accused of exposing hundreds of young women to HIV.[46] This case gained notoriety given the number of women involved and the public health officials' deci-sion, endorsed by a court, to publish his photograph as a way of protecting other women from exposure.[47] Mr. Williams was charged under multiple statutes, including reckless endangerment, sexual misconduct, attempted assault and statutory rape.[48] Some of these charges did not depend on his HIV status, but his HIV status was the motivation behind the prosecution. As one Jamestown official said, 'I had to go after this guy, and I had to get him off the street.'[49] Mr. Williams pleaded guilty to several charges, includ-ing statutory rape and reckless endangerment.[50] After completing his sen-tence, a court ruled that he could be kept civilly confined as a predatory sex offender under New York law.[51]

The more common approach, however, has been for states to adopt HIV-specific criminal exposure statutes.[52] These statutes can define a new crime of HIV exposure or provide enhanced penalties for specific crimes that may expose victims to HIV, typically sex crimes such as prostitution, sexual assault and rape.[53] These are not mutually exclusive, and many states have adopted both (e.g., California and Florida). Nevertheless, some states only have HIV-specific statutes that enhance penalties on existing crimes and other states have only adopted statutes that create the crime of HIV exposure.[54] The prostitution enhancement statutes often include low-risk behaviours within their scope. While some of these statutes apply

[44] L. O. Gostin, 'The politics of AIDS: compulsory state powers, public health, and civil liberties', *Ohio State Law Journal*, 49 (1989), 1017–58, at p. 1041; 'President commission report', p. 130.
[45] Wolf and Vezina, 'Crime and punishment', p. 843, Latham et al., 'Prevalence', p. 12.
[46] Wolf and Vezina, 'Crime and punishment', pp. 822–5 citing Amy Waldman, Guilty Plea in an H.I.V. Exposure Case, *New York Times* B3 (19 February 1999).
[47] Wolf and Vezina, 'Crime and punishment', pp. 822–5, 867–8.
[48] Ibid., p. 824.
[49] A. Z. Galarneau, 'The doctor who dared', *Buffalo News* 1C (11 November 1997).
[50] 'Judge refuses to release sex offender Nushawn Williams', *Rochester Democrat and Chronicle*, 24 August 2010.
[51] C. Ewing and K. Dudzik, Nushawn Williams Remains Confined, *WGRZ (Buffalo) News*, 5 March 2014, wgrz.com/story/news/local/2014/03/05/nushawn-williams-to-remain-confined/6089649; 'Judge refuses to release sex offender'.
[52] Wolf and Vezina, 'Crime and punishment', pp. 845–55.
[53] Ibid., pp. 855–6.
[54] Ibid., p. 855.

only to HIV-infected sex workers, some states also apply the enhancement to HIV-infected people who solicit sex from sex workers.[55]

Although there is significant variation between them, the HIV-specific criminal exposure statutes have some common features. Even though these laws are often referred to as HIV transmission laws, they typically only require that an HIV-infected individual engage in behaviour that *could* lead to HIV exposure. They also generally do not require intent to harm, that is, to intend to expose someone to or transmit HIV. Rather, they generally require only that the person accused know that he is HIV infected, intend to engage in the activity that created the exposure (e.g., sexual activity or needle-sharing), and fail to disclose his HIV status to the person exposed. Thus, the intention requirement is more easily met than in most other crimes.

The statutes treat different classes of people at risk of HIV exposure differently. Twenty-four states require disclosure of HIV status to a sexual partner, whereas only fourteen require disclosure to a needle-sharing partner.[56] Interestingly, the risk of infection based on a single exposure is higher for needle-sharing than from any sexual exposure, with the exception of receptive anal intercourse.[57] Strikingly, the statutes do not focus on activities that most contribute to the spread of HIV, but typically include activities that pose low risk of transmission. Although the majority of states with HIV specific-statutes (twenty-four) include vaginal and anal sexual activity among the prohibited activities, almost as many (twenty-one) include oral sex, which the United States' CDC describes as presenting a low risk of infection.[58] For example, Georgia's statute provides that a person who knows that he is HIV positive who 'knowingly … performs or submits to any sexual act involving the sex organs of one person and the mouth … of another person' is guilty of a felony if he does not disclose his HIV status before engaging in that act.[59] Evidence demonstrating the low risk associated with oral sex came as early as 1984 for male-male oral-penile contact and as early as 1989 for female-male oral-penile and oral-vaginal contact.[60] Similarly, one state

---

[55] Ibid., p. 856–7.
[56] Lehman et al., 'Prevalence', pp. 1000–1.
[57] Patel et al., 'Estimating risk', p. 1513.
[58] Lehman et al., 'Prevalence', p. 1001; CDC, 'HIV transmission'.
[59] O.C.G.A. § 16-5-60(c).
[60] T. Lane and H. Palacio, 'Safer-sex methods', *HIV InSite Knowledge Base Chapter*, December 2003 (content reviewed January 2006), hivinsite.ucsf.edu/InSite?page=kb-07-02-02#S3.4X (*see* Risks Associated with Specific Sexual Practices, Oral-Penile Sex and Oral-Vaginal Sex).

includes masturbation,[61] which is also characterised as presenting a 'negligible' risk of infection, and four include the use of sex objects within their scope, which may present limited risk, depending on use.[62] Eleven states criminalise biting, spitting or throwing of bodily fluid, which, again, the CDC characterises as presenting a 'negligible' risk of infection.[63] This group includes the state of Nebraska, which adopted this as its first and only HIV criminal exposure law in 2011.[64] Nebraska's statute, like most of the biting, spitting or throwing statutes, criminalises this behaviour only with respect to 'public safety officers', which it defines to include peace officers, correctional officers, firefighters, emergency care providers and other public employees in similar positions.[65]

The inclusion of low or negligible risk activities within the scope of the criminal HIV exposure statutes may not be intentional. For example, the Arkansas statute prohibits 'sexual penetration' by a person with HIV without disclosing HIV status. The definition of 'sexual penetration' includes '*any other intrusion, however slight, of any part of a person's body or of any object* into the genital or anal openings of another person's body'.[66] It seems likely that this definition was adapted from the rape statute, which uses similar, although not exact, language.[67] It would not be surprising that the legislature would use existing language that had stood the test of time (and litigation). What makes sense from the perspective of defining rape, however, does not necessarily make sense from the perspective of criminal HIV exposure laws. Indeed, this statute appears to criminalise behaviour that public health would applaud – sexual

---

[61] Colorado's statute provides that a prostitute and his or her client are guilty of a felony if they 'perform[s] any act of sexual intercourse, fellatio, cunnilingus, *masturbation*, or anal intercourse ... with any person not his spouse' if either knows he or she is HIV infected. Colo. Rev. Stat. §§ 18-7-201.7 and 18-7-205.7.

[62] Lehman et al., 'Prevalence', p. 1001. As Galletly and Pinkerton explain, in many circumstances, such activities pose no risk of exposure. C. L. Galletly and S. D. Pinkerton, 'Toward rational criminal HIV exposure laws', *Journal of Law Medicine and Ethics*, 32 (2004), 327–37, at p. 329.

[63] Even at the beginning of the epidemic, the CDC did not consider any of these mechanisms as likely to transmit HIV. Rather, in 1983, it correctly identified sexual contact and exposure to blood or blood products as the mechanisms for HIV exposure. Curran and Jaffe, 'The early years', p. 66. As noted previously, a 1989 study of dental professionals also confirmed that saliva posed little risk of infection. Flynn et al., 'Absence of HIV', p. 441.

[64] Lehman et al., 'Prevalence', p. 1000; R.R.S. Neb. § 28–934.

[65] R.R.S. Neb. § 28–934; Wolf and Vezina, 'Crime and punishment', p. 852.

[66] Ark Code Ann 5-14-123 (emphasis added).

[67] Wolf and Vezina, 'Crime and punishment', p. 851; Ark. Code. Ann. § 5-14-101(1)(A) and (B).

activities that pose negligible risk to an uninfected partner.[68] In contrast, Ohio uses the definition of 'sexual conduct' used in other sex crime statutes, but explicitly exempts the insertion of an instrument, apparatus, or other object that is not part of the body into the vaginal or anal cavity of another, unless the offender knew at the time of the insertion that the instrument, apparatus, or other object carried the offender's bodily fluid'.[69] Thus, legislators can avoid sweeping low-risk behaviours within the scope of criminal HIV exposure statutes with careful drafting and attention to the different goals of statutes.

In addition to the criminalisation of low-risk activities, a remarkable feature of these statutes is the general failure to account for prevention measures. Although condom use has proven efficacy in preventing HIV infection and has been a staple of public health prevention measures from the beginning of the epidemic, only five states discuss condom use as it relates to the crime. Both California and Minnesota account for condom use as part of the definition of the crime; their laws define 'unprotected sexual activity' and 'sexual penetration' that forms the basis of the crime as certain behaviours performed without a condom.[70] Iowa's phrasing is different, but its effect is the same, such that use of condom defeats an element of the crime.[71] North Dakota establishes condom use as an affirmative defence to the crime of exposure, but only 'after full disclosure of the risk of such activity'.[72] The first approach puts the burden on the prosecutor to prove no condom was used, whereas the second puts the burden on the defendant. In contrast, Missouri's statute states explicitly that 'use of condoms is *not* a defense' to sexual exposure to HIV.[73] This provision is

---

[68] Wolf and Vezina, 'Crime and punishment', p. 851. Galletly and Pinkerton noted the same problem with such statutes, concluding 'The irony of these prohibitions is that the use of non-shared sex toys can be a satisfying, risk free alternative to intercourse with an infected partner. Galletly and Pinkerton, 'Toward rational laws', p. 329; See also W. Winkelstein, D. M. Lyman, N. Padian et al., 'Sexual practices and risk of infection by the human immunodeficiency virus: the San Francisco Men's Health Study', *Journal of the American Medical Association*, 257 (1987), 321–5, at p. 324 (the researchers found that of four ancillary sexual practices (rectal insertion of finger, fist, or dildo or douche use before sexual activity), only fisting or douching before sexual activity 'showed significantly elevated relative risks over those with no history of any of the four practices).

[69] Wolf and Vezina, 'Crime and punishment', p. 851; ORC § 2903.11(e)(3).

[70] Cal. Health and Safety Code § 120291; Minn. Stat. § 609.2241; Wolf and Vezina, 'Crime and punishment', pp. 848–9; Lehman et al., 'Prevalence', pp. 1001–2.

[71] Iowa Code § 709D.3(7) (2014) ('a person does not act with the intent required ... or with reckless disregard ... if the person takes practical means to prevent transmission').

[72] N.D. Century Code 12.1-20-17.

[73] Rev. Stat. of Miss. §191.677(4) (emphasis added).

directly in conflict with one of the core public health messages since the beginning of the epidemic – that condoms are an effective HIV prevention measure. Thus, the statute seems to undermine an approach that has a dramatic effect on reducing the transmission of HIV.

Given few HIV exposure statutes have been adopted or amended since 2007, it is less surprising that other proven prevention measures, such as consistent use of HAART and PrEP, generally are not mentioned in the HIV exposure statutes. Some statutes offer broad defences that could encompass these prevention measures. For example, Minnesota's statute provides that '[i]t is an affirmative defense to prosecution, if it is proven by a preponderance of the evidence, that … the person who knowingly harbors an infectious agent for a communicable disease took practical means to prevent transmission as advised by a physician or other health professional.'[74] 'Practical means' is not defined in the statute. Iowa, in its 2014 overhaul of its statute (described in more detail later), takes a similar approach, but defines practical means to include both prophylaxis use (such as condoms) and medical treatment (such as HAART).[75] There are, however, few statutes that contain such broad defences. Moreover, the few statutes that account for condom use do so explicitly. Thus, in most cases, there is no general statutory language that the courts could interpret to extend to newer prevention measures, and statutory amendments would be necessary to include them.

The penalties under the criminal HIV exposure laws are harsher than under traditional sexually transmitted infection laws. The latter are typically defined as misdemeanours, which are punishable by less than one year in jail, whereas the former are typically defined as felonies, which are punishable by more than one year in jail.[76] Criminal HIV exposure laws have maximum sentences ranging from one–ten years (eighteen states) to eleven–twenty (seven states) to more than twenty years (three states).[77] The penalties under these HIV-specific statutes are disproportionately long compared to other crimes, such as driving while intoxicated when no one has been injured.[78]

---

[74] Minn. Stat. § 609.2241. Although the statute does not mention HIV specifically, 'communicable disease' is defined as a 'disease or condition that causes serious illness, serious disability, or death', Minn. State. § 609.2241(1)(a). The only reported case applying this statute involves a defendant who is HIV-infected. *State v. Rick*, 835 N.W. 2d 478 (2013).

[75] Iowa Code § 709D.3(7).

[76] Wolf and Vezina, 'Crime and punishment', pp. 839, 855, 857.

[77] Lehman et al., 'Prevalence', p. 1001.

[78] M. Kaplan, 'Rethinking HIV-exposure crimes', *Indiana Law Journal*, 87 (2012), 1517–69, pp. 1536–9; Wolf and Vezina, 'Crime and punishment', p. 859

Critique of the Criminal HIV Exposure Statutes

Given the historical background and the fears about HIV/AIDS, a fatal, incurable disease, at the time many of the criminal HIV exposure statutes were adopted, it is neither surprising that they were adopted nor that they contain the provisions that they do. Criminal law is an important mechanism for society to define conduct that it deems unacceptable and worthy of punishment.[79] Although practical considerations, including staffing, funding and reporting, may prevent law enforcement agencies from pursuing all violations, criminal laws are intended to have a generalised deterrent effect on the behaviour of the population at large, as well as to remove offenders from society, and to exact retribution for the offence committed.[80]

Those who support criminal HIV exposure laws argue that they play an important role in protecting individuals from physical harm, as well as providing a mechanism for stopping those who will not or cannot comply with prevention measures.[81] Estimates of people arrested and prosecuted for HIV exposure are difficult to obtain, but recent data suggests that there have been a minimum of 440 prosecutions in the United States.[82] Lee's

[79] C. E. Torcia, *Wharton's Criminal Law*, 15th ed. (Deerfield, IL: Clark Boardmen Callaghan: 1993) Vol. 1, §§ 1–5.

[80] W. R. LaFave and A. W. Scott, Jr., *Criminal Law*, 2nd ed. (St. Paul, MN: West Publishing 1986), chapter 1, § 1.5, 22–3 (describing the purpose of criminal law generally). UNAIDS similarly describes the general goals of criminal law in its 2002 report 'Criminal Law, Public Health and HIV Transmission: A Policy Options Paper', data.unaids.org/publications/IRC-pub02/ jc733-criminallaw_en.pdf, p. 20–1. The 1988 President's Commission identified deterrence as a goal of HIV-specific laws, noting that 'Establishing criminal penalties for failure to comply with clearly set standards of conduct can also deter HIV-infected individuals from engaging in high-risk behaviors, thus protecting society against the spread of disease.' 'President commission report', p. 130. See also S. G. Lee, 'Criminal law and HIV testing: empirical analysis of how at-risk individuals respond to the law', *Yale Journal of Health Policy Law and Ethics*, 14 (2014), 194–238, at p. 213 (describing the arguments for criminalisation).

[81] Wolf and Vezina, 'Crime and punishment', pp. 841–3, *citing* Z. Lazzarini, S. Bray and S. Burris, 'Evaluating the impact of criminal laws on HIV risk behavior', *Journal of Law, Medicine and Ethics*, 30 (2002), 239–53, pp. 246 and 239. The use of civil and criminal detention has been used successfully for tuberculosis patients who are noncompliant with their medications. See, for example, T. Oscherwitz, J. P. Tulsky, S. Roger et al., 'Detention of persistently nonadherent patients with tuberculosis', *Journal of the American Medical Association*, 278 (1997), 843–6. M. R. Gasner, K. L. Maw, G. E. Feldman et al., 'The use of legal action in New York City to ensure treatment of tuberculosis', *New England Journal of Medicine*, 340 (1999), 359–66.

[82] *See* National AIDS Manual's (NAM) AIDS map, aidsmap.com/page/1445031#item1445038. As NAM explains, there is no central database for collecting such information, and methods for identifying cases are likely to underestimate the number of cases. Lazzarini, Bray

analysis suggests states' experiences with prosecutions for HIV exposure vary tremendously; while some states have no such prosecutions, some have brought hundreds of cases.[83] In addition, it is not clear whether HIV exposure laws are necessary. On the basis of their analysis of prosecutions, Lazzarini, Bray and Burris concluded that 70 per cent of the cases involved behaviour that was already illegal under other statutes.[84] According to Lee, Texas, which does not have a HIV-specific statute, has had over twenty-two prosecutions, with over twenty convictions.[85] Nevertheless, public health advocates have expressed concerns about criminal HIV exposure statues since they were first adopted; these concerns have only increased as the epidemic has matured, and treatment and prevention options have increased.[86]

An early concern about criminal HIV exposure statutes was that the statutes would deter people from testing for HIV, as the statutes only apply

and Burris identified over 300 prosecutions in their 2002 study. Lazzarini et al., 'Evaluating the impact', p. 244.

[83] Lee, 'HIV testing', pp. 202–5. Interestingly, according to Lee, it is not known whether the states with the highest number of prosecutions (Florida at 239 and Illinois at 100) have been successful. However, even with the gaps in data, Lee found a conviction rate of 60 per cent.

[84] Lazzarini et al., 'Evaluating the impact', p. 244.

[85] Lee, 'HIV testing', pp. 202–5.

[86] For early critiques of criminalisation of HIV exposure, see, for example, L. Gostin, 'The politics of AIDS: compulsory state powers, public health, and civil liberties', Ohio State Law Journal, 49 (1989), 1017–48, 1041–3; K. M. Sullivan and M. A. Field, 'AIDS and the coercive power of the state', Harvard Civil Rights-Civil Liberties Law Review, 23 (1988), 139–97, at pp. 162–5 (noting that an examination of traditional criminal laws reveals doubtful and troubling applications to crimes of AIDS transmission); Kenney, 'Criminalizing HIV transmission', pp. 272–3 (explaining that laws criminalising acts by a person who knows of his or her HIV infection discourages participation in HIV testing and treatment programmes); L. O. Gostin and J. G. Hodge, Jr., 'Piercing the veil of secrecy in HIV/AIDS and other sexually transmitted diseases: theories of privacy and disclosure in partner notification', Duke Journal of Gender Law and Policy, 5 (1988), 9–88, pp. 72–82. For more recent critiques see, for example, Lazzarini, et al., 'Evaluating the impact'; Galletly and Pinkerton, 'Toward rational laws'; Wolf and Vezina, 'Crime and punishment'; S. Burris, L. Beletsky, J. Burleson et al., 'Do criminal laws influence HIV risk behavior? An empirical trial', Arizona State Law Journal, 39 (2007), 467–517, at pp. 481; Lee, 'HIV testing'; R. Jürgens, J. Dohen, E. Cameron et al., 'Ten reasons to oppose the criminalization of HIV exposure or transmission', Reproductive Health Matters, 17(2007), 163–71; Scott Burris and Edwin Cameron, The 'case against criminalization of HIV transmission', Journal of the American Medical Association, 300(2008), 578–81; UNAIDS, Criminal Law, Public Health and HIV Transmission: A Policy Options Paper (2002), data.unaids.org/publications/IRC-pub02/jc733-criminallaw_en.pdf; C. Galletly, Z. Lazzarini, C. Saunders and S. D. Pinkerton, 'Criminal HIV exposure laws: moving forward', AIDS Behavior, 18 (2014), 1011–13; Lehman et al., 'Prevalence'; S. R. Latham, 'Time to descriminalize HIV status', Hastings Center Report, September–October (2013), 12–13, at p. 13.

when someone knows that they are HIV infected.[87] Realisation of this concern may have been more likely early in the epidemic, when many of these statutes were adopted.[88] Before the advent of HAART, there were limited benefits to testing. Knowledge of status could enable individuals to alter their behaviour either to protect themselves from becoming infected (if the tests were negative) or to keep from transmitting the virus to others (if the tests were positive). If the results were positive, people could take steps to plan for the end – spend time with one's friends and family, set one's house in order, make plans for disposition of one's things and identify a surrogate for medical decision making.[89] Without effective treatment, there was no way to alter the course of the disease or to escape the decline towards death. The HAART era dramatically changed that outlook. Given the tremendous benefits to self and others of knowing one's status, getting effective treatment, and living a normal life span, it seems highly unlikely that criminal HIV exposure statutes would deter anyone from testing. A 2010 empirical study supports that conclusion. Using a regression analysis, the study evaluated whether having an HIV-specific statute negatively affected HIV testing decisions. Regression results from four specifications showed that having an HIV-specific law had no statistically significant impact on testing behaviour, although testing rates did decrease in states with HIV-specific statutes with increased media report of HIV criminalisation.[90]

Another concern is that criminalisation of HIV exposure will increase stigmatisation and discrimination against people living with HIV. Early in the epidemic, stigma and discrimination were significant issues.[91] Although such overt discrimination is less common today, stigmatisation of and discrimination against people living with HIV still exists. One-fifth to one-quarter of people living with HIV report experiencing

[87] Wolf and Vezina, 'Crime and punishment', pp. 869–70 and Lee, ' HIV testing', pp. 215–16
[88] The impact of criminal laws on HIV testing was not tested empirically until recently. See, Lee, 'HIV testing'.
[89] People in non-traditional relationships particularly needed to take legal steps if they wanted a partner or friend to make medical decisions on their behalf, because those relationships were not legally recognised. See, for example, R. Steinbrook, B. Lo, J. Tirpack et al., 'Ethical dilemmas in caring for patients with the acquired immunodefiency syndrome', *Annals of Internal Medicine*, 103 (1985), 787–90.
[90] Lee, 'HIV testing', p. 232. Lee notes that the results are consistent with studies of other policies (such as name-based reporting) on testing behaviour, *Id.* p. 235
[91] As described earlier in this chapter, people diagnosed with AIDS risked losing their jobs, housing, medical care and access to school.

discrimination in medical care and employment.[92] A study of employment discrimination claims found HIV/AIDS-related discrimination to be 'the most pervasive in terms of the number and magnitude' compared to the general disability population.[93] Because the majority of state HIV exposure statutes criminalise low risk activities and they suggest that people living with HIV are dangerous, they may reinforce negative perceptions of people living with HIV by suggesting that people living with HIV are dangerous, and that the public needs protection from them.[94]

The disproportionately harsh penalties under criminal HIV exposure statutes may also contribute to stigma and HIV-based discrimination.[95] The heavy punishment, even when effective prevention recommendations are followed, suggests an underlying assessment that people living with HIV should not engage in sexual relations under any circumstances. This approach is both potentially stigmatising and unrealistic.[96] With

[92] See, for example, M. A. Schuster, R. Collins, W. E. Cunningham et al., 'Perceived discrimination in clinical care in a nationally representative sample of HIV-infected adults receiving health care', *Journal of General Internal Medicine*, 20 (2005), 807–13. L. Conyers, K. Boomer and B. T. McMahon, 'Workplace discrimination and HIV/AIDS: the national EEOC ADA research project', *Work* 25 (2005), 37–48; *Bragdon v. Abbott*, 524 U.S. 624 (1998) (dentist refused to care for an HIV-infected patient in office; discrimination lawsuit brought under the Americans with Disabilities Act). In 2010, a school denied admission to a student because he was HIV-infected; it ultimately reversed its decision and settled a discrimination lawsuit against it by the boy and his family. In 2012, Hershey settled HIV suit with fourteen-year-old student denied school admission, 13 September 2012, CBSNews. com, cbsnews.com/news/hershey-settles-hiv-suit-with-14-year-old-student-denied-school-admission/.

[93] Conyers et al., 'Workplace discrimination', p. 47

[94] C. Dodds, A. Bourne and M. Weait, 'Responses to criminal prosecutions for HIV transmission among gay men with HIV in England and Wales', *Reproductive Health Matters*, 17(2009), 135–45, at pp. 136 and 142 (concluding that the movement to more anonymity in sex and decreased disclosure of HIV status by some based on the possibility of prosecution 'demonstrates the capacity for criminalisation to re-inscribe the stigma that is associated with HIV'); C. L. Galletly, W. DiFranceisco and S. D. Pinkerton, 'HIV-positive persons' awareness and understanding of their state's criminal HIV disclosure law', *AIDS Behavior*, 13 (2009), 1262–9, at pp. 1267 and 1268 (citing other commentators' concerns about exacerbation of stigma and noting that 'these laws may reinforce the stereotype of the wanton or desperate HIV-positive person who is a threat to society'); Burris et al., 'Do criminal laws influence?', p. 487.

[95] They also may not achieve another goal of imprisonment, which is to remove offenders from society to keep them from harming the public again. As noted in a 2002 UNAIDS report, the potential for harm may be exacerbated during incarceration, as high-risk behaviours are common in prisons and most prisoners eventually are returned to the community. UNAIDS Report, p. 20.

[96] Burris et al., 'Do criminal laws influence?', p. 487. A study presented at the 2015 Conference on Retroviruses and Opportunistic Infections evaluated the impact of the

treatment advances, HIV positive individuals are living longer, healthier lives. As a result, they are more likely to maintain an active sex life.[97] The US Supreme Court has recognised the importance of sexual activity in human life and has protected decision making about sexual activity as a fundamental right in a string of cases dating back decades.[98]

Another concern is that stigma and discrimination associated with HIV/AIDS will drive prosecutions for behaviour that presents little risk of harm. As described, the vast majority of HIV-specific exposure laws criminalise low or negligible risk behaviours.[99] While extension to these behaviours may not have been intentional, for the most part, states have not moved to change those parts of their laws, despite commentary identifying these problems.[100] Moreover, the vast majority of statutes criminalise behaviours that comply with public health recommendations for reducing risk of HIV transmission. As a result, these statutes may undermine public health prevention messages. The case of Nick Rhoades has highlighted this problem of criminalising low

US President's Emergency Plan for AIDS Relief (PEPFAR) support for abstinence and faithfulness programmes and changes in high-risk sexual behaviour across fourteen PEPFAR funded countries and eight non-PEPFAR funded countries. The study included data from almost 850,000 individuals and found no reduction in high-risk sexual behaviours, including number of sexual partners, age of first sexual encounter or teenage pregnancy. N. Lo, A. Lowe and E. Bendavid, 'The impact of PEPFAR abstinence and faithfulness funding upon HIV risk behaviors in sub-Saharan Africa', croiconference.org/sessions/impact-pepfar-abstinence-and-faithfulness-funding-upon-hiv-risk-behaviors-sub-saharan.

[97] A. O'Leary and R. J. Wolitski, 'Moral agency and the sexual transmission of HIV', *Psychological Bulletin*, 135 (2009), 478–94, at p. 478.

[98] In *Lawrence v. Texas*, 539 U.S. 558 (2003), the Supreme Court struck down state sodomy laws as violating constitutional liberty protections. In doing so, it drew on a long line of cases recognising the fundamental importance relating to decisions about sexual activity, pregnancy and marriage, including *Griswold v. Connecticut*, 381 U.S. 479 (1965) and *Eisenstadt v. Baird*, 405 U.S. 438 (1972) (regarding access to contraception) and *Roe v. Wade*, 410 U.S. 113 (1973) and *Planned Parenthood of Southeastern Pa. v. Casey*, 505 U.S. 833 (1992) (regarding access to abortion). Quoting the latter, the *Lawrence* court highlighted that 'These matters, involving the most intimate and personal choices a person may make in a lifetime, choices central to personal dignity and autonomy, are central to the liberty protected by the *Fourteenth Amendment*. At the heart of liberty is the right to define one's own concept of existence, of meaning, of the universe, and of the mystery of human life.' *Lawrence*, p. 574.

[99] Lehman et al., 'Prevalence', p. 1000.

[100] See, for example, Galletly and Pinkerton, 'Toward rational laws', p. 329 (noting the 'tenuous relationship between the sexual activities prohibited by many states' HIV exposure statutes and actual risk of viral transmission'); Wolf and Vezina, 'Crime and punishment' (similarly identifying problems with HIV exposure statutes and the intended goal).

risk behaviours.[101] Rhoades, an HIV positive gay, man was convicted in 2008 under Iowa's HIV exposure statute after a one-time sexual encounter with another man, A. P. The two engaged in consensual protected anal sex and unprotected oral sex.[102] Rhoades was on HAART with undetectable viral load.[103] There was some evidence that the condom may have broken, but no evidence of exchange of bodily fluids.[104] Nevertheless, the trial court accepted Rhoades's guilty plea and sentenced him to twenty-five years in prison and a lifetime registration as a sex offender,[105] although the court later suspended his sentence and placed him on supervised probation for five years. In 2010, Rhoades sought post-conviction relief on the grounds that his trial counsel had been ineffective.[106] The Iowa Appellate Court affirmed his conviction, noting (wrongly) that 'oral sex is a well-recognized means of transmission of HIV' and, like other courts, considering any possible risk of HIV transmission is sufficient to sustain a conviction.[107] With that mindset and reference to other cases, it concluded 'the decision to engage in *unprotected* sex with another person generally evidences one's intent to expose that person to bodily fluid'.[108]

Fortunately for Rhoades, the Iowa Supreme Court took a different view. Not only did the court indicate that *substantial* risk of transmission was required for conviction under the statute, but it also refused to take judicial notice of the risk of transmission through sexual contact, noting:

> The evidence at the post-conviction relief hearing shows there have been great strides in the treatment and the prevention of the spread of HIV from 2003 to 2008 ... At the time of the plea, Rhoades's viral count was nondetectable, and there is a question of whether it was medically true a person with a nondetectable viral load could transmit HIV through contact with

---

[101] The Rhoades conviction received widespread media attention. A search in the LexisNexis news database yielded 152 news articles, with 122 of them appearing before his conviction was reversed.

[102] *Rhoades v. State*, 848 N.W.2d 22, pp. 25–6 (Iowa S.Ct. 2014).

[103] Ibid., p. 33.

[104] Ibid., pp. 31 and 36.

[105] Persons on the sex offender registry must register their address on a publicly available website and, depending on their crime, may have residency and/or work restrictions; M. Leitsinger, 'Sex offenders no more? Iowa reconsiders tough law on HIV exposure', *NBC News*, 29 March 2014, nbcnews.com/news/us-news/sex-offenders-no-more-iowa-reconsiders-tough-law-hiv-exposure-n53081.

[106] His trial counsel had recommended Rhoades plead guilty. *Rhoades v. State*, 848 N.W.2d, pp. 25–6.

[107] *Rhoades v. State*, 2013 Iowa App. LEXIS 1048 (2013), p. 7.

[108] Ibid., p. 11.

the person's blood, semen or vaginal fluid or whether transmission was merely theoretical.[109]

While technically the court's decision was a narrow one, this recognition of the implications of advances in HIV prevention science to criminal HIV exposure statutes was significant. The attention the case received also prompted the Iowa legislature to revisit and amend Iowa's statute. As described in more detail later in the chapter, these changes take into account the medical advances to which the Iowa Supreme Court referred.

The inclusion of low and negligible risk activities and the failure to incorporate public health prevention messages may also reinforce misconceptions about how HIV is transmitted that have persisted since the beginning of the epidemic. Annual surveys conducted since 1987 have persistently shown a substantial minority of Americans believe that sharing a drinking glass (22–7 per cent) or touching a toilet seat (16–19 per cent) can transmit HIV.[110] Such beliefs are reinforced by news of prosecutions and convictions of HIV positive people who have spat, bitten or thrown bodily fluids. In one recent case, David Plunkett was arrested following some 'bizarre behavior' and 'open possession of marijuana' in his primary physician's reception area. During his arrest, Plunkett, who is HIV positive and also has a long history of mental illness, bit a police officer. He was charged with aggravated assault upon a police officer on the grounds that his saliva was a 'dangerous instrument' within the meaning of the law.[111] Plunkett was sentenced to a ten-year prison term, although that conviction was overturned on appeal.[112]

The statutes may also stand in the way of developing a norm of voluntary disclosure of HIV status as a way of improving health and minimising HIV stigma.[113] When individuals feel safe to disclose their status voluntarily, they are better able to access support and care and to engage in their communities. A substantial percentage (42–8 per cent) of HIV positive men

---

[109] Ibid., pp. 32–3 (footnotes omitted).

[110] The Washington Post/Kaiser Family Foundation, 2012 Survey of Americans on HIV/AIDS, kaiserfamilyfoundation.files.wordpress.com/2013/01/8334-f.pdf, p. 13.

[111] *People v. Plunkett*, 19 N.Y.3d 400 (2012), p. 403. This required a conclusion that saliva from an HIV positive person was 'readily capable of causing death or other serious physical injury'.

[112] S. Sorrell White, 'Ilion man in court for resentencing', *The Evening Times (Little Falls, New York)*, pp. 5, 30 June 2012.

[113] Presidential Advisory Council on HIV/AIDS and CDC/HRSA Advisory Committee on Viral Hepatitis and STD Prevention and Care (PACHA), 'HIV disclosure summit', 28–9 June 2012, aids.gov/federal-resources/pacha/meetings/2013/feb-2013-hiv-disclosure-summit.pdf, p. 2.

who have sex with men reporting unprotected sex do *not* disclose their HIV status to their prospective sex partners, and few have a consistent pattern of disclosure (i.e., always or never tell).[114] Thus, the decision about disclosure is often modulated by a variety of factors, such as the relationship between the parties, the venue, the use of drugs and sense of responsibility. Although some studies have found that some people are more likely to disclose because of fear that failure to do so will subject them to arrest,[115] others have found that people may engage in riskier behaviours, including more anonymous sex without disclosure.[116] Thus, statutes that criminalise sexual activity for those living with HIV, even when taking precautions to prevent transmission of the disease, may create a barrier to voluntary disclosure.

Commentators have also questioned whether HIV exposure statutes are effective. There are doubts about whether they do in fact deter risky behaviour as proponents suggest. In order for them to deter behaviour, people need to know about the statutes. However, there is limited evidence suggesting that they do.[117] Even if people are aware of the statutes, their awareness may not lead to behaviour change. Researchers who conducted a study of knowledge of state laws and on sexual behaviours concluded: '[o]ur research effort as a whole has shown that law is unlikely to

---

[114] P. M. Gorbach, J. T. Galea, B. Amani et al., 'Don't ask, don't tell: patterns of HIV disclosure among HIV positive men who have sex with men with recent STI practicing high risk behavior in Los Angeles and Seattle', *Sexually Transmitted Infections*, 80 (2004), 512–17. See also O'Leary and Wolitski, 'Moral agency', p. 482 (describing studies showing differing responses as to who bears the responsibility to disclose status from a duty to disclose, no duty to disclose, to a shared responsibility to discuss).

[115] Gorbach et al., 'Don't ask, don't tell', pp. 515 and 516.

[116] Dodds et al., 'Responses to criminal prosecutions', p. 142.

[117] Galletly et al. found high awareness (76 per cent) and understanding of one state's HIV exposure statute. They did not ask whether awareness affected behaviour change. Galletly et al., 'Awareness and understanding', p. 1265. However, in another state, these researchers found lower awareness (51 per cent). C. L. Galletly, L. R. Glasman, S. D. Pinkerton et al., 'New Jersey's HIV exposure law and the HIV-related attitudes, believes, and sexual and seropositive state disclosure behaviors of persons living with HIV', *American Journal of Public Health*, 102 (2012), 2135–40, at p. 2137. Dodds et al. found low awareness and understanding (about one-third) about criminalisation. Dodds et al., 'Responses to criminal prosecutions', p. 139. Other studies have suggested a lack of awareness of HIV laws, see, for example, F. M. Hecht, M. A. Chesney and J. S. Lehrman et al, 'Does HIV reporting by name Deter Testing?', *AIDS*, 14 (2000), 1801–8, at p. 1804 (noting that the deterring effects of HIV laws are limited because of the lack of social awareness); S. Schwarcz, J. Stockman, V. Delgado et al., 'Does name-based HIV reporting deter high-risk persons from HIV testing?', *AIDS*, 35 (2004), 93–6 (finding that a small minority were aware of the HIV reporting policy).

be influencing unsafe sexual behaviour under any one of the three leading theories of how criminal law works', that is, incapacitation, deterrence or norm setting.[118] Specifically, neither living in a state with a criminal HIV exposure statute nor knowledge of the law was significantly associated with condom use; that is, the law did not deter people from engaging in risky behaviour.[119] Another research group found 'no evidence that states with or without [HIV exposure laws] differed in HIV risk behaviour reported by HIV positive MSM or MSM in general'.[120] A third study found varied responses to awareness of prosecutions for HIV transmission: although almost half reported no change in behaviour, some indicated positive changes (increased disclosure) and others reported increased risky behaviours (maximising anonymity and decreased disclosure).[121]

In some ways, the recent findings about lack of effectiveness of HIV exposure statues in deterring risky behaviours are not surprising. The sexual behaviours that are the primary subject of the statutes occur in complex social/cultural contexts.[122] While knowing one's status encourages safer behaviour,[123] people – up to 40 per cent – continue to engage in risky

---

[118] Burris et al., 'Do criminal law influence?', p. 505.

[119] Ibid., p. 501. Galletly et al. found a similar lack of reduction in HIV sexual behaviour. Galletly et al., 'New Jersey's HIV law', p. 2138. O'Leary and Wolitski describe research showing that 'disclosure of positive HIV status is not reliably associated with reduced transmission risk behavior'. O'Leary and Wolitsky, 'Moral agency', p. 485.

[120] K. J. Horvath, R. Weinmeyer and S. Rosser, 'Should it be illegal for HIV-positive persons to have unprotected sex without disclosure? An examination of attitudes among US men who have sex with men and the impact of state law', *AIDS Care: Psychological and Socio-medical Aspects of AIDS/HIV*, 22 (2010), 1221–8, at p. 1224.

[121] Dodds et al., 'Responses to criminal prosecutions', p. 141.

[122] The UNAIDS report on criminalisation options notes: '[T]he lessons of history, which show that prohibiting alcohol and other drugs, consensual sex, or prostitution has never succeeded in preventing behaviours, and that the harm that follows from stigmatising them and driving them underground has been greater than any harm (or supposed harm) of the activities themselves.' UNAIDS Report, p. 21.

[123] See, for example, N. Crepaz, C. M. Lyles, R. J. Wolitski et al., 'Do prevention interventions reduce HIV risk behaviors among people living with HIV? A meta-analytic review of controlled trials', *AIDS*, 20 (2006), 143–57, at p. 144; P. H. Kilmarx, F. F. Hamers and T. A. Peterman, 'Living with HIV: experiences and perspectives of HIV-infected sexually transmitted disease clinic patients after post-test counseling', *Sexually Transmitted Disease*, 15(1998), 28–37; G. Marks, N. Crepaz and R. S. Janssen, 'Estimating sexual transmission of HIV from persons aware and unaware that they are infected with the virus in the USA', *AIDS*, 20(2006), 1447–50; L. S. Weinhardt et al., 'Effects of HIV counseling and testing on sexual risk behavior: a meta-analytic review of published research, 1985–1997', *American Journal of Public Health*, 89 (1999), 1397–405, at p. 1403; R. J. Wolitski, R. J. MacGowan, D. L. Higgins et al., 'The effects of HIV counseling and testing on risk-related practices and help-seeking behavior', *AIDS Education and Prevention*, 9: Supplement 3(1997), 52–67.

behaviours, at least occasionally.[124] Many factors may influence whether a person engages in high-risk behaviour. As Burris et al. explain: '[f]actors influencing the choice of whether to engage in dangerous practices include individual-level factors (such as depression, self-efficacy, substance abuse, and comprehension of risk), partner- and group-level factors (such as norms of condom use), and societal-level – or structural – factors (including stigma, social marginalisation, and availability of services).'[125] While there is widespread agreement that people *ought* to disclose their HIV status to their sexual partners, many do not actually do so, especially with casual sexual partners.[126] Disclosure may also be conveyed by non-verbal means.[127] In some cases, an individual may not be able to refuse sex or to require a condom. Women particularly, but not exclusively, may have difficulty negotiating safer sex because of traditional gender norms or even the threat of violence.[128] Other factors, such as a desire for intimacy or

[124] Burris et al., 'Do criminal laws influence?', p. 478, citing G. Marks, S. Burris and T. A. Peterman, 'Reducing sexual transmission of HIV from those who know they are infected: the need for personal and collective responsibility', *AIDS*, 13 (1999), 297–306, 297–308 (reviewing various studies demonstrating that substantial proportions of HIV positive individuals continue to have unprotected intercourse). This is consistent with a meta-analysis among injection drug users, which demonstrated the persistence of sexual risk behaviours. M. M. Copenhaver, B. T. Johnson, I-C Lee et al., 'Behavioral HIV risk reduction among people who inject drugs: meta-analytic evidence of efficacy', *Journal of Substance Abuse Treatment*, 31 (2006), 163–71.

[125] Burris et al., 'Do criminal laws influence?', p. 480 (and citations therein). O'Leary and Wolitski similarly review the numerous studies that have identified factors associated with high-risk practices among those who are HIV positive and HIV negative. O'Leary and Wolitski, 'Moral agency', p. 479. As noted by others, some individuals may not be capable of negotiating disclosure and safer sex. Dodds et al., 'Responses to criminal prosecutions', p. 142

[126] Burris et al. found that only slight majorities of their respondents had disclosed their HIV status to their regular partners or most recent other partners. Burris et al., 'Do criminal laws influence?', p. 496. This is consistent with other studies. Gorbach et al. state that 42–8 per cent of HIV positive MSM reporting unprotected sex do not disclosure their HIV status and also found only 16 per cent of their respondents had consistent pattern of disclosure (which included never and always). Gorbach et al., 'Don't ask, don't tell', pp. 512–13. In an earlier survey, more than 95 per cent of respondents agreed there was a responsibility to disclose sexually transmitted infections with partners, but only a third of respondents with infections actually did so. Kaiser Family Foundation, The 1998 Kaiser Family Foundation/Glamour Survey of Men and Women on Sexually Transmitted Diseases 11 (25 February 1999).

[127] Gorbach et al. 'Don't ask, don't tell', p. 513. This can include leaving medications out, listing HIV status on internet sites and displaying a particular tattoo. Id., p. 516. See also, Burris et al., 'Do criminal laws influence?', p. 480; Horvath et al., 'Should it be illegal?', p. 1225.

[128] See, for example, Z. A. Stein, 'HIV prevention: the need for methods women can use', *American Journal of Public Health*, 80 (1990), 460–2. Microbicide research has been driven

to parent on one end of the spectrum to self-destructive motivations or self-denial on the other – may prevent someone from negotiating for safer sex.[129] Under such complex circumstances, Horvath et al. contend that criminal HIV exposure laws could actually create riskier circumstances because they suggest a norm of disclosure that does not truly exist.[130] Latham also suggests that, given the complex psychosocial factors that may lead to decisions to engage in unprotected sex and failure to disclose HIV status, it is wrong to infer intent to harm others, as the criminal HIV exposure laws typically do.[131]

The statutes' effectiveness may also be limited by the fact that an estimated 20 per cent of Americans living with HIV do not know that they are infected.[132] The statutes typically require that an individual know that he is HIV infected to be prosecuted. Those who are HIV infected but do not know are responsible for an estimated one-third of new HIV infections.[133] The transmission rate from those unaware of their HIV status is estimated to be approximately 3.5 times that of those who are aware that they are HIV positive.[134] A recent study suggests that the reduction in

by the need for a prevention method women can control. World Health Organization, 'HIV/AIDS: microbicides', who.int/hiv/topics/microbicides/microbicides/en/ (indicating their importance of an option 'that women can easily control and do not require the cooperation, consent, or even the knowledge of the partners'.) See also US Department of Health and Human Services, 'Violence, stigma HIV & AIDS [Violence sec.]' (accessed through archived website, web.archive.org/web/20040311013128/http://hab.hrsa.gov/publications/stigma/violence.htm) (explaining that research indicates disclosure of HIV positive status may provoke violence in intimate relationships and that women are five–eight times more likely to be victims of intimate partner assault). Burris et al., 'Do criminal laws influence?', p. 509 (noting that customers may determine whether sex workers engage in protected or unprotected sexual activity, citing L. Cusick, 'Non-use of condoms by prostitute women', *AIDS Care*, 10 (1998), 133–46, at p. 140; Latham, 'Time to descriminalize', p. 13; O'Leary and Wolitski, 'Moral agency', p. 480 (commenting 'Why might an HIV-positive person wish to not have protected intercourse? Some express concerns about reduction in sexual pleasure or intimacy. Requests for condom use can also be taken to signal undisclosed infidelity. Moreover, when norms for condom use are low in a community, social pressure to have unprotected sex is great' (citations omitted)).

[129] O'Leary and Wilitski, 'Moral agency', p. 485.

[130] Horvath et al., 'Should it be illegal', p. 1225.

[131] Latham, 'Time to decriminalize', p. 13.

[132] V. A. Moyer, 'Screening for HIV: U.S. preventive services task force recommendation statement', *Annals of Internal Medicine*, online, 30 April 2013, uspreventiveservicestaskforce.org/uspstf13/hiv/hivfinalrs.pdf, p. 1.

[133] *See* J. Skarbinski, E. Rosenberg, G. Paz-Bailey et al., 'Human immunodeficiency virus transmission at each step of the care continuum in the United, States', *JAMA Internal Medicine*, doi: 10:1001/jamainternmed.2014.8180, published online 23 February 2015.

[134] O'Leary and Wilitski, 'Moral agency', p. 478.

risk behaviour seen after HIV diagnosis 'may be more strongly associated with being engaged in HIV care rather than HIV diagnosis alone'.[135] In any event, to realise any deterrent effect, people must know that they are HIV infected. Thus, exposure statutes will not work on those who do not know that they are infected.[136] Thus, criminal HIV exposure statutes may be ineffective both because the behaviours that they seek to address are too complicated to respond to their provisions and because the population most at risk may fall outside their scope because they do not know that they are HIV infected. They may punish those who deliberately infect others, however.

A Way Forward: The Beginnings of Policy Change

Given the problems with the HIV-specific statues, from a public health standpoint, the best approach is likely to be to repeal them.[137] However, laws tend to be 'sticky' – once they are on the books, it is challenging to remove them; this seems to be the case for these statutes. Moreover, these types of statutes remain popular, with majorities supporting them.[138] Indeed, internationally, a number of countries have adopted HIV criminalisation statutes in recent years, and, in 2011, Nebraska adopted its first HIV-specific exposure statute to biting, spitting and throwing – activities that pose virtually no risk of transmission.[139] Accordingly, perhaps a more realistic approach is to amend the statutes so that they are more supportive of public health prevention efforts. Recent federal policy statements and Iowa's repeal and revision of its criminal HIV exposure statute in ways that minimise the negative impact on public health in the wake of the Nick Rhodes case support the idea that such a shift in approach is possible.

Over the past several years, the US federal government has made several statements suggesting its support for use of criminal HIV statutes is waning. In the 2010 National HIV/AIDS Strategy for the United States, the Obama administration expressed concerns about criminal HIV

---

[135] Skarbinski et al., 'Transmission at each step', p. E6.
[136] Latham, 'Time to decriminalize', p. 12
[137] Burris et al., 'Do criminal laws influence?', p. 515; Latham, 'Time to decriminalize', p. 13. UNAIDS has also recommended against HIV-specific criminal laws. UNAIDS Report, p. 39.
[138] Horvath et al., 'Don't ask, don't tell', p. 1224; S. Hernandez, 'Sex, lies and HIV: when what you don't tell your partner is a crime', *ProPublica*, 1 December 2013, propublica.org/article/hiv-criminal-transmission.
[139] Lehman et al., 'Prevalence', p. 1000 and R.R.S. Neb. § 28–934.

exposure laws and concluded: '[i]n some cases, it may be appropriate for legislators to reconsider whether existing laws continue to further the public interest and public health. In many instances, the continued existence and enforcement of these types of laws run counter to scientific evidence about routes of HIV transmission and may undermine the public health goals of promoting HIV screening and testing.'[140] On the basis of this assessment, the National Strategy recommends that state legislatures 'consider reviewing HIV-specific criminal statutes to ensure that they are consistent with current knowledge of HIV transmission and support public health approaches to preventing and treating HIV'.[141] Yet, to date, few states have done so.

In February 2013, the Presidential Advisory Council on HIV/AIDS (PACHA) took a step further in its Resolution on Ending Federal and State HIV-Specific Criminal Laws, Prosecutions and Civil Commitments.[142] The resolution identifies the problems with the statutes, including the failure to account for prevention measures, the disproportionate sentences and the stigma created by punishing those with HIV, and concludes that such statutes 'are based on outdated and erroneous beliefs about the routes, risks, and consequences of HIV transmission'.[143] The resolution goes on to point out additional problems given the complex psychosocial context in which criminalisation cases may arise, such that criminalisation:

1. Creates a tool for control by abusers who threaten prosecutions of partners who want to leave abusive relationships;
2. Complicates custody disputes and pregnancies;
3. Imprisons women and young people for non-disclosure without regard for the complex reasons such as fear of violence or other situations when disclosure may not be advisable or safe;
4. Over-targets sex workers, against whom condom possession has been used as evidence of intent to commit a crime.[144]

---

[140] Office of National AIDS Policy, 'National HIV/AIDS strategy for the United States', White House, Washington, DC, 2010, whitehouse.gov/sites/default/files/uploads/NHAS .pdf, p. 37.

[141] White House, 'National strategy', p. 37.

[142] PACHA, 'Disclosure summit'. PACHA 'provides advice, information, and recommendations to the Secretary [of Health and Human Services] regarding programmes and policies intended to promote effective prevention of HIV disease, and to advance research on HIV disease and AIDS. The White House asks PACHA to provide, on an ongoing basis, recommendations on how to effectively implement the National HIV/AIDS Strategy, as well as monitor the Strategy's implementation.' aids.gov/federal-resources/pacha/about-pacha/.

[143] PACHA, 'Disclosure summit', p. 1.

[144] Ibid., pp. 1–2.

Joining PACHA's call for the repeal of criminal HIV exposure statutes is Representative Barbara Lee, a congresswoman from California. She introduced the Real Existing Policies that Encourage and Allow Legal (REPEAL) HIV Discrimination Act in the US House of Representatives in May 2013. The Bill calls for a national review of federal and state laws regarding criminalisation of HIV and a public report to determine whether the laws create an 'undue burden' on people living with HIV and their impact on public health, as well as the development of best practices.[145] Senator Christopher Coons of Delaware introduced a companion bill in the US Senate.[146]

Finally, in 2014, the Department of Justice issued its report 'Best Practices Guide to Reform HIV-Specific Criminal Laws to Align with Scientifically-Supported Factors', in which it states:

> the best practice would be for states to reform [HIV-specific criminal] laws to eliminate HIV-specific criminal penalties except in two distinct circumstances. First, states may wish to retain criminal liability when a person who knows he/she is HIV positive commits a (non-HIV specific) sex crime where there is a risk of transmission (e.g., rape or other sexual assault). The second circumstance is where the individual knows he/she is HIV positive and the evidence clearly demonstrates that individual's intent was to transmit the virus and that the behavior engaged in had a significant risk of transmission, whether or not transmission actually occurred.[147]

It is not clear from the guide why the Department of Justice believes that specific laws are necessary to address these cases, rather than relying on general criminal laws. Nevertheless, the Department of Justice advises states to take into account CDC evidence regarding activities posing negligible or low risk of transmission (e.g., biting, spitting or throwing bodily fluids, oral intercourse) as well as on the effect of prevention measures (e.g., condoms and HAART) in reducing transmission when revising their laws.[148]

The federal government is not the only voice calling for changes to criminal HIV exposure statutes. Citing the outdated views of risk, failure to incorporate prevention measures and inconsistency with public health

---

[145] H.B. 1843 (113th Congress 2013–15).

[146] S. 1790 (113th Congress 2013–15). Congress did not pass the Repeal Act. The bill was reintroduced in the 114th Congress. https://www.congress.gov/bill/114th-congress/house-bill/1586.

[147] US Department of Justice, Civil Rights Division, 'Best practices guide to reform HIV-specific criminal laws to align with scientifically supported factors', aids.gov/federal-resources/national-hiv-aids-strategy/doj-hiv-criminal-law-best-practices-guide.pdf, p. 4

[148] Department of Justice, 'Best practices guide', p. 5.

goals, in 2013, the US Conference of Mayors called for the elimination of HIV-specific laws. The group also explicitly expressed its support for legislation, such as the REPEAL HIV Discrimination Act.[149]

In response to the Rhoades' case described earlier, the Iowa legislature repealed the statute under which Rhoades was convicted.[150] The historic nature of the legislature's action is noted in news stories.[151] However, those stories, including verbs such as 'scrapped' to describe the legislature's actions, suggest a more significant action than actually occurred.[152] Although the HIV-specific statute criminalising HIV exposure was eliminated, another statute, the Contagious or Infectious Disease Transmission Act, was adopted in its place.[153]

The new statute applies to HIV/AIDS, as well as hepatitis, meningococcal disease and tuberculosis.[154] It distinguishes between transmission and exposure and between intentional infection and reckless disregard for the possibility of transmitting the disease.[155] 'Exposure' is defined as conduct 'that poses a substantial risk of transmission'.[156] An HIV-infected person who *intentionally exposes and transmits* HIV to someone who is uninfected may still be punished up to twenty-five years in prison.[157] An HIV-infected person who *intentionally exposes* someone who is not HIV infected to HIV, without transmission, or who *recklessly exposes and transmits HIV* to a person who was previously HIV negative is subject to not more than five years in prison, plus a fine of between $750 and $7,500.[158] An HIV-infected person *who recklessly exposes* someone who is HIV negative to

[149] US Conference of Mayors, 'HIV discrimination and criminalization', resolution adopted June 2013, http://www.usmayors.org/resolutions/81st_Conference/csj11.asp.
[150] Senate File 2297, §9, co dified at Iowa Code § 709D.
[151] M. Leitsinger, 'Sex offenders no more? Iowa reconsiders tough law on HIV exposure', *NBC News*, 29 March 2014, nbcnews.com/news/us-news/sex-offenders-no-more-iowa-reconsiders-tough-law-hiv-exposure-n53081; M. Leitsinger, 'Iowa scraps harsh HIV criminalization law in historic vote', *NBC News*, 1 May 2014, nbcnews.com/news/us-news/iowa-scraps-harsh-hiv-criminalization-law-historic-vote-n94946.
[152] Leitsinger, 'Iowa scraps harsh law'.
[153] Senate File 2297. Other states may have made amendments to their laws after the Lehman et al. analysis. For example, Illinois changed its statute in 2011 so that it now criminalises sexual activity without a condom knowing one is HIV infected rather than engaging in intimate contact regardless of condom use. *Compare* § 720 ILCS 5/12–5.01 (current statute) with 770 ILCS § 5/12–16.2 (prior statute). However, these amendments were not as comprehensive as the Iowa statute.
[154] Iowa 709D.2(1).
[155] Iowa 709D.3.
[156] Iowa Code § 709D.2(2). 'Substantial risk' is not defined in the statute.
[157] Iowa Code § 709D.3 and Iowa Code § 902.9(2).
[158] Iowa Code § 709D.3 and Iowa Code § 902.9(5).

HIV, without transmission, commits a serious misdemeanour.[159] In Iowa, serious misdemeanours are punishable by fines, with a minimum of $315 and maximum of $1,875, imprisonment of up to one year, or both.[160] A person convicted for the crime no longer must register as a sex offender, and anyone who was convicted under the prior statute and registered as a sex offender will have that registration expunged.[161]

There are several important features of this new statute. First, it explicitly excludes becoming pregnant while infected with HIV/AIDS from the defined crime; most statutes do not mention pregnancy and, thus, could be applied to HIV-infected women who become pregnant.[162] Second, knowing that one is HIV infected and engaging in behaviour that may expose someone to HIV, 'regardless of the frequency of the behaviour', is not enough to prove intent under the statute. Third, perhaps most significantly, the statute provides that a person does not act with intent or the reckless disregard necessary to establish the crime 'if the person takes practical means to prevent transmission, or if the person informs the uninfected person that the person' is HIV infected, offers to take 'practical means to prevent transmission', and the uninfected person refuses.[163] 'Practical means to prevent transmission' is defined as 'substantial good faith compliance with a treatment regimen prescribed by the person's health care provider, if applicable, and with behavioural recommendations of the person's health care provider or public health officials, which may include but are not limited to the use of a medically indicated ... prophylactic device, to measurably limit the transmission'.[164] Finally, it is an affirmative defence that the person exposed to HIV knew about the infection and consented to the exposure.

Although the Iowa legislature did not go as far as some HIV advocates and commentators want and repeal the statute altogether, it did at least include provisions to avoid the problems of its previous statute and others like it. Specifically, it changes the intention required for conviction to one of harm (or reckless disregard for the potential to harm), rather than simply the intention to engage in the sexual or needle-sharing behaviour

[159] Iowa Code § 709D.3.
[160] Iowa Code § 903.1.
[161] Senate File 2297, § 10.
[162] Iowa Code § 709D.5. See Wolf & Vezina, 'Crime and punishment', pp. 872–3. See also M. L. Closen and S. H. Isaacman, 'Criminally pregnant: are AIDS-transmission laws encouraging abortion?', American Bar Association Journal, 76 (1990), 76–8.
[163] Iowa Code § 709D.7.
[164] Iowa Code § 709D.2(2).

that can expose someone to HIV. It also eliminates low or negligible risk behaviours through its definition of exposure and by incorporating prevention measures. That the prevention measures are not listed, but rather described in terms of treatment and recommendations of a healthcare provider or public health officials also means that the statute may be more likely to keep up with changing science. Moreover, consent *or* prevention measures, rather than both, are now sufficient to prevent conviction.

People living with HIV may still be subject to criminal prosecution as a result of exposing another person to HIV; however, the changes made in the new statute narrow the scope of potential cases. For example, it seems unlikely that charges would have been brought against Nick Rhoades had this law been in effect because Rhoades's non-detectable viral load and use of a condom demonstrated he had taken 'practical means to prevent transmission', as defined in the statute.[165] In addition, the fact that he did not use a condom during oral sex does not constitute a 'substantial risk' of infection as defined in the statute.[166] Thus, under the statute, Rhoades did not have the necessary intent to face charges under the statute. Similarly, Plunkett, who was initially charged with aggravated assault on the grounds that his teeth and HIV in his saliva were 'dangerous instrument[s]', would probably not have been charged because saliva does not pose a 'substantial risk' of infection. Thus, the revised Iowa statute does seem to be a significant improvement over existing criminal HIV exposure statutes.

Conclusion

The state of United States' criminal HIV exposure statutes is disheartening. Despite long-standing critiques about these laws, overall, the statutes continue to criminalise low or negligible risk behaviour, fail to account for prevention measures, fail to incorporate scientific developments and disproportionately punish people living with HIV for exposing others to HIV without requiring specific intent to harm.[167] These problems persist despite some states adopting new laws and amending existing ones after the advent of HAART, which has dramatically changed the prognosis

[165] 'Practical means' does not mean perfect means. Accordingly, with the alleged condom failure, Rhoades may have had a moral obligation to inform A. P. of his infection, though it appears the law may not require it.
[166] Iowa Code § 709D.2(2).
[167] Wolf and Vezina, 'Crime and punishment', pp. 877–83.

for people living with HIV from an almost universally fatal disease, to a chronic disease with a normal life span.[168] However, there is now reason to hope that there may be changes in the future. The federal government has moved from supporting the use of criminal HIV exposure statutes to calling into question their continued existence. Moreover, following a case in which a man was sentenced to twenty-five years in prison for HIV exposure, despite posing essentially no risk of HIV transmission and following prevention guidelines, the Iowa legislature substantially revised its criminal exposure statute. This revision avoids many of the problems associated with its earlier statute and those of other states and provides a model for other states. If the federal government were to exert more pressure on states to reconsider their laws, either through the passage of the REPEAL Act or through the power of the purse (as it has done, in the past, with the Ryan White Act), more states might follow Iowa's lead, bringing their laws in keeping with the current HIV epidemic.

---

[168] Department of Justice, 'Best practices guide', p. 4.

7

Making Science Count: Significant Risk, HIV Non-disclosure and Science-Based Criminal Law Reform: A Reflexive Analysis

ERIC MYKHALOVSKIY

In Canada, the criminal law governance of HIV non-disclosure is produced through complex relations of knowledge in which discourses of risk, individual rights and autonomy are paramount. Drawing on an institutional ethnography, this chapter reflexively explores how Canadian activists concerned about HIV criminalisation have sought to intervene in those knowledge relations. I argue that ambiguities in legal notions of risk have been a central feature not only of the discursive organisation of criminal law regulation of HIV non-disclosure, but of activist efforts to intervene in that governance. I conceptualise those efforts as a form of science-based criminal law reform through which people living with HIV, lawyers, community workers and others have sought to intervene in the text-mediated relations of criminal law regulation by translating epidemiological risk knowledge for criminal justice settings. The chapter explores the writing practices and ethical dilemmas associated with such translation efforts. Through an analysis of the 2012 Supreme Court of Canada decision in *R v Mabior*, it also points to the successes, limitations, complexities and unintended consequences of mobilising scientific knowledge in HIV-related criminal law reform.

Introduction

We live in a time of growing interest in the use of the criminal law to regulate HIV transmission or conduct considered to risk the spread of the

I would like to thank Glenn Betteridge, Ryan Peck, the editors, and an anonymous reviewer for their helpful comments. Todd Sherman and Colin Hastings provided valuable editorial assistance. I thank Aryn Martin, Natasha Myers and Ana Viseu for their comments on a much earlier version of the chapter, which was presented at the Politics of Care in Technoscience Conference, Toronto, 2012.

virus. While the legal mechanisms are varied, in all instances they attach criminal liability to the activities of people living with HIV, whether in the form of spitting, biting, transmitting HIV through sex, engaging in so-called risky sexual activities, or not disclosing an HIV-positive status before sexual activity.[1]

I write from the Canadian context where HIV criminalisation is formulated in criminal law as a disclosure requirement. Following the recent Supreme Court of Canada decisions in *R v Mabior*[2] and *R v DC*,[3] people living with HIV are required to disclose their HIV-positive status before engaging in sexual activities that pose a 'realistic possibility' of HIV transmission. Failure to do so can result in criminal prosecution, typically for the crime of aggravated sexual assault, which carries a maximum punishment of life imprisonment.

Like most other scholars working on the issue, I oppose the criminalisation of HIV non-disclosure.[4] I recognise that there may be circumstances that warrant the use of the criminal law, for example, when a person with HIV deliberately transmits HIV to a sex partner. In keeping with a wide body of scholarship, however, I view any benefits associated with HIV criminalisation as far outweighed by its harms.[5] These harms include

---

[1] Global Commission on HIV and the Law, *HIV and the Law: Risks, Rights & Health*, 2012. Available at www.hivlawcommission.org/resources/report/FinalReport-Risks,Rights &Health-En.pdf

[2] *R v Mabior* [2012] 2 SCR 584.

[3] *R v DC* [2012] 2 SCR 626

[4] For work favouring the use of the criminal law see, for example, U. Schuklenk, 'Review essay: should we use the criminal law to punish HIV transmission?', *International Journal of Law in Context*, 4: 3 (2009), 277–84; C. Mathen and M. Plaxton, 'HIV, consent and criminal wrongs', *Criminal Law Quarterly*, 57: 4 (2011), 464–85.

[5] L. E. Wolf and R. Vezina, 'Crime and punishment: is there a role for criminal law in HIV prevention policy'?, *Whittier Law Review*, 25 (2004), 821–86; C. Dodds and P. Keogh, 'Criminal prosecutions for HIV transmission: people living with HIV respond', *International Journal of STD & AIDS*, 17 (2006), 315–18; S. Burris, L. Beletsky, J. Burleson, P. Case and Z. Lazzarini, 'Do criminal laws influence HIV risk behavior? An empirical trial', *Arizona State Law Journal*, 39 (2007), 467–517; M. Weait, *Intimacy and Responsibility: The Criminalization of HIV Transmission* (Abingdon, UK: Routledge-Cavendish, 2007); C. L. Galletly, L. R. Glasman, S. D. Pinkerton and W. DiFranceisco, 'New Jersey's HIV exposure law and the HIV-related attitudes, beliefs, and sexual and seropositive status disclosure behaviors of persons living with HIV', *American Journal of Public Health*, 102: 11 (2012), 2135–40; P. O'Byrne, A. Bryan and M. Roy, 'Sexual practices and STI/HIV testing among gay, bisexual, and men who have sex with men in Ottawa, Canada: Examining nondisclosure prosecutions and HIV prevention', *Critical Public Health*, 23: 2 (2013), 225–36; T. Hoppe, 'From sickness to badness: the criminalization of HIV in Michigan', *Social Science & Medicine*, 101 (2014), 139–47; C. Sanders, 'Discussing the limits of confidentiality: the impact of criminalizing HIV nondisclosure on public health nurses' counseling practices', *Public Health Ethics*,

the stigmatisation that follows from associating HIV with criminality, as well as the considerable negative impact on voluntary approaches to HIV prevention. They also extend to the potential uneven application of the law. In the 1980s, legal scholars warned about discrimination and legal injustices that might result from criminalising HIV non-disclosure, given public anxiety about HIV and the association of HIV with stigmatised social groups.[6] The current Canadian situation certainly suggests the prescience of their concerns. Canada is widely regarded as a world leader in HIV-related criminal prosecutions.[7] Since 1989, at least 180 people have been charged with criminal offences related to HIV non-disclosure, the vast majority of them since 2004.[8] The most recently published study of Canadian HIV non-disclosure cases indicates that 78 per cent of cases ended in conviction, 40 per cent of convictions occurred in circumstances where there was no HIV transmission, and a disproportionate number of cases involved defendants who are men from African, Caribbean and Black communities.[9]

The high stakes associated with HIV criminalisation invite forms of engaged scholarship that can be useful for activist struggles and that can generate new academic insights and knowledge.[10] My own contribution to such efforts is an institutional ethnography of the social, institutional and discursive relations through which the criminal law governance of HIV non-disclosure in Canada is produced and sustained. Institutional ethnography does not involve investigating a circumscribed organisation, as might be suggested by an ethnography of a particular hospital or school. Rather, it is a mode of sociological inquiry committed to the empirical

7: 3 (2014), 253–60; K. S. Buchanan, 'When is HIV a crime? Sexuality, gender and consent', *Minnesota Law Review*, 99 (2015), Forthcoming.

[6] K. A. Sullivan and M. A. Field, 'AIDS and the coercive power of the state', *Harvard Civil Rights–Civil Liberties Law Review*, 23 (1988), 139–97.

[7] E. Cameron, 'The criminalization of HIV transmission and exposure', Keynote Lecture, First Annual Symposium on HIV, Law and Human Rights. Canadian HIV/AIDS Legal Network, Toronto, 12–13 June 2009.

[8] Cecile Kazatchkine, Senior Policy Analyst, Canadian HIV/AIDS Legal Network, personal communication, 22 October 2015.

[9] E. Mykhalovskiy and G. Betteridge, 'Who? What? Where? When? And with what consequences? An analysis of criminal cases of HIV non-disclosure in Canada', *Canadian Journal of Law and Society*, 27: 1 (2012), 31–53. This study reports that the accused in 69 per cent of known cases in Ontario are heterosexual men. From 2004 to 2010, the period during which most cases have occurred in Ontario, Black men account for 52 per cent of all heterosexual male defendants.

[10] C. R. Hale, 'Activist research v. cultural critique: Indigenous land rights and the contradictions of politically engaged anthropology', *Cultural Anthropology*, 21: 1 (2006), 96–120.

investigation of ruling relations.[11] Within institutional ethnography, ruling relations are conceptualised as a complex of activities through which advanced capitalist societies are governed. Ruling relations reach across a range of institutional sites such as government, the corporate sector, the mass media, the professions and the law, as well as the forms of discourse that interpenetrate them.[12] In my work I have sought to better understand and make visible the ruling relations through which the criminalisation of HIV non-disclosure is organised. This has involved particular attention to how activities taking place in the criminal justice system interact with public health activities related to HIV prevention.[13]

This chapter builds on that work by turning attention to the efforts of activists to intervene in the relations of knowledge that contribute to criminalising HIV. Social science scholarship on the criminalisation of HIV transmission, exposure and non-disclosure has increased in recent years.[14] However, there has been relatively little discussion about how HIV criminalisation has been challenged in particular local contexts, through what practices and with what effect.[15] Some scholars warn against exploring such issues for fear that doing so will expose activist strategies to authorities.[16] Mindful of this concern, I focus only on activist activities that are well known to government authorities.

For the past eight years I have worked with a group of activists who are members of two organisations that have been central to Canadian activism against HIV criminalisation. The first organisation, the Ontario Working Group on Criminal Law and HIV Exposure (CLHE), was established in 2007 in opposition to the Ontario Ministry of the Attorney General's growing use of the criminal law in situations of HIV non-disclosure. CLHE

---

[11] D. E. Smith, *Institutional Ethnography: A Sociology for People.* (Lanham: AltaMira Press, 2005).

[12] D. E. Smith, *Writing the Social: Critique, Theory and Investigations.* (University of Toronto Press, 1999).

[13] E. Mykhalovskiy, 'The problem of "significant risk": exploring the public health impact of criminalizing HIV non-disclosure', *Social Science & Medicine*, 73: 5 (2011), 668–75.

[14] C. Sanders, 'Examining public health nurses' documentary practices: the impact of criminalizing HIV non-disclosure on inscription styles'. *Critical Pubic Health*, Forthcoming; T. Hoppe, 'Controlling sex in the name of 'public health': social control and Michigan HIV law', *Social Problems*, 60: 1 (2013), 27–49; B. Adam, P. Corrievau, R. Elliott, J. Globerman, K. English and S. Rourke, 'HIV disclosure as practice and public policy', *Critical Public Health*, Forthcoming.

[15] Although see Y. Azad, 'Developing guidance for HIV prosecutions: an example of harm reduction?', *HIV/AIDS Policy and Law Review*, 13: 1 (2008), 13–19.

[16] S. Smeltzer, 'Asking tough questions: the ethics of studying activism in democratically restricted environments', *Social Movement Studies*, 11: 2 (2012), 255–71.

members include people living with HIV, lawyers, community workers, researchers and AIDS activists. CLHE receives no state funding and operates on a voluntary basis. For the past five years, CLHE has led a provincial campaign to encourage the Ministry of the Attorney General to enter into a process of consultation with community members and public health, legal, medical and other experts to establish prosecutorial guidance for HIV non-disclosure in Ontario. The second organisation, the Canadian HIV/AIDS Legal Network was established in 1992 and is one of the National Partners in Canada's HIV Response.[17] Through its advocacy, research and public education, the Legal Network promotes the human rights of people living with and vulnerable to HIV/AIDS. The Legal Network has provided national leadership in advocating against HIV criminalisation in Canada for decades. Most recently, it led an intervention before the Supreme Court of Canada in *R v Mabior*,[18] in which CLHE members and the HIV/AIDS Legal Clinic Ontario (HALCO) also participated.

This chapter offers a reflexive analysis of the activities of CLHE and the Legal Network and the 'relations of ruling' these organisations struggle against in their work. As both a scholar and an active CLHE member, my discussion complicates the established academic practice of treating the object of knowledge as external to or independent of the knower. I write a sociology of ruling and activism from within and draw on autoethnographic forms of presentation. Doing so locates my analysis within a range of feminist critiques of scientific objectivity that insist upon occupying an embodied location when writing about relations of knowledge in which one is implicated.[19]

The criminal law governance of HIV non-disclosure is a form of social organisation in which various forms of knowledge and reasoning – epidemiological, legal and popular – are thoroughly implicated.[20] This chapter explores one aspect of those knowledge relations – the role played

---

[17] The National Partners are ten national-level HIV/AIDS organisations working to ensure that Canadian government and private sector responses to HIV/AIDS are informed by evidence and the needs of HIV-affected communities. For details see www.catie.ca/sites/default/files/NP%20pamphlet-ENG.pdf.

[18] [2012] 2 SCR 584.

[19] See, for example, Smith, *Writing the Social*; D. Haraway, *Simians, Cyborgs, and Women. The Reinvention of Nature* (New York: Routledge, 1991).

[20] For a compelling analysis of how extending the law of sexual assault to address HIV non-disclosure gives rise to tensions between discourses of individual rights and risk discourses associated with public health/governmental power, see D. Young, 'Individual rights and the negotiation of governmental power: the risk of HIV transmission and Canadian criminal law', *Social & Legal Studies*, 24: March (2015), 113–34.

by scientific knowledge about risk and the nature of HIV disease – in shaping HIV criminalisation and activist responses to that criminalisation. I give particular attention to how developments in Canadian criminal law are discursively coordinated by the legal concept of 'significant risk'. I argue that ambiguities in what constitutes a significant risk have propelled a form of 'science-based activism', practiced by CLHE and the Legal Network, which seeks to establish epidemiological risk knowledge as a determinative ground of legal decision making about HIV non-disclosure. Drawing on insights from institutional ethnography about the role played by texts in shaping social relations, I conceptualise science-based activism as the recontextualisation of scientific knowledge. I pay particular attention to the writing practices and ethical dilemmas associated with activist efforts to write epidemiological risk knowledge *for* criminal justice settings. Drawing on an analysis of the recent Supreme Court of Canada decision in *R v Mabior*, I also explore some of the consequences of science-based activism. I argue that the Court's response to science-based activism gives rise to new problematic forms of biological citizenship with the potential to aggravate existing forms of structural inequality and social marginalisation.

The Canadian Legal Context: *Cuerrier* and the Ambiguities of Significant Risk

Public Health is the primary governmental authority responsible for preventing the transmission of HIV infection. In Canada, public health authorities enjoy a range of powers that can be used to control the spread of HIV. As is the case in many other jurisdictions, Canadian public health officials privilege the use of voluntary measures, such as HIV testing and counselling, to prevent HIV transmission, over the use of more coercive public health strategies such as the issuing of public health orders.

Voluntary public health approaches to HIV prevention can be understood as a form of risk governance. They are based on forms of epidemiological knowledge that attach a risk gradation to sexual and other activities associated with the transmission of HIV. They invite individuals to govern themselves by adjusting their conduct in relation to public health knowledge. Thus, people are encouraged to avoid high-risk sexual activities, to use condoms, to not share drug paraphernalia and so on. Early critiques of the public health response to HIV focused on the stigmatising consequences of epidemiological 'risk groups' that linked HIV with the 'lifestyles' of marginalised social groups including gay men, sex workers and drug users.[21] More recent, Foucauldian-inspired analyses treat HIV as a site for considering neo-liberal modes of self-governance and active biological citizenship.[22] Here, the emphasis is placed on a form of power that operates through a heightened individual responsibility to care for oneself. In the context of HIV, scholars have drawn attention to novel forms of 'self-governance' that manifest as avoiding HIV infection or, for those who are HIV-positive, carefully adhering to biomedical treatment regimens.[23]

Both early and later critiques of public health reasoning and practice address key elements of the knowledge relations through which efforts are made to protect human populations from the threat of HIV transmission. As important as they are, they fail to address critical changes in the biopolitics of HIV. One of the most important of these is the growing use, in recent years, of criminal law strategies for regulating conduct presumed to increase the risk of HIV transmission. In Canada, a new form of criminal law governance has arisen that treats the presence of HIV in the human body as a basis for new legal norms of sexual conduct and new medico-legal ways of classifying human beings. It too is a form of risk governance, but it is formally grounded in legal risk concepts, not public health risk knowledge. It also compels people living with HIV, through threat of punishment, to reveal their HIV-positive status to others, rather than inviting us all to manage our conduct voluntarily by monitoring our health risks. In order to understand this form of criminal law governance and its relationship to particular activist responses, an understanding of the play of risk discourses within it is required.

Significant Risk

In Canada, transmitting HIV is not the formal focus of criminal law regulation. Instead, criminal liability attaches to the failure to be open about one's HIV-positive status. People living with HIV are required to disclose their status, but only before engaging in certain sexual acts, in certain

21 C. Patton, *Sex & Germs: The Politics of AIDS* (Montreal-Buffalo: Black Rose Books, 1986).
22 A. Petersen and D. Lupton, *The New Public Health: Health and Self in the Age of Risk.* (London: Sage Publications, 1996); N. Rose, *The Politics of Life Itself: Biomedicine, Power and Subjectivity in the Twenty-First Century* (Princeton: Princeton University Press, 2007); N. Rose and C. Novas, 'Biological citizenship', in A. Ong and S. J. Collier (eds.), *Global Assemblages: Technology, Politics, And Ethics as Anthropological Problems.* (Malden, MA: Blackwell, 2005), pp. 439–63.
23 E. Mykhalovskiy, L. McCoy and M. Bresalier, 'Compliance/adherence, HIV/AIDS and the critique of medical power', *Social Theory and Health*, 2: 4 (2004), 315–40.

circumstances. The parameters of these circumstances are modulated by legal notions of risk. The operative concept was originally formulated as the 'significant risk of serious bodily harm' test by the Supreme Court of Canada in its 1998 landmark decision, *R v Cuerrier*.[24] Henry Cuerrier was charged with two counts of aggravated assault for failing to disclose his HIV-positive status to two female partners with whom he engaged in unprotected vaginal intercourse. Neither woman became HIV-positive as a result of her sexual encounters with Cuerrier.

In the majority decision, the Supreme Court held that failing to disclose one's HIV-positive status to a sex partner 'could constitute fraud which would vitiate consent to sexual activity, provided there was a *significant risk of serious bodily harm* to the complainant' (emphasis in the original).[25] Writing for the majority, Justice Cory argued that

> [T]he risk of contracting AIDS [*sic*] as a result of engaging in unprotected intercourse would clearly meet that [significant risk of serious bodily harm] test. In this case the complainants were exposed to a significant risk of serious harm to their health. Indeed their very survival was placed in jeopardy. It is difficult to imagine a more significant risk or a more grievous bodily harm.[26]

Through *Cuerrier*, the Supreme Court linked the criminal law definition of commercial fraud with legal concepts of consent and significant risk to extend existing Canadian Criminal Code offences to HIV non-disclosure before sex.[27] In doing so, it set out the legal reasoning that permits otherwise consensual sex to be treated in criminal law as a sexual assault.[28] In the interest of preventing the trivialisation of the law of sexual assault, the Court formalised the presence of a risk concept in the determination of liability for non-disclosure. Fraud would not be vitiated by any non-disclosure, only by the failure to disclose before a sexual act that posed a *significant risk* of HIV transmission.

There are two features of this formulation that are critical for understanding the social organisation of HIV criminalisation in Canada and activists' response to it. First, the parameters of the significant risk test

---

[24] [1998] 2 SCR 371.

[25] I. Grant, 'The prosecution of HIV non-disclosure in Canada: time to rethink', *Cuerrier McGill Journal of Law and Health*, 5: 1 (2011), 7–59, at p. 9.

[26] *R v Cuerrier* [1998] 2 SCR 371 at paragraph 128.

[27] I. Grant, 'The boundaries of the criminal law: the criminalization of the non-disclosure of HIV', *Dalhousie Law Journal*, 31 (2008), 123–80.

[28] R. Elliott, *After Cuerrier: Canadian Criminal Law and the Non-disclosure of HIV-Positive Status* (Toronto: Canadian HIV/AIDS Legal Network, 1999).

were not clearly articulated by the Supreme Court in *Cuerrier*. The Court was clear that unprotected vaginal intercourse constituted a significant risk, but it only suggested that the use of a condom *might* so lower the risk of HIV transmission that disclosure would not be required prior to protected genital intercourse.[29] The Court also failed to explicitly draw on scientific evidence about the nature of HIV or epidemiological research about transmission risks in establishing the significant risk test. Thus, the test had no clear reference to meaningful public health or scientific guidelines about the risk of sexually transmitting HIV. On balance, the concept of significant risk was far too vague. It failed to provide people living with HIV clear guidance about what sexual activities, in what circumstances, would require disclosure. Unsure about when they faced criminal liability, many people living with HIV, and those working with them, responded to the significant risk test with confusion, anxiety and anger.[30]

Second, *Cuerrier* contributed to a disjuncture between how the criminal law obligation to disclose was formally tied to significant risk and how lower courts decided on individual cases. People living with HIV and their supporters were not alone in dealing with the vagueness of the significant risk test. Crown Prosecutors and lower courts also struggled. Scientific evidence has a complex and varied presence in juridical decision-making processes. Judges and other criminal justice authorities interpret scientific evidence in multiple ways. They resist or ignore scientific risk knowledges or combine them with legal ways of knowing and 'lay' and other forms of risk knowledge when making decisions.[31] The indeterminacy of the significant risk test certainly contributed to the multiple forms of knowledge at work in judicial decision making about HIV non-disclosure cases. It contributed to the inconsistent application of the test, wide variations in the extent to which evidence of risk of transmission was considered in individual cases and, of course, inconsistent outcomes.[32]

The vagueness and inconsistent application of the significant risk test, and the tendency for police and Crown Prosecutors to pursue charges vigorously, even in circumstances when a negligible risk of HIV transmission

---

[29] *R. v. Cuerrier* [1998] 2 SCR 371 at paragraph 129.
[30] Mykhalovskiy, 'The problem of "significant risk"' 668–75
[31] M. Valverde, M, R. Levi and D. Moore, 'Legal knowledges of risk', in Law Commission of Canada (ed.), *Law and Risk* (Vancouver: University of British Columbia Press, 2005), pp. 469–522; S. Jasanoff, 'Just evidence: the limits of science in the legal process', *Journal of Law, Medicine & Ethics*, 34: 2 (2006), 328–41.
[32] Mykhalovskiy and Betteridge, 'Who? What? Where? When? And with what consequences?', 31–53.

had been posed, propelled activism against criminalisation in Ontario. Problems associated with the concept of significant risk encouraged forms of activism that sought to rein in the reach of the significant risk test by mobilising epidemiological risk knowledge. In the section that follows I turn to a discussion of this form of science-based criminal law reform.

Significant Risk and Science-Based Criminal Law Reform

In his writings on institutional ethnography, George Smith, the late sociologist and gay rights and AIDS activist, argued that grass-roots political organising provides a location from which to explore the ruling relations that activists confront and seek to transform.[33] His early research on the management of the AIDS epidemic in Canada treated political confrontation, in particular, meetings with government officials, as a site from which to grasp how ruling practices work. Following his example, I orient to my involvement with CLHE and the Legal Network as an important ethnographic resource.

Since 2007, I have participated in dozens of CLHE and Legal Network meetings and strategy sessions about HIV criminalisation. I have attended and spoken at CLHE workshops and public fora, and written and responded to thousands of e-mails to and from fellow CLHE members. I have attended demonstrations, met with public health officials, worked with criminal defence lawyers, lobbied elected officials and met with staff from the Ontario Ministry of the Attorney General. I have also conducted interview research with healthcare providers, lawyers, front-line community workers, activists and people living with HIV, among others. These activities form an important ethnographic ground from which to explore how the criminal law governance of HIV non-disclosure operates. Through my participation in CLHE I came to understand how the social organisation of criminal law governance is discursively coordinated by the legal concept of significant risk. At the same time, my 'insider's status' offered me a basis from which to reflect on how significant risk conceptually shapes CLHE's activism against HIV criminalisation.

CLHE and the Legal Network draw on a variety of rhetorical strategies in their efforts to restrict HIV criminalisation. For example, they argue that criminalisation harms HIV prevention goals and that the law should be restricted to circumstances when a person living with HIV intentionally and successfully transmits the virus. However, the dominant framing

---

[33] G. W. Smith, 'Political activist as ethnographer', 629–48

of criminalisation they rely upon would restrict the reach of significant risk through the enlistment of science. I refer to this as a science-based approach to criminal law reform. It is an approach that problematises science-criminal law relations and that tries to limit the reach of the criminal law by establishing scientific research about HIV disease and the risk of HIV transmission as the fundamental discursive ground upon which legal decisions about HIV non-disclosure are made.

Activism, Texts and Text-Mediated Relations

As practiced by CLHE and the Legal Network, science-based criminal law reform has many dimensions including public education, working with defence lawyers, political lobbying and educating the judiciary. These activities all require that texts about epidemiological research on HIV transmission risks be created and widely circulated, both within and beyond the criminal justice system. From this perspective, science-based criminal law reform can be understood as an attempt to intervene in the text-mediated relations of the criminal justice system. The importance that texts play in enabling contemporary practices of governance is often neglected or minimised. Scholars typically orient to texts as repositories of meaning or as a site from which to explore the intertextual relations of discourse. Rarely do they fully acknowledge how texts – whether in print, electronic, video or some other material form – shape what people do. Yet texts are central constituents of social action and are critical to organising the nitty-gritty work of governing. Because they are mobile and have a standardised form, texts, including laws, enable similar social practices and forms of organisation to occur across time and place.[34]

Recognising the central role that texts play in everyday practices of governing underscores the potential significance of 'textual work' for activism. Texts and the discourses they bear become something that activists can contribute to, reframe and transform as part of efforts to limit or change problematic forms of governance. In the context of advocacy against HIV criminalisation, such efforts have focused on creating texts about epidemiological research on HIV transmission risks and creating the conditions for their circulation within the criminal justice system.

This is a form of activist work that has resonated for CLHE members. A number of CLHE activists were active during the heyday of Canadian HIV treatment politics in the 1980s and early 1990s. They are accustomed

---

[34] D. E. Smith, *Institutional Ethnography*.

to reading and critiquing scientific research and are well-practiced at enlisting scientific research to make political demands. Advocating for changes in how clinical trials research is conducted is, however, a rather different political engagement with biomedical research than drawing on epidemiological and clinical research in an effort to change criminal law regulation. Early activist efforts aimed to produce better science more quickly, primarily by creating new roles for people with HIV in the design and oversight of clinical trials and by advocating for changes in state drug approval processes. The activities of CLHE and the Legal Network, by contrast, involve fewer direct interventions in the conduct of scientific research and, instead, focus on increasing its organising presence in relations formally external to biomedicine. Primarily a matter of making science 'count' in the criminal justice system, science-based criminal law reform presents a set of challenges about representing and translating science that HIV treatment politics did not.

The framework for a science-based approach to reforming the criminal law governance of HIV non-disclosure was established shortly after *R v Cuerrier*. The conditions of scientific discourse required for it to be fully realised, however, came into being only some years later. Barely a year following *Cuerrier*, the Legal Network produced a widely cited report on the Supreme Court's decision.[35] In the report, the current Executive Director of the Legal Network, Richard Elliott, took issue with the lack of clarity associated with the Court's framing of the significant risk test. At the same time, he laid the groundwork for an activist strategy that used science to problematise significant risk, arguing that legal assessments of significant risk 'should be consistent with available epidemiological conclusions regarding the risks of transmission associated with various sexual activities'.[36]

Epidemiological conclusions of the sort called for by Elliott were certainly available at the time the report was published, but they were not yet informed by research on regimens of effective antiretroviral combination therapy, which had only recently become widely available to people living with HIV. A few years later, a sea-change in scientific knowledge about the effects of antiretroviral therapy on disease progression and HIV transmission had occurred. In the early and mid-2000s, epidemiological studies began to be published that showed that HIV therapy had dramatic population-level health impacts. People undergoing antiretroviral therapy

---

[35] Elliott, *After Cuerrier*, 18.
[36] Ibid., 18.

were living longer and healthier lives. In fact, studies indicated that life expectancy had so increased and morbidity had been so reduced that HIV infection had become a chronic manageable disease.[37]

At the same time, treatment was shown to have a dramatic effect on the risk of HIV transmission. Studies published in the late 2000s and onwards showed that treatment reduced viral load – the amount of HIV in the blood – to such a low level that the likelihood of HIV transmission was significantly reduced. Estimates were released that claimed up to a 92 per cent reduction in the risk of HIV transmission associated with antiretroviral therapy use.[38] Some scientists went so far as to argue that, in optimal circumstances, people living with HIV taking antiretroviral therapy were non-infectious.[39] A recently published systematic review of research involving serodiscordant heterosexual couples (in which only one person is HIV-positive) reports a rate of HIV transmission of 0 per 100 person-years when the HIV-positive partner has confirmed virological suppression. In light of accumulated evidence of the low risk of HIV transmission, over seventy Canadian physicians and medical researchers recently endorsed a consensus statement on HIV transmission expressing concern about the overly broad use of the criminal law in circumstances of HIV non-disclosure.[40]

For CLHE activists, new clinical and epidemiological research on lowered HIV transmission risks was a welcome discursive resource that could be enlisted in efforts to narrow the scope of HIV criminalisation. CLHE members oriented to the new science as evidence of the divide between what was known scientifically about HIV and how the criminal justice system treated HIV non-disclosure:

> There was a judge in Barrie who said some very unfortunate things relating to HIV, that HIV can be brought back to life after being outside the

[37] N. F. Crum, R. H. Riffenburgh, S. Wegner, B. K. Again, S. A. Tasker, K. M. Spooner, A. W. Armstrong, S. Fraser and M. R. Wallace, Triservice AIDS Clinical Consortium, 'Comparisons of causes of death and mortality rates among HIV-infected persons: analysis of the pre-, early, and late HAART (highly active antiretroviral therapy) eras', *Journal of Acquired Immune Deficiency Syndromes*, 41: 2 (2006), 194–200.

[38] S. Attia, M. Egger, M. Muller, M. Zwahlen and N. Low, 'Sexual transmission of HIV according to viral load and antiretroviral therapy: systematic review and meta-analysis', *AIDS*, 23: 11 (2009), 1397–1404.

[39] P. Vernazza, B. Hirschel, E. Bernasconi and M. Flepp, 'Les personnes séropositives ne souffrant d'aucune autre MST et suivant un traitement antirétroviral efficace ne transmettent pas le VIH par voie sexuelle', *Bulletin des Médecins Suisses*, 89: 5 (2008), 165–9

[40] M. Loutfy, M. Tyndall, J. Baril, J. Montaner, R. Kaul and C. Hankins, 'Canadian consensus statement on HIV transmission in the context of criminal law', *Canadian Journal of Infectious Diseases & Medical Microbiology*, 25: 3 (2014), 135–40.

body, can be brought back to life with moisture ... I wouldn't say that's indicative of all judges, but it points towards attitudes in mainstream society and in judges. And judges there are new issues that come up, but HIV non-disclosure is a particularly, this is a particularly new issue because it's using existing criminal law [on sexual assault] in a new kind of way. So for judges that's a big deal, right? And ... all of a sudden you have all this crazy science to do with viral load, to do with condom use, that has to do with the legal test of what is considered a significant risk, and judges are only as educated as the lawyers that appear before them, right, because if the lawyers don't present a good case, then the judges are, especially if they don't know a lot about HIV in the first place, you know, what can they do?[41]

As suggested by the speaker quoted, judges and the courts were framed by CLHE members as dangerously anachronistic and out of touch with the latest scientific evidence. From an activist perspective, criminal justice actors needed to be 'better educated' so that their legal and judicial decisions about HIV could be more fully informed by available epidemiological and clinical research. While a favourable body of epidemiological and clinical research was at hand, the question that presented itself to CLHE and the Legal Network was how best to synthesise, translate and represent it to a juridical readership.

Writing Science for Juridical Readers

The opportunity to work through those issues came in the form of an invitation to CLHE members and Legal Network staff to become co-investigators on a study focused on informing sound public policy responses to the use of the criminal law in circumstances of HIV non-disclosure.[42] I served as the principal investigator of the research. The study linked CLHE's activism, particularly its emphasis on the problematisation of the significant risk test, with practices for producing and writing about research evidence for policy-making audiences. Its principal aim was to provide the Ontario Ministry of the Attorney General with a way to think about what was problematic about the criminalisation of HIV non-disclosure and how to address it.

The study report argued that the criminalisation of HIV non-disclosure presented the Ministry with an urgent problem of legal unfairness that could be addressed by engaging in a process of widespread consultation to

---

[41] Interview, lawyer, 24 December 2009.
[42] E. Mykhalovskiy, G. Betteridge and D. McLay, *HIV Non-disclosure and the Criminal Law: Establishing Policy Options for Ontario.* (Toronto: Ontario HIV Treatment Network, 2010).

create evidence-informed prosecutorial guidance for Crown Prosecutors. In support of claims about the unfairness of HIV criminalisation, we offered analyses of four types of research data. We reported on the demographic, temporal and geographic patterns of criminal HIV non-disclosure cases in Ontario, emphasising the large proportion of cases that involved Black, male defendants. We produced an analysis of inconsistencies in the interpretation and application of the significant risk test by Ontario courts. We also analysed original interview research on the impact of HIV criminalisation on the HIV prevention counselling efforts of public health nurses and front-line service providers. Finally, we reviewed epidemiological research on HIV transmission and on mortality and morbidity associated with HIV infection.

Writing the section of the report dealing with the risks of sexually transmitting HIV infection involved knowledge moves through which we sought to bring science to the courts. Scholars who have written about the enrolment of science in judicial processes have raised concerns about the vulnerability of jurists to unfair manipulation of scientific research, as well as jurists' unfamiliarity with established epistemological critiques of the truth claims that science makes.[43] These concerns call into question what a practical ethics of engagement in scientific research might look like for activists working to limit HIV criminalisation. As noted already, CLHE members were familiar with earlier HIV treatment activism and the challenges associated with the efforts to speed up, democratise and otherwise transform how biomedical research on HIV was conducted. Writing the report, by contrast, was a matter of recontextualising existing epidemiological research, initially intended primarily for public health and clinical readers, for an audience of criminal justice authorities who were being asked to rethink a legal risk concept. In trying to 'convince' criminal justice authorities to reframe their approach to HIV non-disclosure on the basis of science, CLHE members were vulnerable to the charge of overstating scientific certitude in the pursuit of advocacy goals. Writing the report thus posed the dilemma of how to write science for jurists in ways that would not disavow advocacy goals but, at the same time, would not colonise science for political ends:

> I was interested in finding a format that would allow us to place front-and-centre the limits of science, to raise doubts about the transference of epidemiological transmission risk to the risk between two individuals at

---

[43] S. Jasanoff, 'Just evidence: the limits of science in the legal process', *Journal of Law, Medicine & Ethics*, 34: 2 (2006), 328–41.

a point in time. You and I worked closely with David McLay to provide this context, trying to never lose sight of the absolute necessity of impressing upon the reader the low risk of HIV transmission overall. Perhaps we were even inviting or authorizing judges to use scientific language about risk to arrive at a more common sense understanding of HIV risk, grounded in an understanding of science but without being a slave to the competing and confusing numbers.[44]

These comments made by my colleague and report co-author Glenn Betteridge speak to the main ways in which we responded to the challenges of writing science for criminal justice system readers. In order to establish scientific credibility for the review, our first step was to hire an external science writer, David McLay, and to form an advisory board of scientific experts to provide additional direction and guidance. Given widespread criticism that advocacy results in biased knowledge claims,[45] we might have yielded to the pull to reproduce forms of so-called objective scientific reporting. Instead, we worked hard to strike a balance between a concern for what science can and cannot know and remaining transparent about our advocacy goals. While seeking to provide an evidence base that could inform legal decisions about significant risk, we took care not to invoke a premature closure on areas of scientific controversy within epidemiological research on HIV transmission risks. We made strong claims in areas of established scientific consensus, particularly regarding data on condom use,[46] while also bringing forward areas of scientific uncertainty and controversy, for example, about the precise magnitude of risk reduction stemming from an undetectable viral load when engaging in unprotected anal intercourse.[47]

At the same time, we realised that writing the review would not be simply a matter of 'getting the science right'. All scientific writing expresses cultural metaphors and narratives.[48] Our challenge was to situate our analysis of the research on HIV transmission risks and mortality rates within a deliberate narrative strategy that carried forward the politics of criminal law reform we intended. We wanted our review of scientific research to be linked with a history of exaggerating the risk of transmitting HIV that

[44] Glenn Betteridge, personal communication, 5 November 2014.
[45] For a critique of such claims see L. Code, *Ecological Thinking: The Politics of Epistemic Location* (Oxford: Oxford University Press, 2006).
[46] Mykhalovskiy, Betteridge and McLay, *HIV Non-disclosure and the Criminal Law*, 31–2.
[47] Ibid., 32–3.
[48] E. Martin, 'The egg and the sperm: how science constructed a romance based on stereotypical male-female roles', *Signs*, 16: 3 (1991), 485–501.

had contributed to public fear of and discrimination towards people living with HIV, and in which current judicial decisions about non-disclosure were implicated. We therefore framed our review within a common-sense narrative that we came to think of as 'HIV is not as bad as, nor as easy to transmit as, you might think'. In our review, we historicised and problema- tised 'common-sense' knowledge about HIV, noting in the introduction that 'we now know that HIV is difficult to transmit' and 'that even activi- ties considered risky, such as unprotected sexual intercourse, carry a risk of transmission much lower than is often commonly believed'.[49]

The review helped to solidify science-based advocacy against HIV criminalisation by giving it evidentiary weight. It discursively supported CLHE and Legal Network activism by pointing to a body of scientific research that could be used by criminal justice authorities in deliberations about the reach of significant risk. Circulating the review among judges and lawyers resulted in a strategic intervention in the text-mediated rela- tions of criminal law governance and reform. Shortly after the full report was published, the Legal Network excerpted the review and included it as a key component of its curriculum at the Canadian National Judicial Institute Workshop on HIV and the Law held in 2010.[50] Among those in attendance at the workshop were justices from the Manitoba Court of Appeal. In October 2010, a short time after the institute workshop, they would release a decision in *R v Mabior* that drew fundamentally on sci- entific evidence about HIV transmission risks. Included in the evidence they cited in their decision was the review's analysis of condom use and HIV transmission risks.[51]

The Court of Appeal's decision was an important victory for science-based criminal law reform. Mabior, an HIV-positive man, engaged in vaginal intercourse with multiple women without disclosing his HIV-positive status. None of the women became HIV-positive. At trial, he was convicted on six counts of aggravated sexual assault for fail- ing to disclose his status. In its decision, the Manitoba Court of Appeal overturned four of the six convictions. On the basis of a careful review of

---

[49] Mykhalovskiy, Betteridge and McLay, *HIV Non-disclosure and the Criminal Law*, 26.

[50] An updated version of the review was also included in a Legal Network online resource kit for lawyers that focused on HIV criminalisation. At an international level, UNAIDS published the updated review as a chapter in a judicial handbook on HIV. UNAIDS, *Judging during the Epidemic: A Judicial Handbook on HIV, Human Rights and the Law.* (UNAIDS, 2013). www.unaids.org/sites/default/files/media_asset/201305_Judging-epidemic_en_0.pdf

[51] *R v Mabior* (C.L.) (2010) MBCA 93 at paragraph 88.

available scientific research, the Court found that a significant risk of HIV transmission had not occurred when the defendant used a condom for vaginal sex *or* had an undetectable viral load.[52]

Any satisfaction with the Court of Appeal decision on the part of CLHE and Legal Network activists was short-lived. The Manitoba Attorney General appealed the decision to the Supreme Court of Canada. Doing so set the stage for Canada's highest court to revisit *Cuerrier* to determine the circumstances under which people living with HIV can be convicted of a criminal offence for not disclosing their HIV-positive status to a sex partner. The intervention in *R v Mabior*, led by the Legal Network, was an important milestone in Canadian science-based activism to restrict the reach of HIV criminalisation. The Supreme Court's decision in that case introduced important changes to the criminal law's HIV disclosure obligation. In fact, it widened rather than narrowed the scope of prosecution for HIV non-disclosure, raising important questions about the nature of science-law relations and about the unintended consequences of science-based advocacy.[53]

Science-Based Activism Reaches the Supreme Court

By the time *Mabior* reached the Supreme Court of Canada, it was joined by a second case, *R v DC*, which had been brought on appeal by the Quebec Attorney General. *R v DC* involved an HIV-positive woman convicted of sexual assault and aggravated assault for failing to disclose to her boyfriend prior to a single instance of alleged unprotected vaginal intercourse that occurred roughly four years prior to the complaint.[54]

In its written argument to the Supreme Court, the Legal Network and its partners in the intervention repeated arguments that had been

---

[52] Ibid.

[53] In a number of other national jurisdictions, including Denmark, Norway, Sweden and Switzerland, scientific research on HIV disease and HIV transmission risks has also played a central role in judicial reasoning about HIV. In some instances, scientific research has been central to key acquittals and broader criminal law reform. For an example, see E. Bernard, 'Denmark: justice minister suspends HIV-specific law, sets up working group', www.hivjustice.net/news/denmark-justice-minister-suspends-hiv-specific-criminal-law-sets-up-working-group/. For a general 'best practice' discussion of medical and scientific evidence, criminal law and HIV see UNAIDS, *Ending Overly Broad Criminalization of HIV Non-disclosure, Exposure and Transmission.* www.unaids.org/sites/default/files/media_asset/20130530_Guidance_Ending_Criminalisation_0.pdf

[54] S. Claivaz-Loranger, *R. v. D.C. Summary of the Decision of the Court of Appeal of Quebec.* (Montreal: COCQ-SIDA, 2010).

developed as part of its and CLHE's science-based advocacy against HIV criminalisation.[55] They argued that, with proper access to treatment, HIV becomes a chronic manageable infection. They further argued that the significant risk test established in *Cuerrier* was 'an appropriate and necessary limitation on the use of the criminal law', but that its uneven interpretation and application had 'resulted in the unfairness and uncertainty that were cause for concern when *Cuerrier* was decided'.[56] The intervenors called for an incremental clarification and evolution of the law that would be principally informed by ongoing developments in the science of HIV transmission. The factum summarised current findings on HIV transmission risks and proposed a refinement of the significant risk test that articulated a 'bright lines test' attached to specific sexual practices. On the basis of available scientific evidence, the intervenors argued that a significant risk does not occur when condoms are used for genital intercourse, during oral sex or when a person with HIV has a low or undetectable viral load and that, accordingly, people living with HIV should not be held criminally liable for non-disclosure in those circumstances.

In February 2012 I travelled to Ottawa to attend the Supreme Court hearings. I sat with other CLHE members in the audience and listened to the arguments described play out during the proceedings. My fieldnotes capture the rhetorical struggles that ensued at a moment when efforts to consolidate the authority of scientific knowledge within judicial decision making about HIV non-disclosure reached their pinnacle. Those struggles centre on the question of scientific certitude and the broader place of epidemiological knowledge of transmission risks in the criminal law governance of HIV:

> There is a discussion happening about the stability of scientific knowledge about transmission risk and whether it's an appropriate basis upon which to establish criminal liability ... Jonathan Shime, the lawyer for the intervenors from community-based organisations, is trying to answer Justice Abella's question about risk reduction associated with condom use. He's referred to the chart on scientific findings related to condom use and transmission risk from our scientific review. He's explaining that condoms prevent 80% of transmissions that would occur without their use. The risk of HIV transmission for unprotected vaginal intercourse is commonly estimated to be .08% or 8 in 10,000. Condom use drops that to 1 or 2 in 10,000. An unprotected viral load drops it a further 96% ... Jonathan is arguing that the current scientific research on HIV transmission risks

---

[55] Canadian HIV/AIDS Legal Network, *Factum of the Interveners, R v Mabior and R v DC*, Supreme Court of Canada Court File Nos. 33976/34094, 2012a.

[56] Ibid., 1.

makes possible a new 'bright lines' test around non-disclosure. The argument is that the risk for oral sex, vaginal or anal intercourse with a condom, and sex with an undetectable or low viral load is so small that it should not require disclosure.... The Manitoba Crown lawyers are now arguing against Jonathan. In their closing statements they are trying to destabilize the science in ways that imagine a very different HIV-infected body. They are arguing that the condom chart is confusing, with big ranges in scientific findings about transmission risk and far too many variables that affect that risk. They are emphasizing that there are spikes in viral load over time that can't be predicted or measured and that the science hasn't told us that there is no risk. In order for someone to truly consent to sex, a person should know the HIV-positive status of his or her sex partner regardless of the risk posed by the encounter. They want the Court to require full disclosure in all sexual circumstances.[57]

Speaking for the Legal Network and its partners in the intervention, Shime emphasised the authority and security of scientific research on low levels of transmission risk. The Manitoba Attorney General, by contrast, called into question that security, hoping to destabilise science and remove its organising presence from judicial reasoning on matters related to HIV non-disclosure.[58]

In the end, the Supreme Court did not fully accept the position taken by the Manitoba Crown that people living with HIV who do not disclose their HIV-positive status to sex partners, regardless of whether any risk of transmission is posed, should be charged with a criminal offence; however, the Court also rejected most of what had been argued by the Legal Network. It rejected activist claims about the degree of harm posed by HIV infection. The established biomedical representation of HIV as a chronic manageable disease is scarcely present in its decision, in which the Court finds that 'HIV is indisputably serious and life threatening'.[59] The Court also rejected the Legal Network's 'bright lines test' and its science-based arguments about the relationship between research on the risk of HIV transmission and the parameters of the significant risk test. In its decision, the Supreme Court broadened the reach of the significant risk test, finding that people living with HIV are required to disclose prior to sex that poses a 'realistic possibility of transmission of HIV'.[60] It further provided

---

[57] Fieldnotes, 8 February 2012.

[58] For a parallel argument that, in addition, draws on an analysis of 'objectification' to maintain that HIV non-disclosure should be treated as a sexual assault see C. Mathen and M. Plaxton, 'HIV, consent'.

[59] *R v Mabior* [2012] 2 SCR 584 [92].

[60] *R v Mabior* [2012] 2 SCR 584 [84].

only one circumstance when disclosure is not required: prior to vaginal intercourse when condoms are used *and* the HIV-positive person has a low viral load.[61] On this basis, the Court reinstated three of Mabior's four convictions handed down by the trial court.

CLHE, the Legal Network, HALCO and other activists decried the decision, framing it as a repudiation of science and an abandonment of people living with HIV. The decision was described as 'enshrining stigma in the rule of law' by AIDS ACTION NOW[62] and as 'a cold endorsement of AIDS phobia' by the Legal Network.[63] Activists claimed that the decision would invite convictions for HIV non-disclosure even when the risk of transmission is negligible and when people living with HIV followed established public health advice by using condoms. The Legal Network framed the decision as a regressive step that compounded the injustices associated with the *Cuerrier* decision. It argued that the Supreme Court paid mere lip service to concerns about risk and not overextending the reach of the criminal law and that the level of risk established by the new realistic possibility test is so low that it approximates an absolute disclosure obligation.[64]

Conclusion – Unintended Consequences

It is tempting to view the Supreme Court's decision as evidence of the failure of science-based criminal law reform; however, doing so would obscure the complexity of the science-law relations that played out in the decision. There can be no disputing that the *Mabior* decision is a step backwards for activists. While the Supreme Court engaged with science, it did so only minimally and not as those of us who worked with CLHE and the Legal Network had hoped. The Court's engagement with science did not end up clarifying the ambiguities associated with the significant risk test for people living with HIV. For example, *Mabior* provides little guidance about whether other low-risk sexual activities, such as oral sex, might also

61 *R v Mabior* [2012] 2 SCR 584 [94].
62 AIDS ACTION NOW, 'More criminalization, further marginalization: Supreme court's HIV non-disclosure decisions create viral underclass', 2012. Available at: www.aidsactionnow.org/?p=975. Accessed 20 September 2014.
63 Canadian HIV/AIDS Legal Network, 'Unjust Supreme Court ruling on criminalization of HIV major step backwards for public health and human rights'. Press Release, 2012b. Available at: www.aidslaw.ca/publications/interfaces/downloadFile.php?ref=2055 Accessed 20 September 2014.
64 Canadian HIV/AIDS Legal Network, 'HIV Non-disclosure and the criminal law: an analysis of two recent decisions of the Supreme Court of Canada', 2012c. Available at: www.aidslaw.ca/publications/interfaces/downloadFile.php?ref=2083

fall outside of what is considered a realistic possibility of HIV transmission. What sexual activities in what circumstances might be excluded from a realistic possibility of HIV transmission, beyond having a low viral load and using a condom prior to vaginal intercourse, is left unclear in *Mabior*.[65] Furthermore, some fourteen years after *Cuerrier*, and in the face of an accumulated body of scientific research showing that HIV is a less serious medical condition and much harder to transmit given the significant success of antiretroviral therapy, the Court established a standard that is more expansive than the significant risk test. Prior to *Mabior*, a number of trial and appellate courts had ruled that HIV-positive people who use condoms during sexual intercourse are not required to disclose their status. Under the new legal regime they can be found guilty of an aggravated sexual assault.

At the same time, the Court did not fully abandon science or detach scientific reasoning from criminal law governance of HIV non-disclosure. It used scientific risk estimates to establish the realistic possibility threshold. While arguably far too broad in its reach, the 'realistic possibility' test does provide some measure of protection from criminal liability and represents a not insignificant development for those HIV-positive people with access to effective treatments who use condoms for vaginal intercourse. The Court also established that onward modification of the disclosure requirement could occur in response to 'future advances in treatment'.[66] Science-based arguments may also have played an important role in preventing the Court from fully siding with the Manitoba Attorney General's arguments that disclosure should be required prior to any sex, regardless of the risk posed.

Rather than a simple success/failure story, then, the decision of the Supreme Court of Canada in *Mabior* points to the complex, contradictory nature and unintended consequences of mobilising science in HIV-related criminal law reform. Faced with few alternatives, activists turned to scientific reasoning to formulate arguments that might restrict criminalisation and have some impact on the Court's reasoning. Our approach arguably over-estimated the purchase of science in the juridical field and misrecognised the heterogeneity of knowledge relations that hold sway in juridical processes. The public is not privy to the internal deliberations of the Supreme Court and a full analysis of the interdiscursivity of the Court's decision is beyond the scope of this chapter. Still, it is clear that scientific

---

[65] P. Hartford, 'Case comment: a critique of the Supreme Court of Canada's use of statistical reasoning in *R v Mabior*', *Law, Probability and Risk*, 13 (2014), 169–180.

[66] *R v Mabior* [2012] 2 SCR 584 at paragraph 95.

risk evidence was conjoined with and largely subordinated to alternative bases of reasoning in the Court's decision. Most prominent among the latter was an appeal to Canadian Constitutional values of equality, autonomy and human dignity, particularly as guaranteed to women and expressed through feminist and related legal arguments about consent to sex and the nature of sexual fraud.[67]

As the argument goes, in order to protect the sexual autonomy of women, women must have the right to choose when they will have sex, with whom, and under what circumstances. Although the Court provided little analysis of the claim,[68] it justified the realistic possibility of transmission test by arguing that the test supports the values of autonomy and equality enshrined in the Canadian Charter of Rights and Freedoms and 'the interest of a person to choose whether to consent to sex with a particular person or not'.[69] The Court's decision highlights discursive tensions between a science-based approach to determining when the obligation to disclose holds, advanced by HIV activists, and a normative approach based on notions of equality, autonomy, dignity and a subjective approach to consent, held by feminist advocates, among others. It further indicates the persuasive force of the latter approach.

An interesting outcome of *Mabior* was a decision on the part of CLHE and Legal Network activists to establish closer ties with feminist scholars and advocates concerned about sexual assault law. In April 2014, Alison Symington, the Legal Network's Co-Director of Research and Advocacy, spear-headed a national workshop that brought feminist legal scholars, women with HIV, HIV activists, service providers and others together to explore the legal and social implications of using sexual assault law to prosecute HIV non-disclosure. The workshop provided a foundation for extending science-based advocacy with a more radical critique of the criminal law. That critique would preserve a broad definition of consent, needed in the context of violence against women, while calling for legal reforms that address the perverse consequences of using that definition to punish, as rapists, people living with HIV who do not disclose.[70]

[67] Young, 'Individual rights'; A. Klein, 'Feminism and the criminalisation of HIV non-disclosure' in this collection; M. Shaffer, 'Sex, likes, and HIV: Mabior and the concept of sexual fraud', *University of Toronto Law Journal*, 63:3 (2013), 466–74.
[68] A. Symington, 'Injustice amplified by HIV non-disclosure ruling', *University of Toronto Law Journal*, 63: 3 (2013), 485–95.
[69] *R v Mabior* [2012] 2 SCR 584 [89].
[70] The challenges of reconciling a feminist politics of sexual assault with HIV-related anti-criminalisation work surfaced earlier for CLHE, including during community

Understanding science-based criminal law reform as simply failing to fully realise its hoped for outcomes also obscures the unintended effects of anti-criminalisation HIV activism. The concept of biological citizenship provides a useful conceptual resource for thinking through the nature and significance of those effects. The concept as developed by Adriana Petryna[71] refers to how, in the context of post-Chernobyl Ukraine, people whose bodies were biologically damaged by radiation came together to demand access to social welfare and make citizenship claims. The concept was subsequently modified and popularised by Rose and Novas[72] to refer to the growing importance of corporeality for forms of identity that arise in the context of rapid biotechnological development. For Rose and Novas, biological citizenship is about new 'regimes of the self' through which individuals are encouraged to manage and shape their lives through acts of choice that relate to their biology. Their use of the term has helped give rise to the trope of the responsible, well-informed citizen who manages his or her conduct in relation to public health and biomedical expertise in order to maximise good health.

Scholars have recently critiqued the approach to biological citizenship suggested by Rose and Novas, citing its lack of empirical specificity and nuance, its failure to take into account social difference, and its lack of attention to the varied ways that actors make claims or otherwise relate to a broad array of institutional practices that are implicated in the production of biological identities.[73] I take inspiration from that critique to make sense of how one consequence of science-based criminal law reform has been the creation of new forms of problematic biological citizenship. CLHE and Legal Network activists used biopolitical arguments – arguments about how the conduct of a group of people, known biologically, should be governed – in an effort to temper the application of the criminal law in circumstances of HIV non-disclosure. Our arguments mobilised scientific research about the impact of treatment on viral load, the infectiousness of HIV-positive bodies and

consultations held in 2011 on developing prosecutorial guidance for HIV non-disclosure. Women's criminal justice and sexual assault providers were key consultation participants. See *Consultation on Prosecutorial Guidelines for Ontario Cases Involving Non-disclosure of Sexually Transmitted Infections: Community Report and Recommendations to the Attorney General of Ontario.* http://clhe.ca/wp-content/uploads/CHLE-guidelines-report.pdf

[71] A. Petryna, *Life Exposed: Biological Citizens after Chernobyl* (Princeton: Princeton University Press, 2002).

[72] Rose and Novas, 'Biological citizenship', 439–63

[73] S. R. Whyte, 'Health identities and subjectivities: the ethnographic challenge', *Medical Anthropology Quarterly*, 23: 1 (2009), 6–15.

degrees of HIV transmission risk. As taken up by the Supreme Court, they played an important role in changing the discursive landscape of criminal law governance in Canada, notably through the creation of the realistic possibility of transmission test. By requiring that people living with HIV have a low viral load and use a condom to escape criminal liability for HIV non-disclosure before sex, the *Mabior* decision creates new medico-legal subjects that are distinguished in criminal law according to whether their virus is effectively suppressed or not.

Through the intersection of activism, science and the criminal law, a novel form of biological citizenship has arisen that carries forward implications for people living with HIV that were not initially intended by HIV activists. The new medico-legal subject created by *Mabior* does not anchor voluntary forms of self-governance in the pursuit of better health. Instead it situates novel medico-legal subjects within coercive relations of the state. *Mabior* creates new kinds of biological persons – those with or without a particular measured quantity of HIV in the blood – and attaches to that measured quantity possibilities of arrest and conviction for a crime that no other kind of person can commit.

An obvious concern is how this new form of biological citizenship may reinforce existing forms of structural inequality characteristic of criminal law regulation. Following *Mabior*, evidence that an HIV-positive defendant is taking effective treatment and documentation about viral load levels will likely play an increasingly important role in criminal prosecutions and defence strategies. Even though Canada has a system of universal health insurance, access to effective HIV treatments, diagnostic technologies and medical care remains a stratified phenomenon.[74] HIV-positive people who are homeless, use drugs, are prisoners or who live in remote communities, among others, face systematic barriers of access to medical care and social supports that may make it difficult for them to achieve, and document for evidentiary purposes, a low viral load. While it is too soon to tell, new forms of biological citizenship produced through the interface of activism, science and judicial reason may have the effect of aggravating forms of structural inequality that leave people who are most marginalised doubly vulnerable to the coercive powers of criminal justice.

---

[74] E. Wood, J. Montaner, D. Bangsberg, M. Tyndall, S. Strathdee, M. O'Shaughnessy and R. Hogg, 'Expanding access to HIV antiretroviral therapy among marginalized populations in the developed world', *AIDS*, 17 (2003), 2419–27.

8

Feminism and the Criminalisation of HIV Non-disclosure

Introduction

The past few decades have witnessed a worldwide trend towards the prosecution of sexual acts perceived to create a risk of HIV transmission, typically in cases in which an accused fails to disclose HIV positive status to a partner.[1] In response, a vast and diverse literature from scholars, non-governmental organisations and international organisations has emerged, warning of the potential negative impacts of this resort to criminal law. Disclosure and safer sex are important, the argument typically goes, but criminalisation of HIV exposure and transmission is nonetheless wrongheaded. Two arguments tend to figure most prominently in these critiques: first, that criminalisation fuels stigma,[2] which ultimately undermines the fight against the HIV epidemic;[3] second, that it unfairly singles

---

[1] The Global Network of People Living with HIV [GNP+], *The Global Criminalisation Scan Report 2010: Documenting Trends, Presenting Evidence* (Amsterdam: Global Network of People Living with HIV (GNP+), 2010), accessible online at www.gnpplus.net/resources/

[2] C. Dodds and P. Keogh, 'Criminal prosecutions for HIV transmission: people living with HIV respond', *International Journal of STD AIDS*, 17: 5 (2006), 316–18; C. Dodds, P. Keogh, O. Chime, T. Haruperi, B. Nabulya, W. Sanyu Seruma and P. Weatherburn, *Sigma Research Report: Outsider Status Stigma and Discrimination Experienced by Gay Men and African People with HIV* (London: Sigma Research, 2004), pp. 33–4. Available at www.sigmaresearch.org .uk/downloads/report04f.pdf; T. Shevory, *Notorious HIV: The Media Spectacle of Nushawn Williams* (Minneapolis: University of Minnesota Press, 2004); A. Persson and C. Newman, 'Making monsters: heterosexuality, crime and race in recent Western media coverage of HIV', *Sociology of Health and Illness*, 30: 4 (2008), 632–46; K. Buchanan, 'When is HIV a crime? Sexuality, gender and consent', *Minnesota Law Review*, 99: 4 (2015), 1231–342 (on file with author).

[3] K. M. Sullivan, 'AIDS and the coercive power of the state', *Harvard Civil Rights–Civil Liberties Law Review*, 23: 1 (1988), 189–91; M. Weait, 'Unsafe law: health, rights and the legal response to HIV', *International Journal of Law in Context*, 9: 4 (2013), 541; Buchanan, 'When is HIV a crime', 1237–48.

175

out people living with HIV for criminal responsibility for mutually consensual risky sex.[4] Within this literature, concerns about women's vulnerability to prosecution have figured consistently. Women, for example, may
face gender-related barriers to disclosure, which include increased vulnerability to threats of violence and economic abandonment.[5] Yet, the trend
to criminalise has continued essentially unabated. This is driven mainly
by perceptions of the moral blameworthiness of failing to disclose one's
HIV status to a sex partner and the criminal law's role in deterring and
denouncing moral wrongs.[6]

This chapter evaluates the growing criminalisation of HIV
non-disclosure from the perspective of contemporary feminist legal
methodology, focusing primarily on the Canadian context. There are several reasons why the need for this kind of analysis has become urgent.
First, the role of criminal law as a response to HIV non-disclosure is
growing,[7] and consequently, women are at increasing risk of criminal
sanction. Early prosecutions tended to involve a male, often racialised
accused, with a white, often female complainant(s).[8] This may have
been related to the fact that only a small proportion of failures to disclose known HIV status attracts the attention of police and prosecutors,[9]
and prosecutions have depended on whether complainants actually seek
recourse to criminal sanction as well as whether police and prosecutors
view the case as worthy of such prosecution.[10] These early prosecution

---

[4] M. Weait, 'Taking the blame: criminal law, social responsibility and the sexual transmission
of HIV', *Journal of Social Welfare and Family Law*, 23: 4 (2001), 441–57; J. Dine and B. Watt,
'The transmission of disease during consensual sexual activity and the concept of associa-
tive autonomy', *Web Journal of Current Legal Issues*, 1998: 4 (1998); S. Ryan, 'Risk-taking,
recklessness and HIV transmission: accommodating the reality of sexual transmission
of HIV within a justifiable approach to criminal liability', *Liverpool Law Review*, 28: 2
(2007), 244–6; J. Slater, 'HIV, trust and the criminal law', *Journal of Criminal Law*, 75: 4
(2011), 323–4.

[5] Buchanan, 'When is HIV a crime', 16–18; J. K. Stoever, 'Stories absent from the courtroom:
responding to domestic violence in the context of HIV/AIDS', *North Carolina Law Review*,
87: 4 (2009), 1172–7; Global Commission on HIV and the Law, *Risks, Rights and Health*
(New York: 2012), p. 23, accessible online at www.hivlawcommission.org/resources/report/
FinalReport-Risks,Rights&Health-EN.pdf; GNP+, *Global Criminalization Scan*, pp. 32–5.

[6] See, e.g., *R v. Cuerrier*, [1998] 2 SCR 371 (Supreme Court of Canada).

[7] E. Dej and J. M. Kilty, ' "Criminalization creep": a brief discussion of the criminalization of HIV/AIDS non-disclosure in Canada', *Canadian Journal of Law and Society*, 27: 1
(2012), 55–66.

[8] See L. E. Wolf and R. Vezina, 'Crime and punishment: is there a role for criminal law in HIV
prevention policy', *Whittier Law Review*, 25 (2004), 821–48.

[9] L. Beletsky, S. Burris, J. A. Burleson, P. Case and Z. Lazzarini, 'Do criminal laws influence
HIV risk behavior? An empirical trial', *Arizona State Law Journal*, 39: 2 (2007), 510.

[10] Wolf and Vezina, 'Crime and punishment', 871.

patterns may have cemented a perception that HIV criminalisation primarily protects rather than targets women. In Canada, this perception is further reinforced by the fact that the majority of prosecutions are conducted via sexual assault laws.[11] As prosecutions become more routine,[12] however, and as the number of women living with HIV is increasing,[13] the threat of criminal sanction has become a fixture in the lives of all people living with HIV,[14] including women. Further, the seriousness of charges for HIV non-disclosure and the available penalties have escalated over time:[15] from causing a common nuisance[16] to criminal negligence,[17] (sexual) assault[18] and aggravated (sexual) assault. One man has been convicted of first-degree murder for non-disclosure[19] though aggravated (sexual) assault remains the most common charge. Finally, and perhaps most importantly for the purposes of this discussion, the Supreme Court of Canada in 2012 issued the first decision of a highest court justifying the expansion of the scope of criminal liability for failing to disclose one's HIV status to sexual partners in explicitly feminist terms.[20]

In this context, it is important to examine critically the claim that prosecution of HIV non-disclosure in the context of risky sex is consistent with feminist aspirations. There may be retributive, desert-based arguments for criminal sanction, and criminalising non-disclosure sends a message about the importance of ensuring that people can make the most informed choices about the terms on which they have sex. This chapter argues, however, that ostensibly feminist arguments in favour of expanding the

---

[11] I. Grant, 'The prosecution of non-disclosure of HIV in Canada: time to rethink *Cuerrier*', *McGill Journal of Law and Health*, 5: 1 (2011), 42.

[12] A. Symington, 'Criminalization confusion and concern: the decade since the *Cuerrier* decision', *HIV/AIDS Policy and Law Review*, 14 (2009), 1; E. Mykhalovskiy and G. Betteridge, 'Who? What? Where? When? And with what consequences? An analysis of criminal cases of HIV non-disclosure in Canada', *Canadian Journal of Law and Society*, 27 (2012), 31–7.

[13] Public Health Agency of Canada, Chapter 5 in *HIV/AIDS Epi Updates* (Surveillance and Risk Assessment Division, Centre for Communicable Diseases and Infection Control, 2010), accessible online at www.phac-aspc.gc.ca/aids-sida/publication/epi/2010/index-eng .php.

[14] Mykhalovskiy and Betteridge 'And with what consequences?', 31–53.

[15] Symington, 'Criminalization confusion and concerns', 1–5.

[16] *Criminal Code* (Canada), s 180, as applied in *R v. Summer*, 98 AR 191, [1989] AJ 784 QL (Alberta Provincial Court); *R v. Kreider*, [1993] AJ 422, 140 AR 81 (Alberta Provincial Court).

[17] Ibid. s 219, as applied in, e.g., *R v. Wentzell*, [1989] NSJ 510, C.R. No. 10888 (Nova Scotia County Court); *R v. Mercer*, [1993] NJ 198; 110 Nfld. & PEIR. 41 (Newfoundland Court of Appeal), leave to appeal to SCC refused, SCC Bull, 4 March 1994, at 348.

[18] Ibid. s 268, as applied in, e.g., *R v. Cuerrier*.

[19] *R v. Aziga*, [2008] OJ 2431, 78 WCB (2d) 87 (Ontario Superior Court of Justice).

[20] *R v. Mabior*, 2012 SCC 47 at paras 93–4, [2012] 2 SCR 584 (Supreme Court of Canada).

reach of the criminal sanction for HIV non-disclosure fail to take adequate account of insights of more recent feminist critique. In particular, feminist pro-criminalisation arguments rely on under-examined conceptions of agency and autonomy that privilege the interests of HIV negative people at the expense of those more marginalised; they deny that sex can be a site of value as well as danger in the lives of men and women; and they ignore or give insufficient weight to competing anti-subordination goals that ought to be the subject of contemporary feminist concern, including the role of stigma in the context of HIV infection. In short, arguments in favour of an expanded role for criminalisation may find some support in feminist thought, but this feminist thought is an essentialist one that fails to account adequately for the complex power dynamics where HIV sex, and gender interact.

The Rise of Anti-essentialism in Contemporary Feminist Legal Methodology

Of course, feminist legal scholars do not always come to the same conclusions or prescriptions. It may make more sense to designate analysis as 'feminist' based on its methodology or the question it pursues rather than the substantive position it advances.[21] Katharine Bartlett, for one, defines a feminist method in legal scholarship as one that seeks to reveal or address 'bias in the way law relates to women'.[22] That bias can come in many forms: law may perpetuate stereotypes; it may construct gender in more or less hidden ways; it may have unjust effects or impose unfair burdens on women; or it may simply fail to reflect women's interests more generally. What feminist methodologies have in common as they search for this bias is a commitment to women's equality, recognition of the widespread and systemic nature of gender-based injustice and a critical stance toward existing power structures.[23]

Feminist legal methodology has been debated and refined over the years within the common thrust of identifying and responding to gender bias in law. The women's suffrage movement opposed the explicitly

---

[21] K. T. Bartlett, 'Feminist legal methods', *Harvard Law Review*, 103: 4 (1990), 829–88.

[22] K. T. Bartlett, 'Cracking foundations as feminist method', *The American University Journal of Gender, Social Policy & the Law*, 8: 1 (2000), 35.

[23] D. Réaume, 'What's distinctive about feminist analysis of law?: a conceptual analysis of women's exclusion from law', *Legal Theory*, 2: 4 (1996), 271; M. A. Fineman, 'Introduction', in M. A. Fineman, J. E. Jackson and A. P. Romero (eds.), *Feminist and Queer Legal Theory: Intimate Encounters, Uncomfortable Conversations* (Ashgate, 2009), p. 2.

discriminatory exclusion of women from public life by calling into question the prevailing notion that women by their nature were less equipped to vote, to serve on juries and to own property after marriage.[24] In the 1960s and 1970s, feminists challenged both explicitly discriminatory and facially neutral laws that either perpetuated myths or failed to reflect women's lived experience, for example, by demanding equal pay for equal work and workplace accommodations and benefits such as parental leave.[25] Through the 1980s, 'dominance feminists' sought to reveal barriers to women's equality that operated via more insidious, sexualised societal forces, often indirectly supported by law, such as pornography, rape, prostitution and sexual harassment.[26] For their part, 'difference' and 'relational' feminists looked to ways in which law's structures were gendered, in the sense that they were premised on liberal notions of autonomy and individualism that failed to reflect what they argued were more 'female' values of care, mutuality and interdependency.[27]

Beginning in the 1980s, the investigation of gender bias in law and legal scholarship began to turn inward against prevailing feminist methods themselves. Most prominently, 'dominance feminism', associated with Catharine MacKinnon and Andrea Dworkin, was criticised for resting on untested or untestable assumptions that failed to consider adequately the perspectives of all women. In this vein, 'anti-essentialist' scholars[28] argued that prior feminist critiques had ignored the multiple forms of oppression that women endure, myopically measuring law against a prototypical woman who was all too often white, straight, Judeo-Christian and middle class.[29] Similarly, during the 'feminist sex wars' of the 1980s, 'pro-sex' legal scholars challenged dominance feminists' opposition to pornography and prostitution, insisting that it is methodologically bankrupt blithely to

---

[24] Fineman, 'Introduction'.

[25] Ibid.

[26] See for example, C. A. MacKinnon, 'Difference and dominance: on sex discrimination', in *Feminism Unmodified* (Harvard University Press, 1987), p. 40.

[27] See, e.g., L. Bender, 'Feminist (re)Torts: thoughts on the liability crisis, mass Torts, power, and responsibilities', *Duke Law Journal*, 1990: 4 (1990), 848–912; R. L. West, *Caring for Justice* (New York: NYU Press, 1997).

[28] K. T. Bartlett and A. P. Harris, *Gender and Law: Theory, Doctrine, Commentary*, 2nd edition (Aspen Law and Business, 1998), pp. 1007–9.

[29] K. Crenshaw, 'Demarginalizing the intersection of race and sex: a black feminist critique of antidiscrimination doctrine, feminist theory, and antiracist politics', in K. T. Bartlett and R. Kennedy (eds.), *Feminist Legal Theory: Readings in Law and Gender* (Boulder, CO: Westview Press, 1991), pp. 57–80; E. Spelman, *Inessential Woman: Problems of Exclusion in Feminist Thought* (Boston: Beacon Press, 1988); M. Kline, 'Race, racism and feminist legal theory', *Harvard Women's Law Journal*, 12 (1989), 115–50.

dismiss as 'false consciousness' claims that sex, even in the context of gender inequality, might serve as a personal and social good for many women.[30]

These anti-essentialist critiques of feminism and its methods have not necessarily yielded a clear new feminist legal theory or project.[31] Instead, over the past twenty years or so, they have provided the basis for a set of feminist methodological insights and imperatives, or questions that any feminist analysis ought to acknowledge in an honest, grounded search for bias in how law constructs or responds to gender and sex. As these imperatives are applied to particular problems – especially those seemingly most intractable – unresolved tensions are explored and prodded, and various assumptions, fault lines and the risks of competing analyses are exposed.[32] The criminalisation of HIV exposure and transmission is one such problem.

'Significant Risk,' R v Mabior and the Feminist Case for Criminalisation

The basic framework for prosecuting non-disclosure in Canada was established in the 1998 Supreme Court of Canada decision in the R v Cuerrier case. That decision established that failure to disclose one's HIV positive status constituted fraud vitiating consent to sex, rendering such sex an assault, so long as there was a 'significant risk of serious bodily harm' to the complainant.[33] Consequently, merely exposing one's partner to HIV, even in the absence of transmission, could result in conviction for offences ranging in seriousness from assault to aggravated sexual assault.[34] This is in contrast with other jurisdictions such as England and Wales where only actual transmission is prosecuted.[35]

[30] L. Duggan, N. D. Hunter and C. Vance, 'False promises: feminist anti-pornography legislation', *New York Law School Law Review*, 38 (1993), 153–6. See also K. Abrams, 'Sex wars redux: agency and coercion in feminist legal theory', *Columbia Law Review*, 95 (1995), 304–76; C. Meyer, 'Reclaiming sex from the pornographers: cybersexual possibilities', *Georgetown Law Journal*, 83 (1994–5), 1969–2008.

[31] Abrams, 'Sex wars', 314–15; Bridget Crawford, 'Toward a third-wave feminist legal theory: young women, pornography and the praxis of pleasure', *Michigan Journal of Gender and Law*, 99 (2007), 62; A. Gruber, 'Neofeminism', *Houston Law Review*, 50: 5 (2013), 1325–90; M. Kaplan, 'Sex-positive law', *New York University Law Review*, 89: 1 (2014), 89–164; L. Goodmark, 'Autonomy feminism: an anti-essentialist critique of mandatory interventions in domestic violence cases', *Florida State University Law Review*, 37: 1 (2009), 1–48.

[32] See, for example, Fineman et al., *Feminist and Queer Legal Theory*.

[33] *R v. Cuerrier* at para 128.

[34] *Criminal Code* (Canada), §§ 265, 266, 268, 271, 273.

[35] See *Offences against the Person Act*, 1861, § 20.

In the years after *Cuerrier*, courts did not apply the 'significant risk' test consistently.[36] The Supreme Court had stated in *Cuerrier* that 'the careful use of condoms might be found to so reduce the risk of harm that it could no longer be considered significant',[37] and so most, though not all, lower court decisions appeared to restrict criminal sanction to unprotected sex.[38] (Condoms are frequently cited to reduce per-act transmission risks by 80 per cent.[39]) *Cuerrier* was silent, however, on how risk varied by type of sexual activity. Estimates of per-act transmission risk vary, but one recent review estimated per-act risk from unprotected vaginal intercourse at 1 in 1,000, and unprotected anal intercourse at 1 in 100 or 1 in 50.[40] Further, research since Cuerrier reveals that suppression of viral load through antiretroviral therapy reduces the risk of transmission by up to 96 per cent.[41] As the role of viral load in reducing transmission risk was beginning to be understood only in the years following *Cuerrier*, courts came to divergent conclusions about the question of whether a low viral load could reduce the level of risk to below 'significant'.[42]

In light of these divergent applications of the law and of these new scientific developments, the Supreme Court of Canada revisited the 'significant risk' test in *Mabior*, ultimately lowering the threshold at which risk would attract criminal sanction.[43] *Mabior* was a complex case involving nine complainants, some of whom were teenagers. None of the complainants contracted HIV. The accused had a low viral load during some, though not all, of the sexual encounters giving rise to the complaint,[44] and he did not use condoms well or consistently.[45] The Manitoba Court of Appeal

---

[36] See E. Mykhalovskiy, G. Betteridge and D. McLay, *HIV Non-disclosure and the Criminal Law: Establishing Policy Options for Ontario* (Toronto: 2010), available at http://ssrn.com/abstract=1747844; Grant, 'Time to rethink', 9–10.

[37] *R v. Cuerrier* at para 129.

[38] See Grant, 'Time to rethink', 14–16.

[39] S. C. Weller and K. Davis-Beaty, 'Condom effectiveness in reducing heterosexual HIV transmission', *Cochrane Database of Systematic Reviews*, 1 (2002), 2.

[40] Ibid., 27.

[41] D. Donnell, J. M. Baeten, J. Kiarie, K. K. Thomas, W. Stevens, C. R. Cohen, J. McIntyre, J. R. Lingappa, C. Celum and Partners in Prevention HSV/HIV Transmission Study Team, 'Heterosexual HIV-1 transmission after initiation of antiretroviral therapy: a prospective cohort analysis', *The Lancet*, 375: 9731 (2010), 2092–8; M. S. Cohen et al., 'Prevention of HIV-1 infection with early antiretroviral therapy', *New England Journal of Medicine*, 365: 6 (2011), 493–505.

[42] Grant, 'Time to rethink', 20–5.

[43] *R v. Mabior*, at para. 16.

[44] Ibid. at para. 109.

[45] Ibid. at para 6.

had held that there was no significant risk of serious bodily harm where condoms were used *or* where viral load was undetectable, and on that basis quashed four of the six original convictions.[46] The Supreme Court of Canada determined that there is a 'significant risk of serious bodily harm' whenever there is a 'realistic possibility' of transmission. Such a realistic possibility is negated where the accused uses a condom *and* has a low viral load, at least in the context of penile-vaginal sex.[47] In other words, condoms alone could no longer suffice to negate the disclosure obligation. As a result, it restored three convictions against Mabior.[48]

In *Mabior*, the Supreme Court of Canada justified on feminist grounds its decision to broaden the circumstances in which a person must disclose his or her HIV status to partners or be subject to prosecution for sexual assault for exposing an unknowing partner to a risk of transmission. More specifically, it stated that a 'generous approach to the issue of consent and when deceit might vitiate it respect[s] the right of women involved to choose whether to have intercourse or not'.[49] The '[Canadian Charter of Rights and Freedoms] values of autonomy, liberty, privacy and human dignity require full recognition of the right to consent or to withhold consent to sexual relations',[50] concluding that 'to hold that a complainant consents to the risk of an undisclosed disease affronts contemporary sensibilities and contemporary constitutional values'.[51]

Similar arguments have been put forward by Carissima Mathen and Michael Plaxton. Reflecting the traditional concern of feminist legal theorists with laws that embody myths and stereotypes that presume women's sexual availability, they argue that an HIV positive person who fails to disclose objectifies the HIV negative partner and denies that partner's sexual autonomy:

> [T]o automatically proceed on the basis that one's sexual partner is not invested in her own health and well-being and is therefore willing to make herself sexually available in spite of obvious risks ... effectively denies that one's partner has any meaningful autonomy in any sphere.[52]

---

[46] *R v. Mabior*, 2010 MBCA 93 (Appeal Judgement).
[47] *R v. Mabior*, 2012 SCC 47 at paras. 93–4.
[48] Ibid. at para. 110.
[49] Ibid. at para. 31.
[50] Ibid. at para. 43.
[51] Ibid. at para. 110.
[52] C. Mathen and M. Plaxton, 'HIV, consent and criminal wrongs', *Criminal Law Quarterly*, 57: 4 (2011), 464.

In other words, criminal culpability for non-disclosure is understood to affirm, support and reinforce a person's ability to choose for himself or herself whether or not to consent to the risk of HIV transmission.

Non-disclosure is prosecuted through a variety of offences in different jurisdictions including HIV-specific statutes[53] as well as general criminal prohibitions against causing grievous bodily harm,[54] nuisance[55] and recklessly engaging in conduct that may place a person in danger of death or serious injury.[56] Sexual assault is both the primary offence through which HIV non-disclosure is prosecuted in Canada and a primary site of feminist criminal law reforms.[57] As the law of non-disclosure and the law of sexual assault are bound up together, the concern is that the law related to non-disclosure must not undermine the robust conception of consent that has been developed over the years through the law of sexual assault more broadly. The above justifications for criminal sanction clearly draw from feminist contributions in the context of sexual assault.

Feminist reforms to sexual assault law generally have been directed at removing pernicious gender stereotypes from the law.[58] For example, from the 1970s to the 1990s, marital rape became a criminal offence in most common law jurisdictions including Canada, England and all fifty of the United States,[59] after feminists decried the misogyny reflected in and perpetuated by the common law rule that a man cannot be found to have raped his wife.[60] Feminist advocacy also led to the reform of many statutory

---

[53] For example, *Florida Statutes Annotated*, § 384.24; *Tennessee Code Annotated*, § 39-13-109.

[54] Offences against the Person Act 1861 (England and Wales), § 20; Crimes Act (New Zealand), 1961, § 188.

[55] Crimes Act (New Zealand), 1961, § 145.

[56] Crimes Act (Australian State of Victoria), 1958, ss 22–23.

[57] G. P. Fletcher, 'Criminal theory in the 20th century', *Theoretical Inquiries in Law*, 2: 1 (2001), 14.

[58] For example, S. Brownmiller, *Against Our Will: Men, Women and Rape* (New York: Fawcett Columbine, 1975), pp. 427–8; C. Estrich, 'Rape', *Yale Law Journal*, 95: 6 (1986), 1087–184; E. A. Sheehy, 'Legal responses to violence against women in Canada', *Canadian Woman Studies*, 19: 2, 62–73; L. Snider, 'Legal reform and social control: the dangers of abolishing rape', *International Journal of Sociology of Law*, 13: 4 (1985), 337–56. C. Hosek, 'Women and the constitutional process', in K. Banting and R. Simeon (eds.), *And No One Cheered: Federalism, Democracy and the Constitution Act* (Toronto: Methuen Publications, 1983), p. 280.

[59] See T. Fus, 'Criminalizing marital rape: a comparison of judicial and legislative approaches', *Vanderbilt Journal of Transnational Law*, 39 (2006), 481–518; J. E. Hasday, 'Contest and consent: a legal history of marital rape', *California Law Review*, 88: 5 (2000), 1482–1505

[60] R. L. West, 'Equality theory, marital rape, and the promise of the fourteenth amendment', *Florida Law Review*, 42 (1990), 64–5; J. Koshan, 'The legal treatment of marital rape and

and judge-made evidentiary rules unique to the context of rape and sexual assault – rules that relied on 'rape myths', presenting rape victims as wanton, wicked and seeking to entrap innocent men. These included the doctrine of 'recent complaint' or 'fresh complaint', which required a victim to report a rape immediately or face consequences ranging from an adverse inference against the complainant's credibility to a total bar on prosecution after three months;[61] corroboration requirements that needed proof beyond the complainant's testimony to sustain a conviction;[62] and the permissibility of drawing adverse inferences as to both credibility and likelihood of consent to sex based on past sexual history.[63]

In *Mabior*, the Supreme Court of Canada treated broadening the reach of criminalisation of HIV exposure as a natural extension of feminist-driven reforms, as a move towards completion of the project of purging gender-based stereotypes and misogyny from the law.[64] Reforms that are directed at ridding the law of gender stereotypes that made sexual assault harder to prosecute than virtually any other offence and that rendered complainants in such cases more suspect than witnesses in ordinary criminal trials are relatively uncontroversial. They are easily reconciled with basic criminal law objectives to seek truth and to ensure that the law is applied equally.[65] The suggestion at the heart of *Mabior* – that exposing someone to even a minuscule risk of HIV inherently constitutes wrongful sexual exploitation – raises a different question about what ought to qualify as valid consent to sex. This is a question about which feminists may disagree.

As the next sections of this chapter demonstrate, a number of feminist tensions are raised by this question of whether consent ought to be constructed to require HIV disclosure even when the risk of transmission is very small. These tensions flow from two key insights from contemporary criticisms of dominance feminism. The first is the need to take into account multiple intersecting forms of oppression that women experience. The second is the need to recognise sex as a personal and social good for women that should not be dispensed with unless there is good

women's equality: an analysis of the Canadian experience', for the Equality Effect Project (formerly the African and Canadian Women's Human Rights Project) (2010), www .theequalityeffect.org

[61] Estrich, 'Rape', 1139 (noting that this rule is unique to rape)
[62] Ibid., 1137
[63] Brownmiller, *Against Our Will*, p. 433
[64] *R v. Mabior* at paras. 46–8
[65] See contra H. Reece, 'Rape myths: is elite opinion right and popular opinion wrong', *Oxford Journal of Legal Studies*, 34: 4 (2013), 1–29

justification. These tensions surround the feminist understanding of the victim-agent dichotomy; the extent to which feminists ought to support expansions of the criminal law in the name of some women when it may marginalise others; and the more abstract question of the kind of political order that the law constructs in criminalising HIV non-disclosure.

Victimhood and Agency

Interrogating the roles of autonomy and victimhood in justifying the criminalisation of HIV transmission and exposure lays bare some growing fault lines in feminist legal thought. One of the basic premises of the feminist pro-criminalisation argument is that a robust criminal-law-backed disclosure obligation helps to reinforce sexual autonomy and bodily integrity by permitting HIV negative partners to choose whether or not to consent to the risks of HIV transmission. The argument is that without such information, the HIV negative partner is essentially a victim, denied the capacity to have sex under the terms and conditions of his or her choosing.[66]

This notion of autonomy, however, has been criticised as both impoverished and decontextualised. In particular, opponents of criminalisation argue that the unilateral disclosure obligation may deny or obscure the agency that the HIV negative partner may exercise, thereby reducing the HIV negative partner to a passive participant in the sexual encounter.[67] By agency, they mean the ability of a partner to choose whether or not to assume the risks of unprotected sex, or alternatively, to reduce those risks by taking appropriate steps to prevent the possibility of transmission. It is important to keep in mind that not everyone has equal capacity to take such steps. Women in particular may have greater difficulty negotiating condom use for reasons directly related to lack of power in relationships with men.[68] At the same time, however, they also face greater obstacles to disclosing for much of the same reasons.[69] As Matthew Weait argues, the legitimacy of the criminal sanction may best be seen as depending on the

---

[66] Mathen and Plaxton, 'HIV, consent and criminal wrongs', 464

[67] For example, K. Rawluk, 'HIV and shared responsibility: a critical evaluation of *Mabior* and *DC*', *Dalhousie Journal of Legal Studies*, 22 (2013), 22, 29

[68] Stoever, 'Stories absent from the courtroom', 1175–8; H. Amaro, W. De Jong, S. L. Gortmaker, J. Pulerwitz and R. Rudd, 'Relationship power, condom use and HIV risk among women in the USA', *AIDS Care: Psychological and Socio-medical Aspects of AIDS/HIV*, 14: 6 (2002), 789–800

[69] E. M. Arnold, S. Comulada, S. Green, E. Rice and M. J. Rotheram-Borus, 'Differential disclosure across social network ties among women living with HIV', *AIDS and Behaviour*, 13 (2009), 1253–61

context and nature of a particular relationship between sexual partners as well as their knowledge of risk.[70] Weait imagines the example of a husband who knowingly fails to disclose his HIV status to his wife where his infection comes from undisclosed adultery. Here, the autonomy of the receptive partner would seem to be much more compromised by non-disclosure than it would be in the case of, for example, a subsistence sex worker who fails to disclose to a client who himself declines to use a condom.[71] In other words, it may make more sense to conclude that someone chooses to assume a risk when they opt for unprotected sex with a stranger or casual acquaintance than when they have unprotected sex with a partner they reasonably believe to be monogamous.

The preceding discussion evokes a more general tension in feminist thought around the concepts of agency and victimhood, which has served as a central preoccupation of feminist thought since the 1990s.[72] As a number of feminist scholars have observed, once-prevailing conceptions tended to view victimhood and agency as opposites, since agency was understood as the capacity to act with freedom from all forms of oppression.[73] This tendency is traced to dominance feminism, which, with its focus on how subordination constructs identity, denies any possibility of agency within conditions of oppression.[74] Anti-essentialist scholars – who increasingly comprise the majority of contemporary feminist scholarship[75] – however,

[70] M. Weait, 'Harm, consent and the limits of privacy', *Feminist Legal Studies*, 13: 1 (2005), 106, citing J. Nedelsky, 'Reconceiving autonomy: sources, thoughts and possibilities', *Yale Journal of Law and Feminism*, 1 (1989), 7–36

[71] See *R v. Murphy* [2013] OJ 3903 (Ontario Superior Court of Justice), in which a woman was convicted for failing to disclose to a casual acquaintance; a man who paid her $20 in exchange for sex.

[72] E. M. Schneider, 'Describing and changing: women's self-defense work and the problem of expert testimony on battering', *Women's Rights Law Reporter*, 9 (1986), 221; C. S. Vance, 'More danger, more pleasure: a decade after the barnard sexuality conference', *New York Law School Law Review*, 38 (1993), 289–318; M. Minow, 'Surviving victim talk', *UCLA Law Review*, 40 (1992–3), 1411–46; M. Mahoney, 'Victimization or oppression? Women's lives, violence and agency', in M. Fineman and R. Mykitiuk (eds.), *The Public Nature of Private Violence: The Discovery of Domestic Abuse* (New York: Routledge, 1994), pp. 59–92; J. Nedelsky, *Law's Relations: A Relational Theory of Self, Autonomy, and Law* (Oxford: Oxford University Press, 2012).

[73] Mahoney, 'Victimization or oppression', 64; K. Abrams, 'Songs of innocence and experience: dominance feminism in the university', *Yale Law Journal*, 103 (1993–4), 1533, 1552–6.

[74] E. M. Schneider, 'Feminism and the false dichotomy of victimization and agency', *New York Law School Law Review*, 38 (1993), 397.

[75] L. Goodmark, 'Autonomy feminism: an anti-essentialist critique of mandatory interventions in domestic violence cases', *Florida State University Law Review*, 37 (2009), 44–45 (arguing that anti-essentialist feminism is the legal manifestation of 'third wave' feminism); Gruber, 'Neofeminism', 1325–90.

urge a more 'textured and contextual analysis of the interrelationship between women's oppression and acts of resistance within a wider range of women's circumstances'. This requires that we 'reject simple dichotomies, give up either/ors, learn to accept contradiction, ambiguity and ambivalence in women's lives, and to explore more 'grays' in our conceptions of women's experiences'.[76] In a world of such greys, a person who has unprotected sex without knowing his or her partner's HIV status may be both an agent choosing to have sex, even though this carries an unknown risk, and/or a victim being exposed to risk that only the HIV positive partner knows about.

Responding to the simultaneity of opposing experiences may appear difficult in law, particularly in criminal law where the purpose is to demarcate and target morally wrongful behaviour.[77] Put another way, these anti-essentialist critiques, which are post-structural in nature (i.e., 'insisting on contingency around every corner'[78]), are often hard to integrate or reconcile with 'law', which is 'by definition, structuralist'.[79] Yet, the anti-essentialist argument does not claim that classification and categorisation of wrongful behaviour is illegitimate. Rather, it requires recognition of those categories as contingent and urges careful consideration of whether those categories are serving their purposes in law and policy.[80] Anti-essentialist scholarship urges us to question categories, including those of agent/victim, to identify circumstances where such categorisation or over-generalisation 'disappears some experiences in a systematic way'.[81] Further, it demands a careful consideration of what is lost or gained when law's categories (perhaps inevitably) fail to line up with lived experience.[82] Indeed, the uncritical assumption that a criminal-law-backed disclosure

---

[76] Schneider, 'Feminism and the false dichotomy', 397. See, similarly, Abrams, 'Sex wars', 304–76.

[77] See R. A. Duff, *Punishment, Communication, and Community* (Oxford: Oxford University Press, 2003), p. 58. See also Nicola Lacey's discussion of the difficulty of integrating 'cultural defenses' into criminal law in 'Community, culture and criminalization', in W. Kymlicka, C. Lernestedt and M. Matravers (eds.), *Criminal Law and Cultural Diversity* (Oxford: Oxford University Press, 2014), pp. 47–67.

[78] A. Scales, 'Post-structuralism on trial', in Fineman et al. (eds.), *Feminist and Queer Legal Theory*, p. 396.

[79] Ibid.

[80] See A. Campbell, *Sister Wives, Surrogates and Sex Workers: Outlaws by Choice?* (Ashgate, 2013). See also D. Young, 'Individual rights and the negotiation of governmental power: the risk of HIV transmission and canadian criminal law', *Social & Legal Studies*, 24: 1 (2015), 113–34.

[81] See A. P. Harris, 'Race and essentialism in feminist legal theory', *Stanford Law Review*, 42: 3 (1990), 581–616, 586.

[82] For example, Campbell, *Sister Wives*, pp. 195–6.

obligation supports women's autonomy systematically obscures certain experiences.

First, to the extent that it is autonomy-enhancing at all, the unilateral disclosure obligation targets only the autonomy of the complainant, or the HIV negative partner. In this way, it denies the relational aspects of the victim-agent dichotomy,[83] effacing the intersecting forms of marginalisation that complicate disclosure on the part of the HIV positive partner. In the context of 'traditional' sexual assault (i.e., where there is no initial subjective consent to be vitiated by non-disclosure), there are good reasons for emphasising the subjective experience of a complainant, for example, by restricting the availability of defences of honest but mistaken belief in consent.[84] These reasons include the systematic nature in which women are sexually assaulted[85] and the pervasive and destructive myths around women's sexuality that support it.[86] When this logic is transferred to the present context, as Emily MacKinnon and Constance Crompton observe, the non-disclosing partner is uncritically constructed as 'male', the aggressor and the receptive partner as 'female', the victim, as though known HIV infection unambiguously gives one partner power over the other.[87]

The exclusive focus on what the HIV negative partner 'needs to know' eliminates from consideration reasons why the HIV positive partner may fail to disclose. It may be because the HIV positive partner harbours a subjugating view that the HIV negative partner does not deserve to know, or does not care, or is reckless or in some cases vengeful (see Ceri Evans' chapter in this volume). However, research suggests that there are many other reasons why individuals may not disclose. For example, there may be concerns about others discovering one's positive status or about the possibility

---

[83] See Nedelsky, *Law's Relations*, p. 175.
[84] See, for example, *R v. Ewanchuk*, [1999] 1 SCR 330 (Supreme Court of Canada).
[85] The most recent Canadian *Criminal Victimization Report* found that 4,72,000 people had self-reported instances of sexual assault in 2009 and that this rate was more than twice as high for women than men: S. Perreault and S. Brennan, *Criminal Victimization in Canada, 2009* (Canada: Statistics Canada, 2010), Juristat Catalogue No. 85-002-X.
[86] See, for example, Martha Burt, 'Cultural myths and support for rape', *Journal of Personality and Social Psychology*, 38: 2 (1980), 217–30; K. A. Lonsway and L. F. Fitzgerald, 'Rape myths', *Psychology of Women Quarterly*, 18 (1994), 133–64. M. E. Deming, E. K. Covan, S. C. Swan and D. L. Billings, 'Exploring rape myths, gendered norms, group processing, and the social context of rape among college women: a qualitative analysis', *Violence Against Women*, 19: 4 (2013), 465–85.
[87] C. Crompton and E. Mackinnon 'The gender of lying: feminist perspectives on the non-disclosure of HIV status', *University of British Columbia Law Review*, 45: 1 (2012), 423–6.

of rejection.[88] Fear of being stigmatised or discriminated against has also been found to play a role.[89] In general, HIV positive women have greater difficulty disclosing their HIV status to sexual partners than do men.[90] For those women, concerns about violence, abandonment or accusations of infidelity can be seen to flow directly from the intersection of HIV stigma and women's social subjugation.[91] Disclosure difficulties are exacerbated along further axes of oppression and marginalisation over-represented in the context of HIV, including immigrant status, aboriginality, drug use and sex work.[92] One case study, for example, describes how HIV positive Inuit women, overwhelmingly poor single mothers, feared that they would be beaten and that they or their children would be forced to leave their communities, to which they were deeply attached, if they were to disclose that they were HIV positive.[93]

Second, by effectively presuming that no one would autonomously agree to sex that risks transmitting HIV, the argument ignores the social and personal value that sex, even risky sex, brings to the HIV negative partner. This presumption is reflected in the Canadian courts' general failure to grapple meaningfully with the question of whether the failure to disclose – the fraud – in fact induced the consent to sex.[94] In reality, people relatively commonly consent to unprotected sex,[95] which always carries

---

[88] M. A. Schlitz and T. G. M. Sandfort, 'HIV-positive people, risk and sexual behaviour', *Social Science & Medicine*, 50 (2000), 1574.

[89] M. D. Stein, K. A. Freedberg, L. M. Sullivan, J. Savetsky, S. M. Levenson, R. Hingson and J. H. Samet, 'Sexual ethics: disclosure of HIV-positive status to partners', *Archives of Internal Medicine*, 158: 3 (1998), 253–7; Buchanan, 'When is HIV a crime', 14–19.

[90] S. C. Kalichman and D. Nachimson, 'Self-efficacy and disclosure of HIV-positive serostatus to sex partners', *Health Psychology*, 18 (1999), 281–7.

[91] J. Anderson, R. Faden, L. Fogarty, A. C. Gielen, J. Keller and P. O'Campo, 'Women living with HIV: disclosure, violence, and social support', *Journal of Urban Health*, 77: 3 (2000), 480–91; A. Eke, R. R. Faden, A. C. Gielen and P. O'Campo, 'Women's disclosure of HIV status: experiences of mistreatment and violence in an urban setting', *Women and Health*, 25: 3 (1997), 19–31.

[92] Public Health Agency of Canada, *HIV/AIDS Epi Updates* (Surveillance and Risk Assessment Division, Centre for Communicable Diseases and Infection Control, 2010), chapters 8 and 10.

[93] S. J. Ship and L. Norton, 'HIV/AIDS and aboriginal women in Canada: a case study', *Canadian Woman Studies*, 21: 2 (2001), 26–8.

[94] See, for example, *R v. Mabior*, 2008 MBQB 201 (Manitoba Court of Queen's Bench); *R v. Wilcox*, 2014 SCC 75 (Supreme Court of Canada).

[95] Beletsky et al., 'Do criminal laws influence HIV risk behavior', 485; M. Reece, V. Schick, S. A. Sanders, B. Dodge and J. D. Fortenberry, 'Condom use rates in a national probability sample of males and females ages 14 to 94 in the United States', *Journal of Sexual Medicine*, 7: 5 (2010), 266–76.

with it the risk that they may potentially be exposed to HIV. When, in line with dominance feminism, sex is viewed as a site of danger, this 'choice' is treated as coerced, a form of false consciousness, or else of low value and unworthy of protection in light of competing political goals.[96] The agency that a person exercises when he or she chooses to have sex with someone whose HIV status is unknown to him or her (regardless of whether that risk may be known to the HIV positive partner) is denied.

Sex-positive and relational feminists, on the contrary, caution against ignoring the personal and social value of sex, even sex that some might disapprove of, or that presents known or knowable risks.[97] Where law fails to acknowledge that value, it limits the possibilities for honest discussion and appraisal of the goals of legal regulation and how to pursue them fairly.[98] Recognising and grappling with the fact that such sex may, to varying degrees, be autonomously desired and chosen,[99] the question becomes how best to structure the law, as it interacts with societal institutions, practices and beliefs in a way that enhances that autonomy,[100] reduces risk and broadens options and opportunities.[101] As discussed in the other sections of this chapter, the criminal law may or may not have a role to play here.

Marginalisation and the Criminal Law's Unintended Consequences

At a broader level, feminist scholars increasingly urge circumspection about the use of the criminal law to achieve feminist ends.[102] One reason for this scepticism, developed most prominently in the area of violence

---

[96] Abrams, 'Sex wars', 309–10.
[97] K. M. Franke, 'Theorizing yes: an essay on feminism, law, and desire', *Columbia Law Review*, 101: 1 (2001), 199; N. Lacey, *Unspeakable Subjects: Feminist Essays in Legal and Social Theory* (Oxford: Hart Publishing, 1998), p. 50.
[98] Kaplan, 'Sex-positive law', 93, 98; T. Dean, *Unlimited Intimacy: Reflections on the Subculture of Barebacking* (Chicago: University of Chicago Press, 2009), p. 6.
[99] Franke, 'Theorizing yes', 200.
[100] Nedelsky, *Law's Relations*, p. 176.
[101] See Campbell, *Sister Wives*, p. 195.
[102] See, for example, A. P. Harris, 'Gender, violence, race and criminal justice', *Stanford Law Review*, 52: 4 (2000), 777–807; D. Martin, 'Retribution revisited: a reconsideration of feminist criminal law reform strategies', *Osgoode Hall Law Journal*, 36: 1 (1998), 151–88. See similarly, in queer/trans literature, D. Spade, *Normal Life: Administrative Violence, Critical Trans Politics and the Limits of the Law* (Brooklyn, NY: South End Press, 2011); S. Lamble, 'Transforming carceral logics: 10 reasons to dismantle the prison industrial complex using a queer/trans analysis', in N. Smoth and E. A. Stanley (eds.), *Captive Genders: Trans Embodiment and the Prison Industrial Complex* (Oakland: AK Press, 2011) pp. 235–66.

against women,[103] concerns unintended consequences of the criminal law's engagement with women's intimate lives – especially in relation to poor, racialised and marginalised women. A second critique centres on how the criminal law constructs and polices social and sexual roles more broadly.

Planting the seeds for a large body of anti-essentialist, intersectional[104] and critical race feminism,[105] Angela Harris has demanded that feminist scholars move away from abstractions about autonomy reinforcement in rape law reform to a more textured consideration of women's lived experience. In her view, for example, the experience of rape for black women cannot be reduced to that of women 'in general', because black women's experience with rape is intricately bound up with the history of slavery, oppression and exclusion from legal institutions. That is, black women were historically under-protected by the law, particularly when their assailants were white, while black men were disproportionately the targets of prosecution. In these circumstances, black women might reasonably be sceptical about the power of criminal justice institutions to protect them and reinforce their autonomy.[106]

Harris' injunctions to consider the law's consequences in context rather than in the abstract, and to reflect particularly on the lived experiences of marginalised women, have had an important impact on feminist criminal justice scholarship. A substantial body of literature has developed noting ways in which the alliances between feminism and criminal justice have unintentionally disadvantaged women, and particularly poor and racialised women. In a study of domestic violence among poor women of colour, for example, Donna Coker criticises mandatory arrest policies and 'no drop' policies that preclude police and prosecutors from dropping criminal charges for domestic violence once they are laid. These policies had the perverse effect of increasing the risk of violence toward poor women of colour at the hands of the eventually released spouse.[107] They also carried

---

[103] See, for example, Gruber, 'Neofeminism', 1325; D. Coker, 'Crime control and feminist law reform in domestic violence law: a critical review', *Buffalo Criminal Law Review*, 4: 2 (2001), 801, 851–2; L. Snider, 'Towards safer societies: punishment, masculinities and violence against women', *British Journal of Criminology*, 38: 1 (1998), 1–39; J. Suk, 'Criminal law comes home', *Yale Law Journal*, 116: 1 (2006), 2–70.

[104] K. Crenshaw, 'Mapping the margins: intersectionality, identity politics, and violence against women of color', *Stanford Law Review*, 43: 6 (1991), 1241–99.

[105] See S. Razack, M. Smith and S. Thobani (eds.), *States of Race: Critical Race Feminism for the 21st Century* (Toronto: Between the Lines, 2010).

[106] Harris, 'Race and essentialism', 598–602.

[107] D. Coker, 'Shifting power for battered women: law, material resources, and poor women of color', *University of California Davis Law Review*, 33 (2000), 1042.

with them the risk of police brutality against the batterer; the risk of the victim's subsequent arrest; the risk that police involvement would result in extensive intrusion in the life of the victim; and the risk of financial and relationship loss associated with the batterer's arrest.[108] In addition, she notes that these policies embrace a separate-and-prosecute model when in fact many women cannot or may not want to leave their abusive partners.[109] Understood in context, these policies have been considered by some to be 'more about increasing the likelihood of defendants going to jail than about supporting the individual desires, welfare and interests of victims'.[110]

These criticisms need not imply a wholesale rejection of the criminal law in responding to violence against women. Feminist scholars writing about intimate violence in aboriginal communities in Canada, for example, share a commitment to contextualised assessments of law's impacts. They are divided nevertheless about whether conventional, restorative or traditional aboriginal justice systems are most likely to be responsive to the circumstances of aboriginal women who live with violence from their partners.[111] Others may continue to place value on the expressive aspirations of the criminal law.[112] Rather, the concern is that feminist law reform efforts in the area of rape law may slip uncritically from addressing clear stereotypes embodied in law to the unjustified assumption that an expanded role for criminal justice more broadly will protect women from violence.[113] There is reason to be sceptical of such a claim, particularly considering criminal justice institutions' role in controlling and coercing, and their history of often doing so at the expense of the marginalised.[114] Feminist criminal law sceptics therefore insist on careful consideration of whether proposed changes to the criminal law are really about enhancing women's autonomy broadly understood, and whether they sufficiently consider the impacts of reforms on poor, racialised and otherwise marginalised women.[115]

---

[108] Ibid.

[109] Ibid., 1012.

[110] A. Gruber, 'The feminist war on crime', *Iowa Law Review*, 92 (2006), 750.

[111] See A. Cameron, 'Stopping the violence: Canadian feminist debates on restorative justice and intimate violence', *Theoretical Criminology*, 10: 1 (2006), 49–66.

[112] See, for example, D. K. Citron, 'Law's expressive value in combating cyber gender harassment', *Michigan Law Review*, 108: 3 (2009), 373–415.

[113] L. Snider, 'Feminism, punishment and the potential of empowerment', *Canadian Journal of Law and Society*, 9: 1 (1994), 75–104; Gruber, 'Feminist war', 741.

[114] Snider, 'Feminism, punishment', 82. See similarly, Martin, 'Retribution revisited', 155.

[115] Gruber, 'Feminist war', 751; Campbell, 'Sister wives'.

Given that criminalisation of HIV non-disclosure is situated in the context of arguably the most stigmatised disease in medical history,[116] as well as historical public support for quarantining people living with HIV,[117] the fact that the feminist justification of criminalisation is dominated by the perspective of the HIV negative complainant is glaring. The perspective of the HIV positive partner reveals important practical implications for women living with HIV. Women living with HIV have expressed fear that their partners would threaten them with criminal sanction in the event of relationship breakdown, whether or not they in fact disclosed or used adequate protection.[118] *R. v. D. C.*, the companion case to *Mabior* at the Supreme Court of Canada, illustrates this point. The female accused, D.C., disclosed her HIV positive status to her partner following their first sexual encounter. The couple continued to date, practising safe sex, for four years. When D.C. decided to end the relationship, the complainant refused to accept this and became violent (he was eventually charged with assault). In turn, he responded by pressing charges of sexual assault, alleging that on their first sexual encounter four years earlier, before D.C. had disclosed her HIV status, the sex had been unprotected.[119] D.C. was initially convicted. In a rare instance of appellate judges overturning trial judges on questions of fact, the Supreme Court of Canada acquitted D.C. on the basis that the trial judge's finding that no condom was used was based on an unreasonable interpretation of her doctor's interview notes.[120]

Not every woman will be able to resist an unjustified finding of fact the way that D.C. eventually managed to do. Criminalisation submits women accused of non-disclosure to a justice system that is not immune from societal stigma against people living with HIV. As in the domestic violence context, police, prosecutors, judges and juries may not believe accounts about condom use or disclosure depending on whether the accused is

---

[116] P. Aggleton and R. Parker, 'HIV and AIDS-related stigma and discrimination: a conceptual framework and implications for action', *Social Science and Medicine*, 57: 1 (2003), 13–24; C. Parikh and S. Rana, 'The game of fear, blame and shame: stigma of HIV, a major public health debacle', *Journal of Pediatrics and Neonatal Care*, 1: 1 (2014), 00003–00004.

[117] L. Gostin and A. Ziegler, 'A review of AIDS-related legislative and regulatory policy in the United States', *Law, Medicine and Health Care*, 15: 1–2 (2011), 5–16, at p. 11.

[118] A. Perone, 'From punitive to proactive: an alternative approach for responding to HIV criminalization that departs from penalizing marginalized communities', *Hastings Women's Law Journal*, 24 (2013), 365. ('Moreover, perpetrators of abuse aware of their partner's HIV status can use HIV criminalization laws as leverage in a relationship by threatening to tell police that they were unaware unless the partner agrees to stay.')

[119] *R v. D.C.* [2012] 2 SCR 626 paras 4–7 (Supreme Court of Canada).

[120] Ibid., at para. 30.

perceived as 'normal' or 'deviant'.[121] Worth and colleagues observe, for
example, that people who use drugs and sex workers, who are at increased
vulnerability to HIV infection, are less likely to be viewed as credible witnesses, and so 'it is no accident that most cases that are prosecuted pos-
sess strikingly similar characteristics'.[122] Some women have expressed fear
that disclosing will open them up to false accusations of non-disclosure.[123]
Others may choose to forgo sex rather than risk disclosure or criminal
prosecution. Finally, women living with HIV, particularly those most marginalised, may be reluctant to turn to the criminal justice system should
they be victims of criminal acts because of their own vulnerability to
criminal charges. Recently, for example, three women living with HIV
in British Columbia chose not to report their separate sexual assaults to
police out of fear that their assailants would accuse them of non-disclosure. One woman was Aboriginal, the second transgender and the third of
African descent.[124]
    Indeed, HIV stigma – including the idea that people living with HIV
are more likely to be deceitful, that they are responsible for their condition, as well as exaggerated perceptions of the threat of infection – may
explain preliminary research suggesting that conviction rates in HIV
non-disclosure may be higher than for 'traditional' sexual assault, where
stereotype has tended to operate primarily against the complainant.
A recent study in Ontario found that from 1989 to 2009, for example,
68 per cent of HIV non-disclosure cases had resulted in conviction.[125]
By contrast, national-level crime statistics show that only 42 per cent of

---

[121] I. Grant, 'The boundaries of the criminal law: the criminalization of the non-disclosure
of HIV', *Dalhousie Law Journal*, 31 (2008), 161–4. Compare, for example, K. J. Ferraro,
'The legal response to women battering in the United States', in J. Hanmer, J. Radford
and E. Stanko (eds.), *Women, Policing and Male Violence: International Perspectives*
(New York: Routledge, 1989), pp. 155–84.

[122] H. Worth, C. Patton and D. Goldstein, 'Introduction to special issue. Reckless vectors:
the infecting "other" in HIV/AIDS law', *Sexuality Research and Social Policy*, 2: 2 (2005),
3–14, at p. 7.

[123] P. Allard, C. Kazachkine and A. Symington, 'Criminal prosecutions for HIV non-disclosure:
protecting women from infection or threatening prevention efforts?', in J. Gahagan (ed.),
Women and HIV Prevention in Canada: Implications for Research, Policy and Practice
(Toronto: Women's Press, 2013), pp. 195, 204; C. L. Galletly and J. Dickson-Gomez, 'HIV
seropositive status disclosure to prospective sex partners and criminal laws that require it:
perspectives of persons living with HIV', *International Journal of STD and AIDS*, 20 (2009),
613–18.

[124] Personal communication with Melissa Madjuck, Support Worker and Retreat Coordinator,
Positive Women's Network, 1 October 2014.

[125] Mykhalovskiy et al., *HIV Non-disclosure and the Criminal Law*.

traditional sexual assault cases resulted in convictions in Canada.[126] This is particularly telling in Canada, where evidential issues are not all that different in traditional sexual assault cases than in HIV non-disclosure cases. That is, the same basic elements of sexual assault apply to both kinds of offence. There is no need to demonstrate actual transmission to be convicted for HIV non-disclosure. Convictions in both categories tend to turn on the credibility of complainants and the accused around consent.

The Criminal Law and the Construction of Social Order

More abstractly, feminist scholars are increasingly attending to the ways in which the expanding reach of the criminal law in neo-liberal times risks producing and reinforcing hegemonic orders contrary to broader feminist goals.[127] Feminist scholarship has long acknowledged the criminal law's role in constituting social and political relationships. Indeed, early sexual assault and rape law reforms were designed to counter law's (and society's) construction of women as 'promiscuous', as liars or 'asking for it'.[128] Recent feminist scholarship argues, however, that while reforms may mitigate the law's sexist construction of societal orders, it is an unlikely vehicle for promoting feminism's goals of building a social order free of hierarchy and subordination.

On the contrary, through coercion, control, repression and punishment,[129] the criminal law purports to delimit deviant from non-deviant behaviour. In doing so, it cannot avoid constructing certain activities, relationships and ways of living as more legitimate and worthy of protection than others. Sex-positive feminists have been wary of feminist law

---

[126] M. Dauvergne, *Adult Criminal Court Statistics in Canada, 2010/2011* (Ottawa: Statistics Canada, 2012), Juristat Article Catalogue No. 85-002-X, p. 25 (Table 4: 'Cases completed in adult criminal court, by type of offence and decision, Canada, 2010/2011).

[127] Snider, 'Feminism, punishment', 75–104; Martin, 'Retribution revisited', 151–88; A. Gruber, 'Rape, feminism and the war on crime', *Washington Law Review*, 84 (2009), 582–658; J. Halley, P. Kotiswaran, H. Shamir and C. Thomas, 'From the international to the local in feminist legal responses to rape, prostitution/sex work, and sex trafficking: four studies in contemporary governance feminism', *Harvard Journal of Law and Gender*, 29: 2 (2006), 335–424; J. Suk, 'Criminal law comes home', *Yale Law Journal*, 116: 1 (2006), 2–70; L. Gotell, 'Governing heterosexuality through specific consent: interrogating the government effects of R v J.A.', *Canadian Journal of Women and the Law*, 24: 2 (2012), 359–88.

[128] See, for example, M. Los, 'The struggle to redefine rape in the early 1980s', in R. V. Roberts and R. M. Mohr (eds.), *Confronting Sexual Assault: A Decade of Legal and Social Change* (Toronto: University of Toronto Press, 1994), p. 20.

[129] Snider, 'Feminism, punishment', 81–2. See also Gruber, 'Rape, feminism and the war on crime', 614.

reforms that treat sex outside a reproductive context as inherently dangerous, immoral, abnormal or unworthy of consideration.[130] They have noted
how feminist-driven reforms in areas such as rape, domestic violence and
workplace inequality have operated to 'strengthen repronormative ideolo-
gies or increase the constraints experienced by women in their pursuit of
sexual and political agency'.[131] These scholars also tend to question whether
sex is always the most appropriate lens through which to view questions of
gender subordination. Katherine Franke and Vicki Schultz, for example,
suggest that sexual oppression in the workplace comes as much through
dependency, lack of political power and through stereotyped roles. In their
view, policing sexual expression generally in these contexts overshoots the
mark of protecting against discriminatory and destructive behaviour and
fails to address the true sources of gender-based oppression, while denying the possibilities for women's experiences of pleasure.[132]

By protecting one partner's right to presume that the other is HIV negative, the criminalisation of non-disclosure not only reinforces the notion
of sex with any level of unknown risk as deviant, but also denies that
assuming unknown risks may be a legitimate possibility or choice. The
exclusive focus on HIV non-disclosure as inherently *about sex* obscures
other ways in which HIV criminalisation constructs and distributes
power.[133] Meanwhile, it constructs a public order where the responsibility
for any risk of HIV exposure and transmission falls solely on the members of a stigmatised underclass – those already living with HIV – under-
mining notions of shared responsibility.[134] This effectively denies society's
collective responsibility for the factors that drive HIV infection, including the risks associated with migration, social disruption including war,
instability and the effects of colonisation on aboriginal people, and, yes,
gender inequality that leaves women in a diminished position to negotiate

---

[130] Franke, 'Theorizing yes', 204, 205 ('The normativity of white, straight, middle-class wom-
en's repronormative behavior seems to set-off the lesbian / Black / HIV-positive / infertile /
disabled woman's predicament as a marked deviation from the natural order'); E. Craig,
'Capacity to consent to sexual risk', *New Criminal Law Review*, 17: 1 (2014), 113.

[131] R. Dixon, 'Feminist disagreement (comparatively) recast', *Harvard Journal of Gender and
Law*, 31 (2008), 319.

[132] Franke, 'Theorizing yes', 202; V. Schultz, 'The sanitized workplace', *Yale Law Journal*, 112:
8 (2003), 2070.

[133] This insight has led some scholars to suggest that HIV non-disclosure ought not to be
prosecuted as a *sexual* offence: Grant, 'Time to rethink', 7–59; Crompton and MacKinnon,
'The gender of lying', 447.

[134] A. Klein, 'Criminal law, public health, and governance of HIV exposure and transmission',
International Journal of Human Rights, 13: 2–3 (2009), 256–7.

condom use or safer sex.[135] In this context, casting the HIV positive partner as alone responsible for what can be understood as a joint decision,
driven by societal factors, may constitute covertly punishing 'based on status or race or some other prejudicial reason'.[136]

On Striking a Balance

None of the feminist arguments canvassed rejects altogether a role for
criminal law in responding to HIV non-disclosure. Nor do these considerations deny the legitimacy of wanting to know one's sexual partner's
HIV status or of a moral obligation to disclose. Rather, contemporary
anti-essentialist feminist insights – about attending to the lived experience of different (and particularly marginalised) women, to how law
constructs power relationships more broadly and to the positive value
of sex – call into question the *uncritical* expansion of the criminal law to
constrain sexual activity in the name of protecting women reflected in
the Supreme Court of Canada's feminist analysis in *Mabior*. Recognising
the infinite range of contexts in which sexual encounters take place, the
need to consider the autonomy of all actors and the complexity of lived
experiences and intersecting identities demands a complex calculus for
evaluating whether criminalisation of non-disclosure in fact empow-
ers women and promotes their equality in a way that is worth its costs.
A disclosure obligation *can* empower, in the sense that it can facilitate
better-informed choices about who to have sex with and under what circumstances. Such an obligation can also marginalise women, by denying that they act autonomously when they choose to undertake unknown
risks; by making women, and especially HIV positive women, the target
for sometimes unfair prosecution; by reinforcing social hierarchies that
cast HIV positive people as solely responsible for infection; and by denying their sexual freedom while protecting the sexual freedom of those
who are HIV negative.

---

[135] R. G. Parker, D. Easton and C. H. Klein, 'Structural barriers and facilitators in HIV prevention: a review of international research', *AIDS*, 14 (2000), S22–S32.

[136] Compare, V. F. Nourse, 'Reconceptualizing criminal law defences', *University of
Pennsylvania Law Review*, 151: 5 (2003), 1742. ('The real problem with sodomy statutes
is not that they cannot be found to address someone's odd sense of harm, but, rather, that
they are "code" for the oppression of persons based on sexual orientation. That, in turn,
is not only a problem for individuals but for the notion of a liberal order as well. By using
violence to enforce sexual inequality and heterosexist superiority, the state taints its own
claims to democratic legitimacy.')

Anti-essentialist scholars have suggested methodologies for taking into account the marginalising as well as empowering potential of law reform projects. Each involves being 'honest about trade-offs'[137] and frankly acknowledging and debating the goals of any law.[138] In an evaluation of whether it is possible to consent in advance to sex while unconscious, Elaine Craig suggests that criminal responsibility should not be premised on whether a particular sex act is presumptively exploitative, particularly where, as here, context matters so much to that determination. Rather, the law should be viewed as allocating risks of harm – harm to individuals whose sexual agency might be compromised, to disempowered groups who may be stigmatised, to the administration of justice institutions that might be complicit in perpetuating stigma[139] and, I would add, to the political order that the criminal law constructs. Craig suggests that it might be fair to deny a capacity to consent in advance to sex while unconscious or asleep,[140] not on the basis that all unconscious sex is exploitative, but on the basis that there is too great a risk of exploitative sex to some if unconscious sex is legal, given that violence against women is all too common.[141] Such a rule might incidentally criminalise some mutually desired, pleasure-producing, non-exploitative sex. Craig views this as a harm to those who are denied that sex, and a failure of the criminal law. She argues, however, that this failure may represent a justifiable gap between law and justice in the name of protecting those women who may be exploited, and one that allows us to 'point fingers at' and work on addressing a 'social context that produces gendered, racist, ageist and classist sexual violence'.[142] In other words, criminalisation of unconscious sex might actually help to create a world order in which the exploitation that women face is better recognised by drawing attention to how some people's sexual autonomy must be constrained to protect against it.

How, if at all, should the criminal law assign the risk of HIV exposure and transmission? In Craig's discussion of unconscious sex, it may make

---

[137] Kaplan, 'Sex-positive law', 156.
[138] In the context of domestic violence, for example, Donna Coker has urged that domestic violence laws should be measured according to the extent to which they facilitate women, particularly poor and marginalised women's access to material resources, given that it is the lack of material resources that leave women more vulnerable to further abuse. This is based on a consensus that the purpose of domestic violence law is to protect women from abuse. Coker, 'Shifting power for battered women', 1009–55.
[139] Craig, 'Capacity to consent to sexual risk', 120.
[140] R v. J. A., 2011 SCC 28 (Supreme Court of Canada).
[141] Craig, 'Capacity to consent to sexual risk', 125.
[142] Ibid. 131.

sense to prioritise the commonality of women's vulnerability to exploitation when unconscious over the specificity of those who may take pleasure in unconscious sex. In the context of criminalising HIV non-disclosure, however, the risk of exploitation may be less than in the case of unconscious sex, particularly in light of the discussions on agency in this chapter. Meanwhile, the risk of 'collateral damage' to marginalised groups through an expanded role for the criminal law is far greater: leaving the denial of pleasure aside, the health and social consequences of reinforcing stigma against people living with HIV are manifold and well-documented.[143] Thus, a number of considerations will factor into such a risk assignment.

First, whether and when the non-disclosure is exploitative varies and may be difficult to quantify. As discussed, it depends on how sex is valued from the perspective of the HIV negative partner. It depends on the reasons for non-disclosure. It depends on the nature of the relationship between the parties. Finally, it depends on the degree of risk. That is, in agreeing to have unprotected sex, the HIV negative partner may be understood to assume a certain risk. Where the risk of HIV transmission is low – in a lower-risk sex act, or when a condom is used or when viral load is suppressed – the risk level may approach that which the HIV negative partner assumes in a given set of circumstances simply by having unprotected sex with a partner whose HIV status is unknown. With these considerations in mind, the circumstances in which HIV non-disclosure is arguably exploitative narrow, and an accused's knowledge of his or her HIV infection becomes only one among a number of factors that may indicate exploitation.

Moreover, whether to assign criminal responsibility to the HIV positive partner will depend on how prepared one is to sacrifice, or to delay addressing, competing anti-subordination claims. Some feminists have suggested 'strategic essentialism' or uniting feminists of varying orientations around areas of shared concern,[144] such as women's right to dictate the terms on which they will have sex. Intersectional feminists are concerned about that approach, however, noting that it will tend to privilege the interests of wealthy, white and able-bodied women over those of poor, racialised and disabled women, while legitimating or ignoring the factors that led to the latter's subordination in the first place.[145] This concern

---

[143] A. P. Mahajan, J. N. Sayles, V. A. Patel, R. H. Remien, D. Ortiz, G. Szekeres and T. J. Coates, 'Stigma in the HIV/AIDS epidemic: a review of the literature and recommendations for the way forward', *AIDS*, 22:Supplement 2 (2008), S67–S79.

[144] See Dixon, 'Feminist disagreement', 304.

[145] K. Crenshaw, 'Race, reform, and retrenchment: transformation and legitimation in anti-discrimination law', *Harvard Law Review*, 101: 7 (1988), 1366–8.

seems especially true in the HIV context: placing the blame for HIV exposure and transmission on HIV positive partners may arguably protect the sexual autonomy of the HIV negative partner in some circumstances. It may reinforce the idea that standards for consent to sex ought to be as robust and exacting as possible. However, it does nothing to address, and indeed may exacerbate, the social inequality and stigma that drives the HIV epidemic and leaves poor, racialised and queer people more vulnerable to infection in the first place.[146] In addition, it does nothing to address prosecution patterns that will likewise vary along the lines of subordination. In short, it would seem that any contemporary feminist justification for criminalising HIV transmission and exposure ought to at least acknowledge those areas where it is demanding strategic essentialism at the expense of competing anti-subordination goals.

Conclusion

This chapter argues that feminist support for extending the scope of criminalisation of HIV non-disclosure fails to take adequate account of contemporary feminist insights around sex as a site of pleasure as well as danger, and around the need to ensure that the feminist project adequately responds to the concerns of disabled, poor and non-white women. Recognising the complex role of stigma and social subordination in the context of HIV infection casts doubt upon the claim that women's interests in dictating the terms on which they have sex justifies a robust law within which to prosecute HIV non-disclosure. At minimum, any feminist argument in favour of criminalisation – such as that offered by the Supreme Court of Canada in *Mabior* – ought to acknowledge when, where and why it is placing a fragile notion of autonomy for HIV negative people ahead of competing anti-subordination goals.

[146] S. Zierler, '*Reframing* women's risk: social inequalities and HIV infection', *Annual Review of Public Health*, 18 (1997), 401–36; G. N. Wingood, 'Application of the theory of gender and power to examine HIV-related exposures, risk factors, and effective interventions for women', *Health Education and Behaviour*, 27: 5 (2000), 539–65.

9

Criminalising Contagion – Questioning the Paradigm

KARL LAIRD

For over a decade prosecutors in England and Wales have relied upon the Offences against the Person Act 1861 to prosecute those who intentionally or recklessly infect another with a sexually transmitted disease (STD).[1] The first case to state explicitly that the law on non-fatal offences against the person encompassed the transmission of STDs was *Dica*.[2] In his seminal judgment Judge LJ stated:

> The effect of this judgment in relation to section 20 is to remove some of the outdated restrictions against the successful prosecution of those who, knowing that they are suffering HIV or some other serious sexual disease, recklessly transmit it through consensual sexual intercourse, and inflict grievous bodily harm on a person from whom the risk is concealed and who is not consenting to it.[3]

In the intervening ten years, criminalisation has not been limited to the intentional or reckless transmission of HIV.[4] There have been reported

---

[1] Numerous provisions of a regulatory nature exist to contain those who suffer from infectious disease and have done so since at least the Victorian era. These provisions were contained in Part 2 of the Public Health (Disease Control) Act 1984. Section 33, for example, made it a summary offence for someone who knows he is suffering from a 'notifiable disease' to enter any public conveyance. The 1984 Act was amended by the Health and Social Care Act 2008 and the provisions in Part 2 were replaced by a number of statutory instruments. These contain various summary offences. This chapter will not analyse these provisions, but rather will engage with why there seems to be a lack of parity between STDs and non-STDs in the context of offences against the person.

[2] [2004] EWCA Crim 1103.

[3] *Dica*, at [59].

[4] For a helpful timeline, see www.aidsmap.com/Timeline-of-developments-in-the-criminalisation-of-HIV-and-STItransmission-in-the-UK/page/1504201 (Accessed 21 November 2015). See also LCCP 217 *Reform of Offences against the Person – A Scoping Consultation Paper* (2014), chapter 6.

I would like to thank Jonathan Herring and Philip Purvis for their comments on previous drafts. The usual caveat applies.

instances of prosecutions for the transmission of genital herpes[5] and gonorrhoea.[6] In England non-consensual STD transmission has become the paradigmatic example of when it is considered appropriate to criminalise contagion. It is considered appropriate, both by members of the public who demonstrate a willingness to invoke the state when infected with an STD, and by prosecutors who subsequently bring charges. Where, however, are the cases concerning the transmission of other types of contagion, that is, those diseases that are not typically[7] transmitted through sexual intercourse, but rather through non-sexual physical or non-physical contact? It is unclear whether the potential for criminalisation in England is limited only to STDs or if an individual could be liable for intentionally or recklessly transmitting influenza or glandular fever, to take but two examples. While the Crown Prosecution Service (CPS) has produced extensive guidance to assist prosecutors in deciding whether to charge an individual who transmits an STD to a non-consenting sexual partner with an offence against the person,[8] and has a system for central referral, no such provision exists to assist in deciding whether to prosecute the transmission of other types of infectious disease. It may be that no one in England has ever been prosecuted for the transmission of a non-STD: certainly it has not been possible to identify any such cases.[9]

The aim of this chapter is twofold. The first aim is to examine how far the criminalisation of contagion extends. The second aim is to investigate some reasons that might explain why those who administer the criminal law have never been required to evaluate whether it encompasses the transmission of non-STDs. Before proceeding, it is important to clarify a number of points. This chapter does not engage with the deeper, normative question of whether contagion ought to be criminalised at all. Contagion has been criminalised in England for over a decade. The aim of this chapter is to evaluate why a dichotomy seems to exist

---

[5] *R v Golding* [2014] EWCA Crim 889.
[6] *R v Marangwanda* [2009] EWCA Crim 60.
[7] It is necessary to add this caveat to address the case of *Marangwanda* [2009] EWCA Crim 60. The prosecution accepted D's guilty plea on the basis that the two children became infected with gonorrhoea through sharing a towel with D.
[8] *Policy for Prosecuting Cases Involving the Intentional or Reckless Sexual Transmission of Infection.* www.cps.gov.uk/publications/prosecution/sti.html (Accessed 21 November 2015).
[9] The CPS cannot say, from its records, that no such prosecution has ever been mounted, but the team currently responsible for oversight of STD cases was not aware of any such case. Email correspondence on file with author. I would like to thank Tim Thompson for his assistance with this matter.

between STDs and non-STDs. It is also important to point out that it is
not the purpose of this chapter to advocate for the prosecution of everyone who transmits an infectious disease, no matter how trivial. Rather,
this chapter argues that English criminal law is extremely expansive in
this regard, a fact that seems to have been overlooked. It is expansive in
the sense that the criminal law encompasses more than just the transmission of STDs; however, the law in England is narrower than in some
other jurisdictions, such as Canada (see Alana Klein's chapter) because
in England there can be no liability without proof of transmission.[10] The
focus on STD transmission has allowed policymakers to avoid grappling with the broader issue of whether contagion ought to be criminalised at all. This is an area of the criminal law that can be ignored,
because seemingly it has an impact only upon those who are Other.[11]
By illuminating how English law currently has the potential to criminalise all sorts of everyday behaviour, it is hoped that this could act as
a catalyst for a discussion on whether disease transmission ought to be
criminalised at all. Finally, this chapter is confined to analysing why
there have been no prosecutions for an offence against the person for
non-STD transmission and does not consider the multitude of public
health measures that exist to contain infectious diseases.

The Scope of Liability for the Transmission of Disease in English Criminal Law

The Importance of R v Clarence

Any discussion of English law's approach to the criminalisation of disease
transmission must begin with *Clarence*.[12] In order effectively to assess
whether it is an offence against the person to transmit a non-STD it is
necessary to trace the interpretation that has been given to the relevant
provisions of the Offences against the Person Act 1861. The 1861 Act
still governs the law in England on non-fatal offences against the person,

---

[10] Cf. S. Cowan, 'Offences of sex or violence? Consent, fraud and HIV transmission', *New Criminal Law Review*, 17: 1 (2014), 135.

[11] Young explains how despite the fact the law is to a large extent blind to group differences, some people still bear characteristics that signify they are deviant, or Other. Despite the fact they are not unified by a single race, gender, class and so on, those who carry STDs could be conceptualised as being Other because they share this characteristic. See I. M. Young, *Justice and the Politics of Difference* (Princeton: Princeton University Press, 1990).

[12] (1888) 22 QBD 23.

despite the criticisms that have been directed towards it for over 150 years.[13] The relevant provisions are Sections 20 and 47.[14] Section 20 provides:

> Whosoever shall unlawfully and maliciously wound or inflict any grievous bodily harm upon any other person, either with or without any weapon or instrument, shall be guilty of a misdemeanor, and being convicted thereof shall be liable ... to be kept in penal servitude ...

While Section 47 states:

> Whosoever shall be convicted upon an indictment of any assault occasioning actual bodily harm shall be liable ... to be kept in penal servitude...

In *Clarence*, C had sex with his wife when he knew, but she did not, that he was suffering from gonorrhoea. The wife contracted gonorrhoea from C, who was charged with inflicting grievous bodily harm, contrary to Section 20 of the Offences against the Person Act 1861 and assault occasioning actual bodily harm, contrary to Section 47. Clarence was convicted of both offences and appealed. On appeal, by a majority of nine to four, C's convictions were quashed. The reasoning of the majority in relation to Section 20 was explained by Wills J, who suggested that the section:

> clearly points to the infliction of direct and intentional violence, whether with a weapon, or the fist, or the foot, or any other part of the person, or in any other way not involving the use of a weapon, as, for instance, by creating a panic at a theatre...[15]

Given that C inflicted no direct violence upon his wife, it followed that his conviction could not stand. The same analysis also applied to Section 47. Stephen J, who was also in the majority, observed that if an individual caused a pandemic, by carrying a child with smallpox through the streets, for example, he would not be free of moral opprobrium. Such an individual would, however, be guilty of committing public nuisance or one of the offences that were then found in Sections 120–30 of the Public Health Act 1875,[16] rather

---

[13] The Law Commission has concluded that the legislation is 'defective on grounds both of effectiveness and of justice'. See LCCP 122, *Legislating the Criminal Code: Offences against the Person and General Principles* (1992). The Law Commission recently completed a scoping exercise as a first step towards a project to reform the law on offences against the person. Available at www.lawcom.gov.uk/project/offences-against-the-person/ (Accessed 21 November 2015). See LCCP 217, *Reform of Offences against the Person – A Scoping Consultation Paper* (2014) and LC 361, *Reform of Offences against the Person – A Report* (2015).

[14] Section 18 could also be invoked if there was an intention to cause really serious harm.

[15] *Clarence*, at 36.

[16] Ibid., at 41. His Lordship cited *R v Vantandillo* 4 M. & S. 73 as an example of a case in which this occurred.

than an offence against the person. His Lordship warned against 'wide and uncertain extensions of the criminal law'.[17] When considering whether it was possible to inflict grievous bodily harm without a weapon or other instrument Stephen J stated that:

> [t]he words appear to me to mean the direct causing of some grievous injury to the body itself with a weapon, as by a cut with a knife, or without a weapon, as by a blow with the fist, or by pushing a person down. Indeed, though the word "assault" is not used in the section, I think the words imply an assault and battery of which a wound or grievous bodily harm is the manifest immediate and obvious result.[18]

His Lordship held that transmission of an STD was analogous to poisoning. Given that poisoning could not constitute an offence under either Sections 20 or 47, C's convictions had to be quashed. Importantly, it was held that this remained the case despite the fact that a poisoning could be conceptualised as grievous bodily harm; it was the method by which the harm was inflicted that precluded liability. It was for this reason that the 1861 Act was thought to pose only a technical bar to prosecution.

The judgment was not a unanimous one, however. Hawkins J explained the minority's disagreement in the following terms:

> In my opinion the legislature in framing the various sections of the statute already and hereafter referred to, used the words 'inflict', 'cause', and 'occasion' as synonymous terms...[19]

So long as the disease in question constituted actual or grievous bodily harm, in the minority's interpretation of the statute, the absence of force did not preclude C from being guilty of either offence. For the minority, the means by which the requisite harm was caused were immaterial, so long as the defendant caused it recklessly or intentionally.

Analysing the basis of the disagreement between the majority and the minority in *Clarence* is instructive. There seems to have been a consensus that gonorrhoea itself could be conceptualised as actual or grievous bodily harm. There was disagreement about whether the language of the 1861 Act was capacious enough to encompass the *method* by which disease is transmitted, that is, where there is an absence of violence or force applied to the body of the victim. The majority adopted a literal interpretation of the statutory language, while the minority seems to have taken a more

---

[17] *Clarence*, at 39.
[18] Ibid., at 41.
[19] Ibid., at 48.

purposive approach. How does this assist with the present enquiry? It is important to understand what was decided in *Clarence* as it dominated this area of the law for over a century and therefore sets the scene for what follows. It is also interesting to note that, aside from the technical reason for why the transmission of gonorrhoea could not constitute an offence against the person, Stephen J was satisfied that this issue was best left as a matter for public health rather than the criminal law. As will become evident, a shift has taken place in the judicial attitude towards the transmission of contagious disease. What was considered a matter for public health in the Victorian era has now become one of individualised criminal responsibility.

The Vindication of Hawkins J and an Act 'That Is Always Speaking'

The passage of time has proved Hawkins J's dissenting judgment to be prescient. A number of decisions in the twentieth century adopted his interpretation of Sections 47 and 20 and paved the way for the Court of Appeal's decision in *Dica*. In *Wilson*[20] the issue the House of Lords had to resolve was whether the trial judge had been correct to direct the jury that if they did not find W guilty of inflicting grievous bodily harm they could nevertheless find him guilty of the lesser offence of assault occasioning actual bodily harm.[21] Lord Roskill, with whom the other Law Lords agreed, held that an allegation of inflicting grievous bodily harm necessarily included an allegation of actual bodily harm. This was the case because infliction of the more serious injuries was held to include the infliction of the less serious. The question that remained, however, was whether an allegation of 'inflicting' included an allegation of assault in the technical sense.[22] Relying upon the Australian case of *Salisbury*,[23] it was held that

---

[20] [1984] AC 242.

[21] Relying upon Section 6(3) of the Criminal Law Act 1967, which provides: 'Where, on a person's trial on indictment for any offence except treason or murder, the jury find him not guilty of the offence specifically charged in the indictment, but the allegations in the indictment amount to or include (expressly or by implication) an allegation of another offence falling within the jurisdiction of the court of trial, the jury may find him guilty of that other offence or of an offence of which he could be found guilty on an indictment specifically charging that other offence.'

[22] Although the House of Lords states that the question is whether there must be an assault, what it really means is whether there must be a battery, that is, some unlawful force. These terms are often used interchangeably, but they denote distinct offences with different *actus rei*.

[23] [1976] VR 452.

'inflict' does not necessarily imply a technical assault, although it often will. This case was important as it had the practical impact of widening the *actus reus* of Section 20. It did not, however, pave the way for the criminalisation of disease transmission, whether of those of a sexual nature or otherwise. Lord Roskill accepted the view of the Supreme Court of Victoria that 'inflict' has a narrower meaning than 'cause'. It was held that this term embodies the requirement that 'force be violently applied to the body of the victim'.[24] This is reminiscent of what the majority held in *Clarence* and would have precluded liability under both Sections 20 and 47 for disease transmission, given that it is difficult to conceptualise the transmission of any disease as involving the application of force to the body.

It was not until *Burstow*[25] that the 1861 Act, and specifically Section 20, was interpreted in such a way as to permit liability for an offence against the person without the use of force. The issue for the House of Lords to consider was whether causing another to develop a psychiatric condition (as a result of a series of silent telephone calls) was an offence under Section 20. The House of Lords examined the majority's reasoning in *Clarence* and observed that the criminal law had moved on in the light of a more sophisticated understanding of the link between physical and psychiatric injury. Indeed the 1861 Act was characterised as 'always speaking'.[26] It was for this reason that the House of Lords held that *Clarence* was no longer of much assistance in interpreting the Act. For Lord Steyn, who delivered the majority judgment, the issue was one of construction, that is, whether as a matter of current usage the contextual interpretation of 'inflict' could embrace the idea of one person *inflicting* psychiatric injury upon another. His Lordship held that: 'One can without straining the language in any way answer that question in the affirmative.'[27] His Lordship did, however, add the caveat that 'inflict' and 'cause' are not exactly synonymous, although there was no elucidation of what the distinction between the two might be. The conviction was therefore upheld. Lord Hope, who delivered a concurring judgment, was less circumspect in seeking to maintain a distinction between 'cause' and 'inflict' and held that for the purposes of a criminal statute the two terms ought to be seen as being interchangeable.[28] His Lordship held that this would be the case provided it was understood that

---

[24] D. Ormerod and K. Laird, *Smith and Hogan's Criminal Law*, 14th edition (Oxford: Oxford University Press, 2015), 742–4.

[25] [1998] AC 147.

[26] *Burstow*, at 158.

[27] Ibid., at 161.

[28] Ibid., at 164.

'inflict' implies that the consequence to the victim involved something detrimental or adverse.

Burstow was of crucial importance to the present enquiry, as it confirmed the obsolescence of *Clarence*. The House of Lords, by interpreting 'inflict' as being largely synonymous with 'cause', dismantled what had by then become the final obstacle that had precluded liability for transmitting disease.[29] The reason why the convictions in *Clarence* were quashed was because the statutory term 'inflict' was interpreted as requiring the application of force to the body of the complainant. If 'inflict' simply means 'cause', then so long as disease could be conceptualised as actual or grievous bodily harm, there was the potential for criminal liability under the 1861 Act. For that reason, it is necessary to consider the extent to which the judicial conceptualisation of 'bodily harm' evolved in the years since *Clarence*.

The Changing Conception of 'Bodily Harm'

In *Chan-Fook*,[30] a case concerning Section 47 assault, Hobhouse LJ examined the meaning of 'bodily harm' with reference to how the term had been utilised in a succession of cases and statutory provisions. In an earlier case, *DPP v Smith*,[31] the House of Lords had held that 'grievous bodily harm' ought to be given its 'ordinary and natural' meaning. It was held by the Court of Appeal that the same applied to the meaning of 'actual bodily harm'. Hobhouse LJ observed that:

> These are three words [actual bodily harm] of the English language which require no elaboration and in the ordinary course should not receive any. The word 'harm' is a synonym for injury. The word 'actual' indicates that the injury (although there is no need for it to be permanent) should not be so trivial as to be wholly insignificant.[32]

The purpose of Section 47 was said to be to define an element of aggravation in a common assault or battery. Hobhouse LJ made a number of observations that are relevant to the present enquiry. His Lordship stated that:

> ... an injury can be caused to someone by injuring their health; an assault may have the consequence of infecting the victim with a disease or

---

[29] The judgment was not without criticism, specifically on the basis that it constituted an example of (inappropriate) judicial legislation. Cf. S. Gardner, 'Stalking', *Law Quarterly Review* (1998), 33. Contrast, C. Wells, 'Stalking: the criminal law response', *Criminal Law Review* (1997), 463.

[30] [1994] 1 W.L.R. 689.

[31] [1961] AC 290.

[32] *Chan-Fook*, at 694.

causing the victim to become ill. The injury may be internal and may not be accompanied by an external injury. A blow may leave no external mark but may cause the victim to lose consciousness.[33]

Hobhouse LJ took an expansive interpretation of 'bodily harm', although this was not necessarily a novel approach, given that there was consensus in *Clarence* that gonorrhoea could potentially constitute actual or grievous bodily harm. Although *Chan-Fook* was not a decision of the House of Lords, it was cited with approval in *Burstow*.[34] The House of Lords relied upon Hobhouse LJ's judgment in arriving at the conclusion that psychiatric harm could constitute bodily harm and so causing it could be considered an offence against the person. If intangible forms of injury, such as that of a psychiatric nature, came within the scope of the 1861 Act, then it was only a matter of time before the transmission of disease did so too.

The problem, however, is that it could be argued that seeking to draw an analogy between tangible forms of harm, such as a stab wound, and intangible forms of harm, such as psychiatric illness, is problematic. An intangible harm is one that does not involve D making physical contact with the body of V. While someone who is not an expert might be able to appreciate the relative seriousness of the former using simply his or her common sense, the same is not necessarily true of the latter. As will become evident, there has been a marked reluctance to grapple with the normative question of what forms of harm ought to be sufficiently serious to fall within the scope of the 1861 Act. The problem is compounded in the context of disease transmission, given that the relative seriousness of a disease depends to a large extent on the physical characteristics of the complainant. Although the various obstacles to criminalising contagion had been dismantled, it would be another decade before the Court of Appeal in *Dica* confirmed what earlier cases had made possible.

Dica and the Expanding Criminalisation of Contagion

The Court of Appeal's decision in *Dica* has been the subject of a number of insightful analyses.[35] The focus here will be on how Judge LJ relied upon the cases discussed in the previous sections to justify imposing liability under the 1861 Act for the transmission of HIV. The facts can be simply

---

[33] Ibid.

[34] *Burstow*, at 158–9.

[35] See, for example, M. Weait, 'Criminal law and the sexual transmission of HIV: *R v Dica*', *Modern Law Review*, 68:1 (2005), 121; H. Law, 'Offences against the person: reckless transmission of HIV', *Journal of Criminal Law*, 69:5 (2005), 389; S. Leake and D.C. Ormerod, 'Grievous bodily harm', *Criminal Law Review* (2004), 944.

stated. D was HIV positive and engaged in unprotected sex with the two complainants. D did not inform either of them of his HIV positive status. Both women contracted HIV and D was convicted of recklessly inflicting grievous bodily harm. D then appealed his convictions.

Referring to *Clarence*, Judge LJ observed how a succession of judgments in the intervening hundred years had vindicated Hawkin J's dissenting judgment. *Wilson*, his Lordship remarked, 'represented a major erosion of the authority of *Clarence* in relation to the ambit of Section 20 in the context of sexually transmitted disease'.[36] As has already been discussed, the House of Lords' decision in *Wilson* had an impact upon the ambit of Section 20 not only in the context of STDs, but all forms of disease. Judge LJ also averred to *Chan-Fook* and how that judgment had withstood the criticisms directed at it by the appellant in *Burstow*. His Lordship relied upon this latter decision in holding that:

> this decision confirmed that even when no physical violence has been applied, directly or indirectly to the victim's body, an offence under section 20 may be committed ... If psychiatric injury can be inflicted without direct or indirect violence, or an assault, for the purposes of section 20 physical injury may be similarly inflicted.[37]

Dica effectively overturned *Clarence*, although it merely confirmed what *Wilson* and *Burstow* had earlier implied was possible. Although Clarence did not intend to infect his wife with gonorrhoea, he was reckless as to whether she would be so infected, and Judge LJ held that he would now be guilty of an offence under Section 20. As was mentioned previously, this judgment marked a shift in the judicial attitude towards contagious disease. The majority in *Clarence* thought that the transmission of gonorrhoea was a matter for the Public Health Act 1875, while Judge LJ in *Dica* took the opposite view. His Lordship did take cognisance of the fact the government, in response to a Law Commission consultation paper,[38] had earlier taken the view that the criminalisation of disease transmission was inappropriate unless D intended to cause really serious harm.[39] His Lordship stated, however, that if Parliament disagreed with the court's interpretation of the law, it was free to intervene.[40]

---

[36] *Dica*, at [26].

[37] Ibid.

[38] *Legislating the Criminal Code: Offences against the Person and General Principles* (1993) (Law Com No 218) (Com 2370).

[39] Home Office, *Violence: Reforming the Offences against the Person Act 1861* (1998).

[40] Arguably the judgment in *Dica* obviated the necessity for Parliamentary intervention. It is submitted that, as has been argued before, an issue as policy laden and complex as the

The Current State of the Law

As the previous sections have established, possible criminal liability in England is not confined to the transmission of STDs, given that the changing interpretation of sections 20 and 47 applies to the transmission of any disease, not just those of a sexual nature. Whether an individual ought to be charged under section 47 or section 20 would depend upon the seriousness of the disease in question. The threshold that harm must cross before it is sufficient to constitute actual bodily harm is in fact extremely low, which opens up a broad vista of potential criminal liability. In *Chan-Fook*, Hobhouse LJ stated that actual bodily harm refers to an injury that is not so trivial as to be wholly insignificant. There are two caveats that must be added to this statement, however. In relation to actual bodily harm, there is the technical requirement to first prove a battery (some unlawful touching).[41] Does this preclude liability under section 47 for transmitting disease? The *actus reus* of battery is the application of unlawful force to the body of the victim, and there is authority to suggest that this application of force must be direct.[42] There are, however, a number of cases confirming that the concept of an indirect battery[43] is not alien to English criminal law.[44] It would not require a great deal of ingenuity to conceptualise the transmission of disease as constituting the indirect infliction of harm and therefore actual bodily harm. This of course depends upon the mode of infliction. If D sneezes on V (or maybe spits on him), infecting him with influenza, then it would be possible to draw an analogy with *DPP v K*, in which D placed acid in a hand dryer that caused injury to V when he used it.

There is no requirement to prove a battery under section 20, which makes this provision a more viable route by which to prosecute the transmission of disease. This is somewhat counterintuitive given that it is

---

criminalisation of disease transmission is not one that lends itself well to the incremental method of the common law. The literature on the appropriateness of invoking the criminal law to punish HIV transmission is voluminous. Cf. A. Ahmed, M. Kaplan, A. Symington and E. Kismodi, 'Criminalising consensual sexual behaviour in the context of HIV: consequences, evidence, and leadership', *Global Public Health*, 6: Supplement 3 (2011), S357.

[41] Ormerod and Laird, *Smith and Hogan's Criminal Law*, p. 714.

[42] Ibid., p. 714.

[43] This refers to the indirect infliction of harm. Examples of this include causing a panic in a theatre leading to a crush, *Martin* (1881) 8 QBD 54. See also *Lewis* [1970] Crim LR 647 in which V barricaded herself in a room to escape D and jumped out of a window when she thought he was breaking through. Both convictions were upheld.

[44] *DPP v K* [1990] 1 WLR 1067.

generally considered to be the more serious offence.[45] It is perhaps this difference between sections 47 and 20 that explains why it is the latter that has featured in all the reported instances in which an individual has been charged with an offence against the person for disease transmission, rather than because the disease in question was considered so intrinsically injurious that it justified prosecution for the more serious offence.

Prosecutorial discretion has a role to play here. The CPS invokes a two-stage test to determine whether prosecution is appropriate.[46] The first stage, the evidential stage, requires the prosecutor to assess whether there is a realistic prospect of conviction if the suspect were to be charged with the offence. The second stage requires the prosecutor to assess whether prosecution would be in the public interest. There are various factors that are weighed when considering whether prosecution would be in the public interest. This is relevant because it could be argued that the two-stage test is simply not satisfied in the context of non-STD transmission. The next section considers the evidential difficulties that might be encountered, but one issue that it is necessary to consider at this stage is of what offence an individual might be guilty. It has been established that the transmission of disease could fall within either section 47 or section 20, but how is the prosecutor to determine which is the more appropriate?

Whether an individual is potentially guilty of actual bodily harm or grievous bodily harm for transmitting disease would be dependent upon the nature of the disease in question (subject to the indirect battery point) and upon the personal characteristics of the victim. In England there have been sporadic prosecutions for the transmission of an STD, but anecdotal evidence suggests there have been none for the transmission of a non-STD. Is influenza, for example, sufficiently serious to constitute actual or grievous bodily harm? This depends upon the meaning of these terms, but it has already been established that the requisite threshold of harm is a low one. The CPS in its guidelines recommends that an individual who inflicts 'serious' injuries ought to be charged with an offence under section 47. This, of course, begs the question of what 'serious' means in this context. The CPS provides a list of factors to assist prosecutors in determining whether an injury can be classified as being serious. Comparisons can be difficult to make. One example is whether stitches are needed. Is influenza

---

[45] See *Offences against the Person, Incorporating the Charging Standard*. Available at www.cps .gov.uk/legal/l_to_o/offences_against_the_person/ (Accessed 21 November 2015).

[46] *The CPS: The Code for Crown Prosecutors*. Available at www.cps.gov.uk/publications/docs/ code_2013_accessible_english.pdf (Accessed 21 November 2015).

analogous to a wound that needs suturing with stitches? If the person to whom influenza is transmitted is elderly or suffers from a compromised immune system, it could potentially be life threatening, unlike a relatively superficial slash across the arm from a knife. If she dies then there might be liability for manslaughter. Since the abrogation of the Year and a Day Rule, this is possible no matter how long it takes the victim to die from the harm in question.[47] Influenza, therefore, is sufficient to come within the statutory definition of actual bodily harm.[48]

The problem is that the law of England in this context proceeds by way of analogy with physical harm. The 1861 Act was drafted for the purpose of criminalising those who inflict tangible forms of harm. Whether it is possible to draw an analogy between tangible and intangible forms of harm is questionable, but it is a necessary exercise to engage in to ascertain what the appropriate charge ought to be. It is also an exercise the jury must engage in. The Court of Appeal has recently confirmed that in the context of the 1861 Act, 'the assessment of harm done in an individual case in a contested trial will be a matter for the jury, applying contemporary social standards'.[49] This remains the case even in the context of disease transmission. The issue, however, is that the law in this context relies too much upon the jury's common sense in order to assess the relative seriousness of harm. Although this might work well enough in the context of tangible forms of harm, something more is needed when considering intangible forms of harm. Expert evidence is required, as is guidance from the judge.[50]

Given that the scope of the 1861 Act is sufficiently capacious to encompass the reckless or intentional transmission of non-STDs, what is it that explains why prosecution has hitherto been confined to STDs? Perhaps there would be insurmountable evidential difficulties, making it impossible for the evidential threshold to be crossed. Another explanation may be that ordinary people perceive STD transmission differently from

---

[47] At common law, death had to occur within a year and a day of the defendant's unlawful act. This rule was abolished by the Law Reform (Year and a Day Rule) Act 1996. The Act requires the consent of the Attorney General to the prosecution of an individual when the injury that it is alleged to have caused was sustained more than three years before death occurred. See Ormerod and Laird, *Smith and Hogan's Criminal Law*, p. 563.

[48] It is important to bear in mind that according to law, an injury that might be trivial if inflicted upon a robust twenty-year-old can be serious if inflicted upon a baby. In determining the relative seriousness of the injury, regard must be had to the effect of the harm on the particular individual. Cf *R v Bollom* [2003] EWCA Crim 2846.

[49] *R v Golding* [2014] EWCA Crim 889, at [64].

[50] See K. Laird, 'Case comment on R v Golding', *Criminal Law Review* (2014), 889.

non- STD transmission and do not perceive non-STD transmission as something that warrants state intervention.[51] This might explain why there has seemingly been no opportunity for those who administer the criminal law to consider the latter.

Four Explanations for the Paradigm

The following sections examine four possible explanations for the situation that pertains in England and Wales. They are:

- The difficulty proving causation;
- The difficulty proving *mens rea*;
- That the reckless or intentional transmission of an STD involves a breach of trust, not present in the context of non-STD transmission;
- That there are feelings of disgust and shame associated with the transmission of an STD.

A Matter of Causation?

Is it simply the case that it is more difficult to prove causation in cases concerning the transmission of non-STDs? Simon Bronitt has pointed out that there will often be difficulty establishing who was the source of the disease in question.[52] Some diseases are so ubiquitous, such as influenza, that the source of the complainant's infection could be very difficult to ascertain. The same difficulty could, however, be encountered in cases concerning the transmission of an STD.[53] Nevertheless this has not proved to be a barrier to prosecution and ultimately conviction. English law, unlike Canadian law, does not criminalise an individual for exposing another to the risk of harm, so it must be proven in each case that the disease has been transmitted and that the defendant was the source of the infection.[54] A number of cases illustrate how these evidential difficulties have been overcome in the context of STD transmission.

---

[51] Anecdotal evidence suggests that people find the type of behaviour that can lead to non-STD transmission extremely irritating, as a Google search of the phrase 'hate people sneeze over me' demonstrates.

[52] S. Bronitt, 'Spreading disease and the criminal law', *Criminal Law Review* (1994), 21.

[53] As has been pointed out on more than one occasion, the difficulties of proof will often be insurmountable, which perhaps explains the relative lack of prosecutions. See M. Weait, *Intimacy and Responsibility: The Criminalisation of HIV Transmission* (Routledge-Cavendish: Oxford, 2007), pp. 100–7

[54] For further analysis of the law in Canada, see Chapter 8 in this volume. For a review of recent case law, see J. Loveless, 'Criminalising failure to disclose HIV to sexual partners:

In *Dica*, D's counsel disputed that the complainants had contracted HIV from him. The Court of Appeal does not go into any detail about the complainants' sexual history, but in the context of the transmission of STDs, much will turn on this.[55] For example, there are instances when it could be possible that the complainant contracted the STD in question from a sexual partner other than the one in the dock. If the complainant undertook an HIV test that proved negative before she began her sexual relationship with D then that would be evidence from which it could be inferred that D was the source of the transmission. Given, however, that most people do not undergo regular HIV testing,[56] such evidence is unlikely to be forthcoming. Even if such evidence could be adduced, the prosecution would still have to prove that D was the only person with whom the complainant was having sex within the relevant time frame. The more people with whom the complainant has had unprotected intercourse, the less likely it will be that this defendant is the source of the transmission of the STD in question.[57] Just because the defendant has been open about admitting that he is suffering from an STD and therefore might have transmitted it to the complainant does not necessarily mean that he is the source of the infection. The consequence of failing to appreciate this fact is that the law might punish those who are honest, rather than those who have in fact transmitted disease. Of course, discharging the evidential burden when the STD in question is HIV is made somewhat easier by virtue of the fact that blood tests can establish whether the defendant and the complainant have the same strain of HIV.[58] Even this, however, is far from conclusive.

Reported cases in which a conviction has been obtained for the transmission of an STD have been 'easy' cases from an evidential perspective.

a short note on recent lessons from the Canadian Supreme Court', *Criminal Law Review* (2013), 214.

[55] Cf. J. Rogers, 'Criminal liability for the transmission of HIV', *Cambridge Law Journal*, 64: 1 (2005), 20.

[56] See www.hpa.org.uk/webc/hpawebfile/hpaweb_c/1316424799217 (Accessed 21 November 2015).

[57] The CPS has noted how important the complainant's sexual history will be in this context in its legal guidance on prosecuting STD transmission. See *Policy for Prosecuting Cases Involving the Intentional or Reckless Sexual Transmission of Infection*. Available at www.cps.gov.uk/publications/prosecution/sti.html (Accessed 21 November 2015).

[58] The CPS notes how phylogenetic analysis may demonstrate that the strain of the infection in the complainant is consistent with the strain of the suspect, but that this is insufficient on its own. See *Policy for Prosecuting Cases Involving the Intentional or Reckless Sexual Transmission of Infection*. Available at www.cps.gov.uk/publications/prosecution/sti.html (Accessed 21 November 2015).

For example, in *Konzani*,[59] K was HIV positive and had unprotected sex with the three complainants, each of whom contracted HIV. In relation to two out of the three complainants, even if K had disputed that he was the source of the infection, there was evidence making it clear beyond doubt that K had transmitted HIV to them. DH was a virgin before having sex with K and had two sexual partners after him, both of whom tested negative for HIV. Provided DH had not received a blood transfusion or otherwise been in contact with potentially contaminated blood or needles, the evidence was such that it was relatively straightforward to establish that K was the source of the infection. One of the other complainants, LH, had an HIV test before having sex with K, as did her partner at the time. Both of them tested negative. As LH did not have sex with anyone other than K after having sex with this partner, the evidence that K was the source of the infection was incontrovertible. There was little in the judgment about the third complainant's sexual history, perhaps because K did not dispute that he had transmitted HIV to her.

This analysis demonstrates that there are evidential difficulties inherent in prosecuting instances of STD transmission, but they have been overcome. When the focus is on non-STD transmission, the question is whether the evidential difficulties are insurmountable. This is an inherently context-dependent question and much turns on the non-STD in question. If the disease is influenza or something else that is ubiquitous, then it could be very difficult indeed to trace the source of the infection. The less prevalent the disease, however, all things being equal, the easier it will be to prove who transmitted it to the complainant. For example, if an individual goes on holiday, contracts dengue fever and then transmits it to everyone in the office upon his return, it would be relatively straightforward to establish the source of the infection.[60] Subject to proving *mens rea*, should the overly eager office worker not be guilty of causing grievous bodily harm? Perhaps, therefore, the difficulty lies not in establishing causation, but in proving the requisite *mens rea*?

---

[59] [2005] EWCA Crim 706. It is important to note that K did not dispute that he had infected each of the complainants with HIV. The facts are, nevertheless, instructive.

[60] According to NHS Choices, there were only 343 reported cases of dengue fever in England, Wales and Northern Ireland in 2012. Available at www.nhs.uk/Conditions/dengue/Pages/Introduction.aspx (Accessed 21 November 2015). By contrast in 2012, 6,360 people were newly diagnosed with HIV in England alone. It is estimated that 21,900 people in England remain unaware that they are HIV positive. See www.nat.org.uk/HIV-Facts/Statistics/Latest-UK-Statistics.aspx (Accessed 21 November 2015).

Recklessness and the Transmission of a Non-STD

In order for D to be guilty of an offence under the Offences against the Person Act 1861, he must have intentionally caused harm or been reckless as to whether harm would be so caused.[61] The focus here is on recklessness, given that all of the reported cases in England and Wales have involved recklessness rather than intention.[62] Recklessness has two components.[63] The first is that the defendant appreciated there was a risk that he would cause some harm to the complainant; since the decision in G[64] this is a subjective question. The difficulty encountered here might be in establishing how much of a risk there has to be before the defendant can be liable. The answer to this enquiry depends upon whether the risk must be a significant one or just more than de minimis. In Brady the Court of Appeal rejected the contention that the risk had to be 'obvious and significant'.[65] It seems therefore that the threshold is a low one.[66] Whether this is desirable is open for debate, but it seems tolerably clear that any level of risk, above de minimis, seems to suffice. Establishing that D was reckless has not proven to be an insurmountable barrier to prosecution and ultimately conviction in those cases in which an individual has been accused of grievous bodily harm for transmitting an STD, such as HIV. Contrary to popular assumption, the risk of HIV being transmitted during unprotected vaginal intercourse, for example, is in fact extremely low.[67] Despite the remoteness of this risk, it

---

[61] To be guilty D need not be reckless as to causing the actual harm, just some harm. Cf. Mowatt [1968] 1 QB 421.

[62] There are some cases that have been reported in the media concerning intentional transmission. See www.dailymail.co.uk/news/article-391418/Woman-jailed-deliberately-infecting-lover-HIV.html (Accessed 21 November 2015). All of the reported cases, however, involve reckless transmission.

[63] Ormerod and Laird, Smith and Hogan's Criminal Law, pp. 129–41.

[64] [2004] 1 AC 1034.

[65] [2006] EWCA Crim 2413.

[66] For discussion of this in the Scottish context, see V. Tadros, 'Recklessness, consent and the transmission of HIV', Edinburgh Law Review, 5:3 (2001), 371.

[67] This is an extremely complex issue. The Centres for Disease Control and Prevention estimate that the per-act probability of acquiring HIV from an infected source by way of penile-vaginal intercourse varies from 4–8 per 10,000 exposures. This figure depends upon a number of variables, such as viral load. Available at www.cdc.gov/hiv/policies/law/risk.html (Accessed 21 November 2015). The risk depends on the type of sexual activity involved. For example, in the case of anal sex, the risk of transmission for the 'receptive' party is significantly higher than in vaginal sex. For the difficulties that have been encountered in the Canadian context, see D. Hughes, 'Condom use, viral load and the type of sexual activity as defences to the sexual transmission of HIV', Journal of Criminal Law, 77: 2 (2013), 136.

is sufficient to establish recklessness. If this is a sufficient basis to establish the first limb of recklessness in the context of STD transmission, it should suffice when the disease in question is a non-STD.

The second limb of recklessness warrants more in-depth consideration, as it could pose more of an impediment to prosecution. This limb requires D to have unreasonably taken the risk that he would cause the complainant to suffer some harm. It is important to point out that it is possible that a relationship might exist between the first and second limbs. If the risk of the harm eventuating is extremely remote, does it follow that it is a reasonable risk to take? The courts have not addressed this issue directly, but in *Chief Constable of Avon and Somerset Constabulary v Shimmen*[68] it was held that it is not reasonable to take even a miniscule risk. It seems, therefore, that the foresight of any degree of risk may be sufficient to render the taking of it unreasonable. This seems to be the case in relation to STD transmission. As has already been discussed, the risk of transmitting HIV during unprotected vaginal intercourse, to give but one example of sexual activity, is extremely low. This does not, however, render it a reasonable risk to take. Perhaps the reason is because it is so easy significantly to reduce the risk, by using a condom.[69] How does this principle apply to non-STDs? It is axiomatic that taking certain risks is an inherent part of everyday life. If I am suffering from a cold and get on a crowded bus, it does not seem unreasonable for me to take the risk that I will transmit my cold to someone on the bus. Why might this be the case? Two potential explanations may be given. It could be argued that everyone who boarded the bus has tacitly consented to taking this risk, given that it is one that is an incident of everyday life.[70] The existence of that tacit consent precludes

---

[68] (1987) 84 Cr. App. R. 7.

[69] Although there may be reasons why a condom is not used, in *Dica* Judge LJ gave the examples of the Christian couple who do not use contraception for religious reasons and the couple who are trying to conceive, at [49].

[70] English law has demonstrated an aversion to the idea of implied consent. Cf *H v CPS* [2010] EWHC 1374 (Admin.). Nevertheless, in *Collins v Wilcock* [1984] 1 W.L.R. 1172 it was recognised that: 'Generally speaking consent is a defence to battery; and most of the physical contacts of ordinary life are not actionable because they are impliedly consented to by all who move in society and so expose themselves to the risk of bodily contact. So nobody can complain of the jostling which is inevitable from his presence in, for example, a supermarket, an underground station or a busy street; nor can a person who attends a party complain if his hand is seized in friendship, or even if his back is, within reason, slapped.... Although such cases are regarded as examples of implied consent, it is more common nowadays to treat them as falling within a general exception embracing all physical contact which is generally acceptable in the ordinary conduct of daily life.' (At 1177)

liability.[71] This remains the case despite the fact that the risk of my transmitting the cold is not insubstantial. The second potential reason invokes a cost–benefit analysis. The risk I pose is relatively minor, compared with my need to go about my daily business.[72] Judge LJ in *Dica* alluded to the same point. His Lordship indicated that he did not think it appropriate to criminalise citizens who take risks for socially beneficial reasons.[73]

There will be instances, however, when it would be unreasonable to take such a risk. Consider D, who is suffering from influenza. D works in a nursing home and comes into contact with people whose immune systems he knows to be compromised. Would it not be unreasonable for him to go into work because he does not want to lose his overtime pay? Intuition seems to indicate that this would be an unreasonable risk for D to take. Intuition can be supplemented by two more principled reasons, however. First, the element of tacit consent is not present. It cannot be presumed that those who reside in nursing homes consent, tacitly or otherwise, to running the risk of contracting infectious diseases, given that a nursing home, like a hospital, is typically thought of as being a sterile environment. Second, D knows that the consequences of the risk eventuating could be dire. There is nothing that justifies D taking such a potentially deleterious risk. All things being equal, the reason for taking the risk (not losing overtime pay) is outweighed by the reason for not taking it (jeopardising the lives of the residents of the home).

To summarise, there are some instances when it is not reasonable to take the risk of transmitting a non-STD. This is the inverse of the approach the law takes to STDs, given that it seems that it is always unreasonable to take the risk of transmitting an STD.[74] Why there should be this distinction

---

[71] English law's approach to consent in the context of non-fatal offences against the person is heavily policy based; cf Lord Woolf CJ's judgment in *Barnes* [2004] EWCA Crim 3246. The House of Lords confirmed in *Brown* [1994] 1 A.C. 212 that an individual cannot consent to the infliction of harm that constitutes actual bodily harm or above. The Court of Appeal subsequently held in *Konzani* [2005] EWCA Crim 706 that an individual could validly consent to the *risk* of contracting HIV. This must be informed consent to the specific risk. For discussion see S. Cowan, 'Offences of sex or violence? Consent, fraud and HIV transmission', *New Criminal Law Review*, 17: 1 (2014), 135.

[72] As Victor Tadros states: 'To put the matter crudely, high risks might be warranted where those risks are necessary for the performance of a very valuable activity. Lower risks are warranted for less valuable activities.' V. Tadros, 'Recklessness, consent and the transmission of HIV', *Edinburgh Law Review*, 5:3 (2001), 371, at p. 378.

[73] *Dica*, at [50]. Cf. G. Mawhinney, 'To be ill or to kill: the criminality of contagion', *Journal of Criminal Law*, 77: 3 (2013), 202.

[74] Although informed consent operates as a defence, it remains unclear whether D could avoid liability for STD transmission when he sought to minimize the risk by using a condom.

between the two is not entirely clear. In the same way that an individual tacitly consents to take the risk of contracting the cold when getting on the bus, the same could be said of the individual who engages in unprotected sex[75] but the Court of Appeal has emphatically rejected this argument.[76] In the context of non-STD transmission, the approach to consent that is adopted outside the context of HIV transmission ought to be the appropriate one.[77] This does not require 'informed consent'. The reason it is appropriate is that there are no public policy concerns that justify imposing a different conception of consent. Put simply getting on the bus with a cold conforms with the social expectation of what types of risks people tacitly consent to taking.

Given that the issues examined in this section have not proven to be a barrier to prosecution in the context of STDs, they should not necessarily prove insurmountable in relation to non-STDs either. Perhaps the reason for the paradigm is that the CPS and the judiciary have had to react to complaints for transmission of the former but not the latter. Although there is a lack of empirical information to substantiate this assertion, it is not wholly implausible to surmise that members of the public perceive STDs as being somehow different from non-STDs. Assuming such a perception does exist, it is necessary to evaluate the extent to which it provides an appropriate reason for action.

The Transmission of Disease as Breach of Trust

Annette Baier undertook important work on the ethics of trust, which has been influential in recent debates over the role that it might play in justifying punishment. Although Baier was not concerned with trust as the justification for punishment, her definition of trust is nevertheless a good starting point when considering that concept in this context. Baier defines trust as the 'acceptance of vulnerability to harm that others could inflict but

---

[75] Cf. M. Weait, 'Harm, consent and the limits of privacy', *Feminist Legal Studies*, 13: 1 (2005), 97, at p. 117: 'couples who pursue sexual pleasure outside established and socially legitimized relationship structures may be assumed to have consented to the risk of infection if it occurs'.

[76] *Konzani*, at [41].

[77] As Gurnham points out, consent has a special legal status in the context of HIV transmission. Cf D. Gurnham, 'Risky sex and "manly diversions": contours of consent in HIV transmission and rough horseplay cases', in A. Alghrani, R. Bennett and S. Ost (eds.), *Bioethics, Medicine and the Criminal Law – The Criminal Law and Bioethical Conflict: Walking the Tightrope* (Cambridge: Cambridge University Press, 2011), pp. 88–101.

which we judge they will not in fact inflict'.[78] This has an obvious resonance when considering the transmission of disease. An individual who knows he is carrying a transmissible disease will not, except for the example discussed, ordinarily be expected to expose others to the risk of contracting it. We ought to be able to 'trust' someone who is carrying an infectious disease to make concerted efforts to keep it to themselves. David Hoekema has considered trust explicitly in the context of punishment. He states that:

> A criminal act, an act deserving punishment, consists in taking advantage of others' trust in a way that undermines the network of vulnerability without which life in the society of others would be intolerable.[79]

Hoekema, however, qualifies this somewhat, as he expresses the belief that not all abuses of trust are, or should be, deserving of punishment. The breaches of trust that Hoekema believes ought to be criminalised are those that take place in the context of 'involuntary trust relationships'. For him, the less voluntary the trust relationship, the greater the interest the state has in preserving and enhancing trust within it.[80] It is this, rather than the gravity of the harm caused, that justifies punishment. Hoekema argues that the reason the law does not punish a failure to take a friend to hospital, for example, is that it is not interested in the degree to which one relies on friends and other intimates. What the law is interested in is preserving the trust upon which contractual and other non-intimate relationships are contingent. This is characterised as 'the trust that strangers extend to each other in order to make life in society possible'. Hoekema argues that children provide the greatest example of this correlation. He states that children have no choice but to rely upon their parents, and it is for that reason that the law punishes severely serious breaches of children's trust, such as neglect.[81]

---

[78] A. C. Baier, *Trust*, the Tanner Lectures on Human Values, delivered at Princeton University, 6–8 March 1991. Available at http://tannerlectures.utah.edu/_documents/a-to-z/b/baier92.pdf (Accessed 21 November 2015).

[79] D. A. Hoekema, 'Trust and obey: toward a new theory of punishment', *Israel Law Review*, 25 (1991), 322, at p. 347.

[80] Ibid., at p. 343. Whether a clear delineation can be drawn between involuntary and voluntary trust relationships may be open to doubt. An individual might not wish to be in love with their abusive spouse, but nevertheless feel unable to leave them. Is being in love voluntary? Hoekema's conceptualisation of voluntariness exists when the trusting person has the means of checking the basis of her trust and so has no need of the law. Friendship is the example he gives.

[81] It could, however, be argued that the harm caused is magnified because of the especial vulnerability of children and this is why offences against children are punished so severely.

Although Hoekema's conceptualisation of trust seems attractive, it has not been without its critics. Susan Dimock, for example, states that there are objective and subjective conditions of trust and criticises Hoekema for focusing only on the latter.[82] The subjective conditions are those that are harmful only to the individual in question and, for Dimock, these ought not to be the concern of the law. Objective conditions are those which are the concern of the law because they serve 'basic trust', that is, meta trust or 'trust in trust'. If society did not punish breaches of such trust, everyone would be made less trustworthy in the objective sense. Dimock gives the example of the spouse who is infected by her partner with HIV. She may have good subjective reasons to mistrust the person who infected her. That is besides the point. What is more important is that if society acquiesced in her being treated in this way, then this would make everyone less trustworthy in an objective sense. The point she makes is that trust in society would become less objectively reasonable if behaviour of this kind was not condemned.

Although there are differences in their respective theories, what unites them is that neither Hoekema nor Dimock base their conception of the role trust plays in justifying punishment on the severity of the harm involved in the trust violation. On their account, even if the tangible harm was relatively trivial, punishment would still be justified provided it entailed a trust violation.

James Slater has explicitly examined theories of trust in the context of HIV transmission. In 'HIV, trust and the criminal law',[83] Slater limits his focus to the transmission of STDs and HIV in particular.[84] Slater criticises Hoekema's thesis on the basis that what matters is not the voluntariness of the relationship, but rather the voluntariness of the trust. For Slater, the two are not necessarily synonymous. Slater argues that just because a relationship is voluntary does not necessarily mean that it is one giving rise to an expectation of trust. In a casual relationship, where the parties are strangers, Slater contends that the ignorant party has no reason to trust the other. It is for this reason that he states that those who engage in casual sex have no justified reason for trusting each other. The ignorant party should either ensure the trustworthiness of her partner or accept the risks that are the potential consequence of failing to do so.[85] Slater does recognise the

[82] S. Dimock, 'Retributivism and trust', *Law and Philosophy*, 16:1 (1997), 37.
[83] J. Slater, 'HIV, trust and the criminal law', *Journal of Criminal Law*, 75:4 (2011), 309.
[84] It is unclear, however, why Slater confines his analysis to HIV, as it could apply to other STDs.
[85] Slater, 'HIV, trust and the criminal law', 323–5.

criticism that is made of this argument by Jonathan Herring.[86] Herring contends that acceptance of this proposition entails accepting that the law protects property to a greater extent than it protects sexual autonomy, given that the law criminalises those who obtain property by deception. Slater counters this by arguing that such offences exist to protect an 'important social good'. For Slater, sex is a social good only 'when reinforcing loving and trusting relationships'.

Given that they focus on a breach of trust as constituting an intrinsic harm, could these theories, provided they resonate outside a theoretical context, explain why non-STD transmission has not been a feature of the English legal landscape? The jurisprudence of courts in England sheds light on this issue, as trust does seem to be a feature of the reported cases. In *Konzani*, for example, LH stated that the reason why she had unprotected sex with K was because she 'trusted him'.[87] In *Dica* Judge LJ envisaged a spectrum with casual sex between strangers at one end and sexual intercourse between couples at the other.[88] When sentencing David Golding, who transmitted genital herpes to his partner, the trial judge stated as follows:

> Because [the transmission] was in a relationship, it was particularly mean and one which amounted to a betrayal – a betrayal in a relationship in which you professed love.[89]

It is instructive that all of the reported prosecutions for STD transmission have occurred in the context of relationships. This could perhaps indicate that it was not necessarily (or solely) the intrinsic harm of becoming infected with the STD in question that made these individuals deem it appropriate to invoke the state, but the fact that the transmission took place in a relationship, one in which there was an expectation of trust. Although the precise contours of the ethics of trust are the subject of much debate and the role it plays in justifying punishment is contested, it is possible to conceptualise the transmission of an STD as entailing a breach of trust of some kind. Even if Slater is correct in his – by no means uncontroversial – assertion that those who engage in casual sex have no justification for trusting each other, this does not mean that trust has no role to play in this context, as his analysis demonstrates. If one party in a relationship

[86] J. Herring, 'Mistaken sex', *Criminal Law Review* (2005), 511.
[87] *Konzani*, at [16].
[88] *Dica*, at [47].
[89] Available at www.theguardian.com/commentisfree/2011/aug/19/jail-herpes-sexually-transmitted-infection (Accessed 21 November 2015).

recklessly transmits an undisclosed STD to the other, it can be said that there is a breach of trust that is distinct from the intrinsic harm caused by the STD in question.

Assuming that trust does play some role in explaining why those who become infected with an STD deem it appropriate to invoke the apparatus of the state, is such a breach of trust confined to STD transmission or might trust have the same role to play in the context of non-STD transmission too? There is an expectation that those who know they are carrying an infectious disease will make concerted efforts not to transmit them to others. In the same way that the ethics of trust dictates that an individual who knows he is infected with gonorrhoea ought to disclose that fact and wear a condom when engaging in sex and will breach his sexual partner's trust if fails to do so, the care worker with potentially deadly influenza ought to refrain from going to work. Margaret Brazier argues that those who are ill bear responsibilities, one of which is to refrain from harming others, by minimising the risk of transmitting their illness. She states that:

> Being ill does not absolve a person of her normal legal and moral responsibilities to other people unless the very nature of that illness deprives her of mental capacity. If I ignore medical advice and expose my students involuntarily to the risk of contracting tuberculosis my conduct is morally indistinguishable from assault.[90]

One of these responsibilities is to take steps to minimise the chance that an infectious disease will be transmitted, for example, by not going to work. To return to Baier's definition, we accept the risk that others could infect us with non-STDs, but we judge that they will not do so because they are aware that they owe obligations to others. For this reason, it is recognised that there ought to be no distinction as to how the transmission of disease is perceived. Depending on the circumstances, both can be conceptualised as constituting a breach of trust. Of course, not every instance of a failure to take precautionary steps entails a breach of trust. There is no expectation of trust when the person with the cold gets on the bus, given that, as has already been discussed, everyone who boards the bus tacitly consents to taking the risk of contracting everyday illnesses. Similarly, there is no breach of trust if the infected partner discloses the fact that he is suffering from an STD and seeks his partner's consent to taking the risk that it will be transmitted.

---

[90] M. Brazier, 'Do no harm – do patients have responsibilities too?', *Cambridge Law Journal*, 65:2 (2006), 397, 406.

Slater might, however, argue that there is no breach of trust because as strangers there is no reason for one anonymous person on the bus to trust the anonymous person sitting beside him. Although our daily encounters with each other are voluntary in the sense that we choose to leave the house in the morning, this seems to be a very thin conception of 'voluntary'. To function as a human being is to interact with others and so we cannot avoid encounters with those who may be ill. For this reason, our relationships with others who may be infected with disease are not truly voluntary (outside our relationships with loved ones, friends and other intimates).

In conclusion, depending upon the circumstances, the criminalisation of any disease can be conceptualised as constituting a breach of trust.[91] Of course, there may be a distinction between STDs and non-STDs in this regard, but it is a matter of degree. In quantitative terms, the breach of trust that follows when one individual surreptitiously transmits a non-STD to another might be considered less grave than the transmission of an STD, but there is a breach of trust nevertheless.

Feelings of Disgust?

Perhaps the reason why STDs could be perceived as being different from non-STDs is a sense of disgust that is associated with the former but not the latter? Assuming such a distinction is drawn, it is necessary to investigate whether it provides an explanation for criminalisation at an unconscious level. The first question that must be addressed is what is meant by 'disgust'. The *Oxford English Dictionary* states that the meaning of the noun 'disgust' is:

> Strong repugnance, aversion, or repulsion excited by that which is loathsome or offensive, as a foul smell, disagreeable person or action, disappointed ambition, etc.; profound instinctive dislike or dissatisfaction.

Although this definition is instructive, of greater relevance is the work that Martha Nussbaum has done on disgust and its relationship with the law.[92]

---

[91] This is a different issue from the one that exists in the context of sexual offences regarding the level of openness that ought to be expected between sexual partners. See, for example, the divergent views taken in Herring, 'Mistaken sex', 511 and H. Gross, 'Rape, moralism, and human rights', *Criminal Law Review*, (1997), 220. For the most recent literature, see the references contained in K. Laird, 'Rapist or rogue? Consent, deception and the sexual offences act 2003', *Criminal Law Review*, (2014), 492.

[92] M. C. Nussbaum, *Hiding from Humanity – Disgust, Shame, and the Law* (Princeton: Princeton University Press, 2004).

Nussbaum states that disgust is a powerful emotion that in many ways shapes both our daily lives and our social relations. She observes:

> [Disgust] shapes much of our intimacies and provides much of the structure of our daily routine, as we wash our bodies, seek privacy for urination and defecation, cleanse ourselves of offending odors with toothbrush and mouthwash, sniff our armpits when nobody is looking, check in the mirror to make sure that no conspicuous snot is caught in our nose-hairs.[93]

Nussbaum's work is especially illuminating for the present enquiry as she is examining disgust within a particular context, a legal one. It is axiomatic that the notion of disgust shapes much of our daily routine, but does it have significance when it comes to determining what type of behaviour we think ought to be the concern of the criminal law? The very idea of an STD itself could in some sense be 'disgusting'. Although the intrinsic harm caused by influenza and gonorrhoea might not be too dissimilar, it could be argued that the latter is somehow debasing in a way that the former is not. The literature on the social construction of illness is voluminous. An important distinction is made between disease and illness: illness is a social designation, rather than a biological one.[94] There is a significant amount of evidence to suggest that the social designation given to STDs is distinct by virtue of the fact they are typically[95] transmitted via sexual intercourse. As Nussbaum notes: 'Sex involves the exchange of bodily fluids, and it makes us bodily beings rather than angelic transcendent beings. So sex is a site of anxiety for anyone who is ambivalent about having an animal and mortal nature, and that includes many if not most people.'[96]

Does this social designation, informed by disgust, explain some unconscious reason for criminalisation? Relying upon a number of psychological studies, Nussbaum argues that it has been definitively established that disgust bears no relationship to danger and risk perception.[97] Disgust is therefore invoked when there is no danger posed by the conduct in question, or at least not as much as it is perceived to pose. This has been a feature of cases in the United States in which defendants have sought to

---

[93] Ibid., p. 72.
[94] P. Conrad and K. K. Barker, 'The social construction of illness: key insights and policy implications', *Journal of Health and Social Behaviour*, 51: 1 Suppl. (2010), S67.
[95] Not all instances of STD transmission involve sexual intercourse. See *Marangwanda* [2009] EWCA Crim 60.
[96] M. C. Nussbaum, *From Disgust to Humanity – Sexual Orientation and Constitutional Law* (New York: Oxford University Press, 2010), p. 17.
[97] Nussbaum, *Hiding from Humanity*, chapter 2.

mitigate their liability for murder by testifying that they were disgusted when observing the victims' same-sex intercourse or at being perceived as homosexual themselves by the victim.[98] It is for this reason Nussbaum states that appeals to disgust are better replaced by principles that in fact correspond with danger and harm. Nussbaum also makes the point that disgust has been invoked in the past to justify excluding certain groups from society by labelling them as 'disgusting', such as Jews, women and homosexuals. Nussbaum therefore concludes that disgust 'does not respond to harms that are alleged and well supported by evidence'.[99]

Although there is evidence to suggest that there exists a perception that non-STDs lack the element of disgust thought to be inherent in STDs, this is not something the law ought to condone. As Nussbaum argues, in the context of the law, disgust is a dangerous social sentiment that should be contained rather than given effect to. The current situation in England is especially problematic as it has the potential to permit people to give effect to their notions of disgust. This is because the Court of Appeal has confirmed that the question of whether an STD constitutes grievous bodily harm is one for the jury.[100] Each juror's perception of harm could be distorted by disgust, such that they are likely to find that the threshold of harm has been crossed even though expert evidence might suggest otherwise.

Implications and Conclusion

Given that the criminalisation of contagion has been a feature of the English legal landscape for over a decade, are we now in a position to explain why there has never been a prosecution for the transmission of a non-STD? It has been demonstrated that English law is broad enough to encompass the reckless or intentional transmission of any type of disease. Although evidential difficulties and the public interest might preclude prosecution in the vast majority of instances of non-STD transmission, it is possible to conceive of circumstances in which prosecution would be both possible and justified. It is true that the public might not perceive non-STD transmission as being something that justifies state intervention. Once these

---

[98] Ibid., pp. 126–34. This defence became known as the 'Portsmouth defence' in England and Wales. See H. Power, 'Provocation and culture', *Criminal Law Review*, (2006), 871. Owing to the objective and justificatory nature of the partial defence of loss of control (which replaced the defence of provocation in England and Wales), it is highly unlikely the defence would be left to the jury on this basis.

[99] Nussbaum, *Hiding from Humanity*, p. 143.

[100] *R v Golding* [2014] EWCA Crim 889.

perceptions are investigated, however, it becomes evident that they do not always withstand scrutiny.

Does the paradigm matter? The focus on STDs obscures how all-encompassing English criminal law is in this regard. The Offences against the Person Act 1861 is broad enough to encompass all sorts of everyday behaviour. The only bulwark against this is prosecutorial discretion. The failure to appreciate the breadth of potential criminal liability has allowed the law to stagnate. The government in the mid-1990s expressed the view that only intentional transmission accompanied by an intention to cause really serious harm ought to be an offence. English law is now much more expansive than this and sets a lower threshold of culpability. In *Dica* Judge LJ expressed unease with the notion that the criminal law might encompass the situation where the parent comforts the child who is suffering from a serious contagious disease. His Lordship stated that, 'interference of this kind with personal autonomy, and its level and extent, may only be made by Parliament'.[101] The law does, however, encompass circumstances such as this. The perception that English law criminalises only those who surreptitiously transmit STDs is predicated upon the notion of Otherness. The law in this area has stagnated because of the commonly held perception that it criminalises only those who are deemed to be deviant. It is hoped that the recent work of the Law Commission of England and Wales will ignite debate over reform of the offences against the person and that the question of whether disease transmission ought to be criminalised will feature prominently on the agenda.

---

[101] *Dica*, at [52].

INDEX

Acquired Immune Deficiency
  Syndrome (AIDS). *See* HIV/AIDS
activist networks
  biological citizenship and, 173–4
  legacy of science-based reforms
    for, 170–4
  science-based criminal law reform
    and, 160–7
actor network theory, agency and, 27–9
advocacy for decriminalisation of HIV/
    AIDS, science-based strategies
    for, 160–7
Africa, criminalisation of HIV/AIDS
    in, 105
agency
  feminist perspectives on, 185–90
  in HIV transmission, 26–33
alcoholism, free will linked to, 38–9
Altman, Lawrence K., 48–9
American Medical Association,
    opposition to lethal
    injection, 39–40
anti-essentialism in feminist legal
    methodology, 178–80, 185–90
  disclosure *vs.* non-disclosure in,
    197–200
  violence against women and, 190–5
Armstrong, Sarah, 46, 54
Armstrong, W. N., 62–3
Arning, Eduard, 66
Ashworth, A., 2–3
Asia, criminalisation of HIV/AIDS
    in, 105
Australia, history of leprosy in, 57
autonomy principles, criminalisation
    of non-disclosure of HIV/AIDS
    and, 185–90

avian influenza, military/criminal
  metaphors concerning, 51–2

Bad Blood: A Cautionary Tale
  (film), 42–3
Baier, Annette, 220–5
Ban Ki-moon, 41–2
Bartlett, Katharine, 178–80
Bashford, Alison, 57
battery, *actus reus* of, UK
  criminalisation of transmission
  and, 211–14
Bayonet Constitution of 1887 (Hawaii),
  58–9, 66
Beacon: Magazine of Hawaii, 74
behaviour
  inefficacy of U.S. HIV/AIDS statutes
    concerning, 139–43
  low-risk behaviours, criminalisation
    in U.S. statutes of, 27,
    128–30, 136–8
  medicalisation/demedicalisation of
    deviance and, 41–2
  scope of, in Norwegian Penal
    Code, 115–16
  U.S. exposure statutes and liability
    based on, 125–31, 134–9
Bell, Joseph, 46
Bennett, Jane, 27–9, 30
'Best Practices Guide to Reform
  HIV-Specific Criminal
  Laws to Align with
  Scientifically-Supported Factors'
  (U.S.), 145–7
Betteridge, Glenn, 165
Bible, illness as punishment in, 36–8
bioinformationist metaphor, 48–9

William W. Lowrance
Privacy, Confidentiality, and Health Research

Kerry Lynn Macintosh
Human Cloning: Four Fallacies and Their Legal Consequence

Heather Widdows
The Connected Self: The Ethics and Governance of the Genetic Individual

Amel Alghrani, Rebecca Bennett and Suzanne Ost
Bioethics, Medicine and the Criminal Law Volume I: The Criminal Law and Bioethical Conflict: Walking the Tightrope

Danielle Griffiths and Andrew Sanders
Bioethics, Medicine and the Criminal Law Volume II: Medicine, Crime and Society

Margaret Brazier and Suzanne Ost
Bioethics, Medicine and the Criminal Law Volume III: Medicine and Bioethics in the Theatre of the Criminal Process

Sigrid Sterckx, Kasper Raus and Freddy Mortier
Continuous Sedation at the End of Life: Ethical, Clinical and Legal Perspectives

A. M. Viens, John Coggon and Anthony S. Kessel
Criminal Law, Philosophy and Public Health Practice

Ruth Chadwick, Mairi Levitt and Darren Shickle
The Right to Know and the Right Not to Know: Genetic Privacy and Responsibility

Eleanor D. Kinney
The Affordable Care Act and Medicare in Comparative Context

Katri Lõhmus
Caring Autonomy: European Human Rights Law and the Challenge of Individualism

Catherine Stanton and Hannah Quirk
Criminalising Contagion: Legal and Ethical Challenges of Disease Transmission and the Criminal Law

Printed in the United States
By Bookmasters